T0308862

In the Jaws of the
Crocodile

Other Books by Emil Draitser

In the Jaws of the Crocodile

A Soviet Memoir

Emil Draitser

THE UNIVERSITY OF WISCONSIN PRESS

The University of Wisconsin Press
728 State Street, Suite 443
Madison, Wisconsin 53706
uwpress.wisc.edu

Gray's Inn House, 127 Clerkenwell Road
London ECIR 5DB, United Kingdom
eurospanbookstore.com

Printed in the United States of America
This book may be available in a digital edition.

Library of Congress Cataloging-in-Publication Data
Names: Draitser, Emil, 1937– author.
Title: In the jaws of the crocodile : a Soviet memoir / Emil Draitser.
Description: Madison, Wisconsin : The University of Wisconsin Press, [2021]
Identifiers: LCCN 2020010782 | ISBN 9780299329006 (cloth)
Subjects: LCSH: Draitser, Emil, 1937– | Jews—Soviet Union—Biography. |
Jewish journalists—Soviet Union—Biography. | Jewish authors—
Soviet Union—Biography. | LCGFT: Autobiographies.
Classification: LCC PG3549.D7 Z46 2021 | DDC 305.892/404772092 [B]—dc23
LC record available at https://lccn.loc.gov/2020010782

Excerpts of this book appeared in a somewhat different form in the
*Los Angeles Times, Studies in Contemporary Satire, Jewish Literary Journal,
Prism International*, and *Odessa Review*.

To the memory of
ARKADY POLISHCHUK

The human race has only one really effective weapon,
and that is laughter.
—MARK TWAIN

Even he who doesn't fear anything else in the world fears ridicule.
—NIKOLAI GOGOL

We need [Soviet] Gogols. . . . We need [Soviet Saltykov-]Shchedrins.
—JOSEPH STALIN

We are all for [satirical] laughter!
But we need kinder Shchedrins
And such Gogols that wouldn't bother us.
—YURI BLAGOV, *Soviet writer*

To truly laugh, you must be able to take your pain and play with it.
—CHARLIE CHAPLIN

Contents

Illustrations

Preface

Chronologically (if not thematically), this volume is a sequel to my memoir *Shush! Growing up Jewish under Stalin* (University of California Press, 2008). By the same token, it is a prequel to my autobiographical novel, *Farewell, Mama Odessa* (Northwestern University Press, 2020), in which I describe my emigration experience.

It takes a village to raise a child; so it does to bring a manuscript to maturity. My former comrades-in-satirical-arms Arkady Polishchuk and Grigory Kroshin (né Kremer) helped to revive many details of events and circumstances of bygone years me for and shared their recollections of adventures in the Soviet satirical scene.

My friends Dr. Richard Sogluizzo, Dr. Anthony Saidy, Dr. Gary Kern, and Nina Prays read several chapters of the manuscript and offered their feedback.

I also appreciate Emily Corvi's fine-tuning my command of idiomatic English.

Gena Fischer served as my beta reader of the whole manuscript to ensure that it was ready to face the outside world.

I also enjoyed the help of my brother, Vladimir, especially his expertise in picture file formatting and in fighting computer glitches, which spring up in the most critical moments.

A separate thank you goes to Dr. Jolanta Kunicka. Being months on end next to a writer going through creative torments isn't an enviable lot by any means. I appreciate her patience and care, as well as her hands-on assistance with the manuscript.

Gwen Walker, the former executive acquisition editor at the University of Wisconsin Press, became enthusiastic upon reading my proposal, asked for the whole manuscript, and passed it on to my peer reviewers,

Dr. Jarrod Tanny, Dr. Boris Dralyuk, and Dr. Anna Shternshis. Their appraisal of my manuscript helped it to take its current shape. Whatever mistakes might spring up in the final text are of my making.

I am also thankful to Grigory Kroshin, Arkady Polishchuk, Nancy I. Suslov, Mark Russell, and Joel Buchwald for their permission to use their (or their loved ones') pictures in this book. For various reasons, some names of real people described in this book are altered.

Notes on Languages and Translation

All translations of excerpts from the Russian texts in this book are my own. I transliterated Russian words according to the Library of Congress system for the Cyrillic alphabet. For some names, however, I keep their traditional rendering in British-American literature.

All Yiddish words in this text are rendered the way my aural memory holds them. In my family, the language was spoken in two different versions. My mother and all relatives on her side spoke the Yiddish of their youth in Uman, Ukraine. My father and all relatives on his side were born and raised in Minsk and therefore spoke Yiddish with a northwestern accent (known as a Litvak accent). Also, some of the Yiddish words and expressions I have used have meanings different from those found in current dictionaries. In this book, I adopted the YIVO standard of Yiddish transliteration.

In the Jaws of the
Crocodile

Prologue

"Hey, Dad," my son Max says during our lunch at a Westwood Village café, basking in the proverbial Californian sun. "Is it true that, back in your Soviet days, you wrote what . . . satires? Did I get it right? Well, forgive me, but it's weird. . . . 'Soviet satire' sounds like a contradiction in terms."

Talk about a generation gap! In my case, it's not even a gap; it's an abyss. Though born in Moscow, Max was just fifteen months old when, in October 1974, we left the former Soviet Union. He is as American as apple pie! (If not pie, then strudel—that's what his grandmother used to bake for him while he was growing up on American soil.)

Max visited his native land only when he was in his late twenties. It happened after the Soviet Union had already collapsed under its own weight. My son saw a land quite different from the one his father had inhabited before emigrating. The Moscow he visited as an adult was a far cry from the Moscow I knew during the Soviet era. Mine was a land of perennial shortages of goods and services. The Moscow he arrived in had already been populated with McDonald's, Burger King, and department stores rivaling Macy's. This doesn't even include nightclubs or other trappings of capitalism. Back in my Soviet life, I saw such things for a split second when watching the newsreels of the *Foreign Newsreel* (Inostrannaya kinokhronika). They were filled with heartbreaking stories of life in the rotten West.

As an American, my son finds it hard to fathom that such a thing as "Soviet satire" existed. How could a totalitarian state tolerate public criticism? How could it encourage this criticism by putting professional satirists on its payroll?

The truth of the matter is that, in my time, there was a plethora of satirical outlets in the country. Many Soviet newspapers published satirical columns, called feuilletons. The main satirical magazine, *Crocodile*,

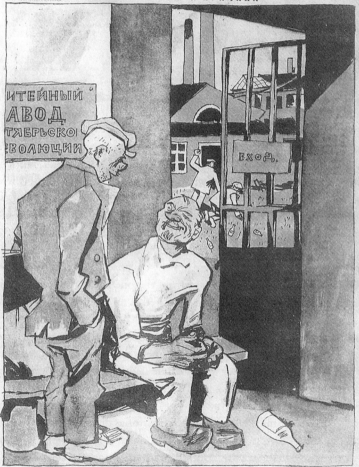

A cover of *Crocodile* magazine

came out three times a month, six million copies each time. It was way more popular than its American counterparts *National Lampoon* and *Mad Magazine*, even in their heydays. And that's not counting the several *Crocodile* spinoffs published in the languages of the Soviet republics. There were also satirical programs on Moscow Radio and on local and central TV stations. Beginning in the early 1960s, the Mosfilm Studios produced the satirical newsreel *The Wick* (Fitil'). Its name derives from the expression *vstavit' fitil'*, to give somebody a good working over. Screened in movie theaters before the main features, the newsreels enjoyed tremendous popularity.

An army of satirists worked in the censored Soviet media. Like its namesake—the real-life beast whose jaws crunch over its prey with several dozens of constantly replaceable saber-sharp teeth—besides its forty-some staff members, the satirical magazine *Crocodile* used more than two hundred freelancers. Many more contributed to other satirical outlets—newspapers, radio, movies, and TV programs. For the ten years of my life before emigrating in late 1974, I was one of the foot soldiers in that satirical army. Besides *Crocodile* and *The Wick*, my work appeared in such

The title sequence of the satirical newsreel *The Wick* (Fitil')

All-Union publications as the magazine *Youth* and the newspapers *Literary Gazette*, *Izvestiya*, *Komsomol Pravda*, *Labor* (Trud), in Republican ones (*Soviet Russia*, *Literary Russia*), and in local publications in Moscow, Kazan, Saratov, Riga, and my home town, Odessa. I also wrote scripts for short satirical features for TV and Central Radio.

Only recently, after living in America half of my life, I pondered that part of my career. It took a while to figure out how it all had happened. Why had I attached myself to the strange animal called "Soviet satire"?

It took some relentless soul-searching to realize it had happened because, early in my life, I had given in to my secret passion, which was irrational and all-consuming—as all passions are.

PART I

Hopes and Dreams,
1953–55

1

Imagine You

"You know, Draitser," says your Russian literature teacher, Victoria Nau-movna, returning your homework, "you have something there." She looks at you through the lenses of her enormous, horn-rimmed spectacles on the tip of her nose. "I mean, I see promise. You write well."

She says it without a trace of a compliment in her voice. She utters this phrase with the same concern doctors do when they inform a patient about cancer.

The year is 1953, mid-September, and you are fifteen years old. It is a typical fall day. The leaves of the trees in Odessa, Ukraine, are already touched with soft yellow ocher, and chestnuts fall to the sidewalks with a light thud, their green skin broken, flashing their shiny brown core.

You are in the eighth grade of School #43 in the Water-Transportation District in Odessa. Your teacher is a serious woman. She is old, almost forty. She is short, a head shorter than you. A large birthmark on her cheek undermines her good looks. After the war, times are hard; there are things more pressing than cosmetic surgery.

Your teacher's words catch you off guard. Nobody has ever praised you. Not for your abilities or for anything else either. Never your mom or dad, let alone any of your aunts or uncles. Nobody has scolded you much: you have made little trouble for anyone. But it is post–World War II, a time of food shortages and other hardships. Everyone leads a stress-ful life; there is no room for sentimentality. And here your teacher says that you write well. . . .

At first, you are dumbfounded. If it is a good thing to be able to write well, then why does your teacher frown while telling you this? It is as if she were saying that since this fact is established, you are under an obligation to do something about it. To put your newly discovered skill to good use . . .

Now, recalling this episode of your youth, you have no idea on what basis the teacher made such a fateful conclusion. Because it happened in September, you can only guess that it was the homework essay you wrote on a topic she had given when the school year began—something like how you had spent your summer break.

However, to write about something as innocent as summer vacation isn't easy at all. You have to be politically correct. As a teenager, you are expected to read more and help your family with chores. You can go swimming and sunbathing but expressing joy while doing it isn't acceptable. Physical pleasure is for the bourgeoisie, languishing in their idleness. It isn't proper for a Komsomol (Young Communist League) member in good standing.

So, even to this day, you are curious: What had you written that impressed your teacher so much? You hardly had much choice. You couldn't write that your mom doesn't care about the Young Pioneer camps, recreational outlets for schoolchildren of all ages. You've been there for only one session; she prefers to improve your health in her own way. During the summers of your early school years, your mom placed you in the care of one Clara Fritzovna. Like all private enterprises, her daycare center functioned underground, without letting the authorities lay their hands on it. Her patronymic, Fritzovna, showed that her father was German (Fritz). So, people assumed she was a true follower of her compatriot Friedrich Froebel (they called her *frebelichka*), who, back in the nineteenth century, had come up with the idea of kindergartens. If children are the flowers of life, he thought, then it is better to grow them together in a single flowerbed.

After you got older, for the summers, you and your cousins went with your mothers to the countryside to drink fresh milk and gorge on ripe fruit. To get there, you traveled a few hours by train, heading northwest from Odessa to the village of Domanevka in the Kryzhopol district, near the city of Vinnitsa.

You couldn't write about your parents in your composition, either. You had to be careful not to reveal that your dad, together with your uncle, runs a private business. They painted houses and hung wallpaper. It is the Soviet Union; they prohibit any private enterprise. Like Clara Fritzovna, the daycare lady, every day your father and uncle risk being caught and facing a huge fine or even incarceration.

You wouldn't also mention your mom was a mere housewife. The ideal Soviet women are expected to be working shoulder to shoulder with men. They should wield if not hammers, at least sickles, just like in the giant Vera Mukhina statue. An image of the sculpture lights up the screen at the beginning of Mosfilm movies while triumphant fanfares of socialism blare from the theater's speakers.

So, it is unlikely your school essay was about something you could be proud of. It probably belonged to the literary genre the scholars of Soviet literature later referred to as "varnishing reality" (*lakirovka dejstvitel'nosti*). The teacher's praise makes you feel good. After all, writing fiction is much more difficult than reporting. You couldn't write such an essay without using your imagination. So, you take your teacher's approval seriously.

Praise can go to the head of an adult, let alone the mind of a teenager.

"*Vey iz mir!*" your mom says hearing your report. She gives you an alarmed look as if a snake had just bitten you. What if it's poisonous? She'd have to do something about it right away. "Woe is me! You write well, that's what it's all about? Are you sure she said that?"

Her face expresses a faint hope you've misheard your teacher.

You shrug, "Yes, she said that."

"Well, here's my advice to you, young man—forget about it! Don't get any ideas. Trust me; it won't do you any good," she utters prophetically.

Since her warning doesn't have much effect on you, she adds, "Well, fine! Let's assume she said that. So, what are you thinking of doing with *that?*"

It looks like she avoids repeating the teacher's praise of my essay writing.

"I'll apply to the Literary Institute," you say. "Or to the Faculty of Journalism at the Moscow State University."

That such an idea has gotten into your head is not your fault. It has come from that part of your brain that hasn't been fully developed yet. After all, it's not by chance insurance companies inflate premiums for drivers under twenty-five.

The utopian nature of your dream to embark on a literary path, and the truth of your mother's warnings, will come to you much later. At the time, there was only one literary institute in the country, and, like the Faculty of Journalism, it was an elite school. A real, proved talent, not just a hint of it, was hardly enough to be accepted there.

However, you live in a country where, whichever way you turn, they remind you how fortunate you are to be born in the fairest society in the world. Twenty times a day—more often than the national anthem—

radio plays the invigorating song from the Soviet blockbuster film *The Circus*: "The young have all opportunities open to them!" (*Molodym vezde u nas doroga!*) These words come to you on the streets from the loud-speakers mounted on the lampposts and at home through your wired radio. (This innovation by Stalin had delighted Hitler; even he hadn't come up with such an effective way to brainwash his people in the privacy of their homes.)

In that film, the superstar of Soviet cinema Lyubov Orlova plays the part of an American circus performer who runs away from her country because they would persecute her for having a black baby. She finds her happiness in the Soviet Union. During the finale, the marching rows of young men and women sing and wave to the American woman, "Don't you worry, transatlantic beauty! We have no racists here, in our great country, as you do in America! Here, all people can do whatever they like with their lives."

Literature and history classes are the only ones you are interested in, and you wait for them impatiently. Though you have As in other subjects, your success comes from cramming and forcing yourself to remember information. For literature, you read every book that comes your way, especially those that aren't on the class list. They give you almost physical pleasure. They make you drift away into another reality, otherwise unreachable. Especially historical novels. Plenty of room for imagination! You still remember how, in *Peter the First* by Alexei Tolstoy, the fresh snow crunches under the felt boots of the two boys running on it. They laugh and throw snowballs at each other. One of them is the future Emperor of All of Russia, and the other is his childhood friend Menshikov, his future minister and closest adviser.

Or take *Genghis Khan* and *Batu Khan* by Vasily Yan. Both novels take your breath away. The vast sunbaked steppes. . . . The Mongolian cavalry rushes through it. The muscular horses try to break free from their bits. They snort, foaming at their mouths. The reckless riders bounce on their backs to the beat of the gallop. They wave their curved, steel Damascus swords over their heads. Under the hooves of the horses, dust spreads across the steppes. It rises until it obscures the sun, turning it into a bloody yolk, high in the sky. . . .

While you have no inkling of the fact that neither the times nor the circumstances of your life are suitable for this youthful daydreaming, your mother is painfully aware of it. She has no time for any musing. While your father is at work all day long, concerns about where to buy food and clothes for her family fill every waking hour of her life. In the grocery store, at the corner of Preobrazhenskaya and Deribasovskaya Streets, they sell wheat flour in the morning, two packs per person, and it won't last for too long. In the department store on Rishelievskaya Street, they've received a batch of decent men's jackets, and a line already stretches around the block. The kiosk on Gavannaya Street is about to get some foreign-made blouses. Where should she run first? If only she could clone herself!

As if all these worries aren't enough, a disease worse than eczema inflicts her son. She can't just cure it with some ointment. After listening to your mutterings about the Literary Institute and the Faculty of Journalism, she waves her hand.

"What are you talking about!" she says. "They won't accept you in either of them."

"Why won't they? If I have good grades . . ."

"They still won't," your mother says, nodding her head with conviction. "Don't forget that you're a Jew."

"So, what of it?" you frown. You're annoyed by the lamentations you hear at home all the time that being a Jew is a curse, that it is time for you to stop believing what you read in the papers. Only according to them, the Soviet Union is the most just country in the world, one where all people are equal, regardless of their race, ethnicity, or creed.

Yes, you recall that, a few years ago, your parents and other relatives freaked out during the campaign against the so-called rootless cosmopolitans. These people lacked Soviet patriotism. They didn't pay our Soviet culture its due. They looked up to the West, admiring its cultural and technological achievements. The papers treated them as internal enemies. Your mom and dad turned pale when they read a spiteful article in *Pravda* about some literary critic. He had a Russian-sounding pen name, say, Petrov, but, as the article revealed, his true surname was Goldberg.

In January of this year, there was another scare. A big one. *Pravda* announced the unveiling of the "Doctors' Plot." A group of prominent physicians, mostly Jews, had conspired to assassinate the country's leaders.

That news hit home hard. Your mother's close friend Tanya, a pediatrician, found herself boycotted by her patients' mothers. She was heartbroken when they told her point-blank that they didn't want her to hurt their children.

Yes, that was bad. However, less than two months later, on March 5, Stalin died, and, shortly after, the Kremlin doctors were exonerated and freed.

Case closed. So, why worry now?

Closed for you, but not for your parents and other relatives. In fact, everyone around you is still on their toes regarding what will happen in their lives next. Stalin had ruled the country with a heavy hand for a quarter of a century. It's only natural to expect that not much change would come about overnight. In fact, they've made one of his henchmen, Georgi Malenkov, the Chairman of the Council of Ministers. All your relatives perceive that, over there, in Moscow, Stalin's heirs fight each other with the fierceness of dung beetles in a glass jar. A rumor has just reached Odessa that they arrested Lavrentiy Beria, the KGB's head honcho. Now, it is anyone's guess where the turmoil among Kremlin's big wigs will lead.

However, you, a fifteen-year-old youth, care little about all those higher considerations that make the adults anxious. In late spring, together with other members of your immediate family, you've relocated. From a two-hundred-square-foot room in the communal apartment on the third floor in the courtyard's rear of Deribasovskaya Street, 18, where you had lived with your father, mother, and five-year-old brother, Vladimir, you have moved to a two-room apartment two blocks away, around the corner, on the first floor of the courtyard on Lastochkina Street, 21. One bigger room with two windows facing the courtyard is about the same floor space as your old apartment. It serves as both a dining room and a living room and, in the evening, as your parents' bedroom. The room next to it, about half the size, is windowless. With two couches fenced off by bookcases, it is your and your little brother's bedroom. There is another tiny room, also windowless, which your father and your uncle Misha have converted into a kitchen. The restroom at the end of the corridor is communal; your family shares it with your neighbors.

While your new living quarters are hardly a godsend by American standards, for your family, it feels like the Palace of Versailles. Your mother threw a big party. Although the formal occasion was her birthday, June 4, the family gathering was also a housewarming. Your parents celebrated the move with such pride and joy that it was as if the new quarters were a fairy-tale castle built to their design.

However, what in fact they were celebrating was the death of Stalin and the dismissal of the Doctors' Case. Overjoyed by the tyrant's untimely demise, the guests kept repeating the same joke that had been making circles since the day the leader had kicked the bucket:

An old Jew knocks on the gate of the Kremlin.

"May I see Comrade Stalin?" he says to the guard.

"What's with you, gramps? Haven't you heard? Comrade Stalin's died."

"Thank you, thank you," the Jew bows and leaves, only to return in a moment.

"Sorry to bother you, comrade," he says. "I have to have a word with Comrade Stalin."

"Haven't I told you already? Comrade Stalin's died."

"Thank you, thank you," says the Jew and leaves.

Soon he comes back.

"Just one brief word with Comrade Stalin, please!"

"Gosh!" the guard says. "Have you lost your marbles, gramps? How many times should I tell you, Comrade Stalin is dead, dead, dead!"

"Oh, thank you so much!" says the Jew. "Please forgive me. I can't hear it enough."

Yet, your parents have a hard time letting go of all the fears and anxieties of the postwar time. Like hoarding junkies, they didn't leave that dreadful yesteryear baggage in the old dwelling place. It seems they took it along.

However, as a fifteen-year-old, you don't want to have anything to do with the old life still on the minds of your parents. In the new apartment, not only is there a bit more space and air but there is also plenty of room for hope and belief in a brighter future.

~

Now, your mother sees it is useless to argue with you. She finds you brainwashed by school and by the ubiquitous state propaganda machine—newspapers and radio (Moscow's Central Television hasn't reached Odessa yet). However, she isn't a person who gives up easily.

"Well," she says, "you heard it from your teacher. Teacher-schmeacher! I want a second opinion."

She contacts the local paper and asks the book review department for an appointment. A tall, sad man with graying temples scans a few pages of your writing and shrugs. "Well, lady," he mutters, scratching his head, "it's hard to know how much of a literary gift your son has. There are good lines here and there, some striking metaphors. . . . Well, he's a young fellow. Let him try. See what happens. Besides, there's such a thing as a passion. Only time will tell whether he has enough of it. You know, if a baby's born with strong leg muscles, it doesn't mean it will grow up to be an Olympic medalist in track and field. He or she still needs to run, eager to win."

Then, he sighs and delivers a non sequitur: "Well, it's easier to become a writer than a literary critic. You need to know so much about so many things."

After the visit, your mom considers looking for a third opinion.

Then she gives up.

"Okay," she says, "since you're so stubborn, let's make a deal. If you receive a gold or silver medal, then you can try to apply wherever you feel like applying."

To improve the secondary education in the country, shortly after the end of the war, the authorities reinstated the incentive from tsarist time, abolished by the October revolution; they awarded medals to the most distinguished school graduates. Your mom looks at you with the compassionate gaze of a casino dealer who has noticed a poorly dressed man at his table, clutching a single dollar bill in his hand. Well, well, go ahead, chap, play for a while. Amuse yourself.

"When that fails," she continues, "you will forget about the things your teacher told you. Once and for all! And you'll go to an engineering school. At least it'll give you a piece of bread on the table. Okay?"

"What's there to try?" I mumble. "Why try? They accept anyone who gets a medal for high school to a college of their choice without exams. Those are the rules."

"Well," your mother says, "get a medal for your school studies first. Gold or silver. Worry about which college to apply to later. You have two more years of school, young man. So, get busy. Don't waste your time. Have you studied today?"

"Yes."

"Do more!"

"I've done enough," you say, annoyed.

"There is no such thing as enough for studying. Go!"

You argue with your mother no more. She issued her verdict. She's not a person you would want to mess with. Her decision is final, not subject to appeal.

2

The Evil Commas

In my youthful wanderings in the clouds of obscure daydreams and nebulous hopes, I have no inkling why my Mom is so obsessed with my
getting a medal at school. It will be several years down the road before I
will understand her anxiety around the time for my state exams.

The point of her worrying is not the medal itself, gold or silver, but
what lies ahead if her son doesn't receive a medal. I might not get into a
college. Not just the one in which I hope to enroll (i.e., the one with
courses in literature) but any institution at all. She hopes that with the
help of a medal, her son can force his way in. It has already been over two
years since Stalin died, but his unwritten anti-Semitic discriminatory
policies are still in place, and it seems they will remain forever. Whenever
my relatives get together, they talk about how hard it is for their children
to get accepted into college.

It is well known that school authorities manipulate entrance exams to
cheat Jewish applicants. There are jokes on the subject, but they are hardly
funny. Too much bitterness and anger in them, Jewish bitterness and
Jewish anger:

At the entrance exam in a prestigious college, they try to disqualify
a young Jewish man. They ask him a question that no one could
answer:
"Can you explain how Leo Tolstoy remembered himself from
the age of forty days?"
"So what!!" the applicant says. "I remember myself from the
time I was eight days old."
"So, tell us what you remember."

"I remember how an old Jew with a long gray beard came to our apartment, washed his hands, took a blade in his hand . . . and cut off my chances of being admitted to your college."

But why do I need to get into college, and why as soon as possible? Here's the catch—serving in the army is mandatory, but if you're enrolled in college before you turn nineteen, then you'll be saved from being a soldier and will be trained to serve as a reserve officer in the army. That means just taking classes on military equipment and two summers of training camp.

Mom thinks three years in the army is a sheer waste of time. It is better to get a degree, and the earlier you do it, the better. In her book, a Jew without a college degree is no Jew at all but some fruitcake. (A few years later, someone who is hardly fond of Jews will express the same opinion. In March 1958, in his interview with the Parisian newspaper *Le Figaro*, Nikita Khrushchev noted that a characteristic mark of the Jews is that they "are intellectuals by their very nature. . . . They never consider themselves educated enough. As soon as the opportunity arises, they want to enroll at a university, no matter what it takes.")

What makes Mom truly anxious about whether or not you are accepted to a college is that she knows very well what will happen to her son if, as the expression goes, they "rake him into the army." The verb in the saying accurately represents the nature of the action. You rake trash under your feet; the army treats its recruits the same way—like lowlife human trash. Rumors abound about what happens to them, one more frightening than the next. In the middle of the 1950s, *dedovshchina*, the brutal hazing in the army, was a horrendous phenomenon. For young Russian men, it began in the 1960s and 1970s, but for minority recruits, mainly Jews, it had existed for a long time before that.

It arose after World War II when those who had been drafted into the army had not been discharged. Some of them had served six or eight years. These soldiers came to be known as "the old guard," and from the army slang came words like "old man" (*starik*) and "grandfather" (*ded*). They had already smelled their fair share of gunpowder. Sometimes wounded and decorated for their valor in war, the grandfathers considered it their God-given right to lighten their service by placing most of their responsibilities on the shoulders of recruits.

Everyone from the officers down to the recruits empathized with the grandfathers. They had endured all the great burdens of the war. Therefore, as soon as a young soldier stepped into the garrison, he fell into slavery under these soldiers and sergeants. Besides direct military duties, other grandfather duties fell to the rookie, including such extra chores as cleaning latrines or tending to the livestock under the army's care. The recruit became a servant of the grandfather. He made his bed, washed his socks, stitched his collars, cleaned his boots, and ran on the double to the garrison shop for his smokes or liquor.

If only it had ended there! It was a matter of course to mock the rookie in every imaginable and unimaginable way. Grandfathers came up with tasks for him to complete, one more degrading than the next. Scrub the floor of the quarters with bottle shards. Measure the barrack's length and width with matchboxes. . . . The never-ending chores amounted to more than just mocking ridicule: there was poking, slapping, manhandling, and boxing of the rookie's ears. He was lashed with a belt and rewarded with boot blows to the ribs. Injuries occurred.

That is how it was during the day. At night, they granted the recruit neither respite nor peace. Quite the opposite: during the day, if an officer noticed the harassment getting out of hand, he could stop it. At night, the perpetrators could do as they pleased with their subordinates. They would take away his pillow after he fell asleep. They'd urinate in his boots. They'd start a "bicycle," placing a piece of cotton soaked in cologne between his toes and setting it afire. Sometimes they pulled down the sleeping re-cruit's trousers and tied a thread around his phallus.

If the greenhorn dared to ask why, what followed was the classic harasser's answer, "If we had a reason, we'd kill you. This is just to teach you a lesson."

So that was the mid-1950s. A decade later, nothing had changed for a young Jew sent to the army. The Odessan poet Igor Pototsky would write about his own experience from that time:

> For me, a Semite, being a nuisance to him,
> My Master Sarge beat me up at will,
> So I would obey his orders,
> As if my mama's given them.
> He was skilled in the beatings
> That leave no bruises.

Nobody wants to send offspring to the army, not just Jewish parents. Only a father belonging to the elite class could protect his son from the military. His child would be accepted to college without trouble by being put on the secret Rector's list. For everyone else, there was only one way to run from the army: get into college on one's own merits. So, Mom is dead serious about this. I, her son, must become a college student, and that's final. By any means, at any cost, through thick and thin.

My mother's hopes rest on the rule that those students who get a high-school distinction award, a gold or silver medal—and there is a good chance that, being a straight-A student for all ten school years, I would earn one—are spared from taking those treacherous college entrance exams.

(It would take me several years down the road to learn that my mother's hopes were quite naïve. To get rid of unwanted applicants, the admission committee subjected the high achievers to one-on-one interviews. Should any of the fellows turn out to be undesirable for any reason—being Jewish was one of them—they would reject them.)

~

The timing of the graduation exams is most unfortunate for Odessa high school students. It is mid-June; the summer's well under way, and this affects the senses of a young man. The buds on the trees have burst, and the foliage has wrestled its way through. Jasmine, lilac, and acacia have already blossomed, and the admixture of floral scents leaves me dizzy.

It is hard to concentrate for yet another reason. Now and then from the street, through the open windows of the classroom, comes girlish laughter. I and my classmates at my all-male school are seventeen years old already, some even older. A girl's voice excites me far more than any topic on the Russian literature final, be it "The Image of the Oppressed People in the Works of Alexander Pushkin" or "Oleg Koshevoy as a Typical Representative of Soviet Youth in Alexander Fadeev's *Young Guards*."

The examiners bring the list of these topics to the classroom in a wax-sealed envelope. Before breaking the seal and writing the questions out on the blackboard, the chairman of the state examination commission, a tall, middle-aged man sweating in his two-piece suit, plods around the desks, his nostrils flaring wider than those of a sniffer dog. He peers into the faces of the graduates-to-be. He guesses who among us has stocked up on cheat sheets.

The fact is that, despite the efforts of the public education officials, from year to year the same activity takes place. On the eve of the state exams, the classified questionnaires appear on the black market. Though everyone in town knows where they sell them, the authorities fail in catching the criminals.

Everyone knows they sell the questionnaire "at the Duke," that is, at the statue of the Duc de Richelieu, a French aristocrat who fled his country's bloody revolution and who was the first mayor of Odessa. They erected this monument at the top of the long, wide staircase that leads to the port of the city, made famous by Eisenstein's *Battleship Potemkin*. "The Duke" faces the sea, holding a blueprint of the future town in his outstretched hand. However, as an Odessa legend has it, it is not a blueprint of any kind; it is the high-school exam questionnaire, each year renewed.

"At the Duke" or not "at the Duke," come what may, my mom would get her hands on those classified questions for her son. But she knows it would hurt my self-esteem. I have received ten letters of commendation, one for each school year, so let the real flunkeys tremble on the eve of the exams, not me.

State exam time is also unsettling because the city is affected by the excitement of another annual tradition. In late May, after a year's voyage in the Antarctic, the whaling flotilla named "Glory" returns to its home port. The entire city is out in the streets greeting the fleet with pomp, just as the ancient Greeks cheered their warriors returning from the battle-fields, the heroes who saved the country from the invaders. Here, in Odessa, the whalers receive a heroes' welcome even though they hunt peaceful sea creatures. Peaceful, that is, if you do not hurl harpoons at them. They do not take it amicably.

Before entering the port, stretched out in the harbor, the squadron of ships roar as loud as they can. It all looks like a scene from Pushkin's *Tale of Tsar Saltan*: "Cannons with a mighty roar / Bid the merchants put to shore." The steamers moored in the port greet them with blasting sirens; following them, the Odessa factories blow their whistles. My heart skips a beat from the hum filling the Odessa sky. The noise reminds me, a child of war, of the German bombers and the air raid sirens.

At the pier, an orchestra blares, and champagne corks pop. While the whalers descend their ships' gangplanks, lush bouquets of Odessa's flowers—peonies and hyacinths—fall on their shoulders. Radio reporters shift from foot to foot, their microphones tilted toward the seafarers. As soon as the greeters spot Alexei Solyanik—the captain-director of the flotilla, Hero of Socialist Labor, and Member of the Central Committee

of the Communist Party—and the harpoon champion Piotr Zarva, everyone freezes.

When ordinary whalers appear on the ladder, they cannot be mistaken
for regular seamen. They wear suits made of some fabulous silver cloth,
never seen in our Spartan, postwar life. The crowd cheers enthusiastically
as if witnessing interplanetary visitors.

After leaving the port, the whalers head to the city center, to Deribasovskaya Street. A crowd swirls around each mariner. Schools of nimble
young men, their little cigarettes sticking out from the corners of their
mouths, rush to the sailors from all sides. They try to get close to the
whalers so they can whisper something in their ears while reaching for
the bags slung over their shoulders. These are black marketers, second-
hand dealers of foreign-made clothes. Police whistles blow. They try to
break up the gatherings: street trade is prohibited in the country.

The whalers waddle the way all sailors do when stepping ashore after a
long voyage. They stagger to the sidewalk edges with the unpredictability
of cannons dislodged from the decks of an old-time frigate in a storm.
Coming ashore, exhausted by hard labor in the holds of their flotilla ships,
the whalers pounce on alcohol and women, having spent many months
at sea without either. Wasted, they try pestering the passersby. Now and
then, the fights flare up. Sailors clench their belt buckles in their fists.
What would Russian festivities be without a scuffle!

Amid all this commotion, I am just thinking about my exams. It is not
only the students who are worried but the teachers too. A week before
exams start, they arrange extra class sessions to skill and drill us.

∼

The exams are over. Three exhausting weeks pass. Every now and again,
Mom runs to our school where the teachers post the exam results on a
board in the hallway. Finally, the day arrives when two lists appear. One
of them has the names of everyone who has passed the graduation exam
and the other—the names of those who have been awarded medals. My
mom does not even look for my name on the first list; she has no doubt
my name is on it. She peeks at the short list.

She stops breathing. She scans it again and again. She cannot believe
her eyes; her son's name is not on that list! How can that be? No medal
at all? No gold or even silver?

Horrified, my mom rushes to the principal, Vasyli Petrovich, a middle-aged man wearing an embroidered collarless shirt called a *kosovorotka*, which is part of the Ukrainian folk costume. His walrus mustache, à la Taras Shevchenko, the great Ukrainian poet, is gray. He throws up his hands after listening to my mother's concerns. More precisely, he throws up the one hand that survived the war. As if to say, *what* am I supposed to do? The regional commission decides the grade. He is not part of that commission.

My mother's face, pale with grief, causes him to dig through his file cabinet. He reports to her that her son has not one but two Bs—one in composition and the other in trigonometry. According to the rules, he is ineligible to receive any medals. If he received a B for one exam and an A for the second, then he could have earned a silver medal. But, as it stands, no medal at all, either gold or silver . . .

"Why!" Mom screams as if they have shoved a knife up to its hilt into her heart. "Why have they slaughtered him?"

She does not ask; she demands proof of why her son does not deserve a medal. She does it in the same voice, full of terrible quakes, in which Othello, suspicious of his wife's infidelity, demands the handkerchief treacherous Iago had slipped to him.

Though a war veteran, Vasily Petrovich tenses up while being confronted by my mom. He knows her well. She has been on the school's parent council for all ten school years. All this time she has tried to stay close to the school to be sure nothing unfair happened to her son. Now, it seems to her, her intuition proved to be right.

"Sofia Vladimirovna," says Vasyli Petrovich, wiping his bald head with a handkerchief. The sweat pours forth whenever his students' mothers attack him. "Please understand, nothing depends on me. The State Board . . . the Regional Board . . . look here, in the comments. In trigonometry, your son has earned a B, not an A, because his solution to the problem isn't the best possible. And, in his essay exam, he made two syntactic errors."

(Now, after over thirty years of teaching in America and recalling this episode from my youth, I find it hard to believe the rules for grading schoolwork in the Soviet Union in my time were so draconian. For one error in syntax, they reduced a pupil's grade by half a point, to A-; for two, by a whole point.)

"Syntactic!" my mom exclaims in disbelief. "What do you mean, syntactic?"

"I don't know, Sofia Vladimirovna," said the director. "Perhaps, some commas or dashes. . . . Maybe some colons or semicolons. I've never seen the tests. You know, it's the Commission's business . . . I'm not allowed."

"What! You've deprived my son of a well-deserved medal because of some lousy commas? What sort of commas? I want to see them with my own eyes."

"How do I know about those commas? Believe me, Sofia Vladimirovna, I would tell you if I knew. All the papers are at the Regional Board of Education. . . . Excuse me, I have to close my office now. They've summoned me to the Party district committee."

He wipes the sweat from his bald head again.

My mom comes home in turmoil. She walks around the apartment, wringing her hands. Her active nature abhors inactivity. What to do? How can she prove what she is sure of—that they graded her son's work unfairly? It does not occur to her I may have made a blunder: I am an excellent student. In desperation, she grabs her head, running her hands through her thick hair. She pulls it, trying to relieve her mental pain with the physical one. What does "not the best solution" mean in math? What is the criterion? Who can prove it one way or another? Where to find an independent and authoritative expert? Should she call some member of the All-Union Academy of Science, some PhD in mathematics from Moscow, for expert analysis? Like hell they would rush at the beck and call of some regular Sonya from Odessa!

In those years, when one clashed with the local authorities, it was common to flaunt state-issued awards to sway the government into treating you fairly. The awards for wartime effort were considered particularly powerful. Mama was proud of earning two medals, one for "Defending the Caucasus," the other for "Victory over Germany." When the war began, she had worked as a civilian in the repair shop of the Second Air Force, where my father was a serviceman. After being attacked by German planes, the shop workers rode five hundred miles on the freight train with the retreating troops from Odessa to the Caucasus and then another eight hundred miles to the northeast, all the way to Stalingrad. From there, they evacuated Mama and me with other refugees to Central Asia.

Mom decides her medals are not weighty enough to ensure that I will be admitted to college. Perhaps not a medal but an order would help.

Maybe the Red Star order or the Order of the Great Fatherland War would do. But these had been awarded to the military commanders. After Stalingrad, Mom spent most of the war fighting to save her only son from the cold, from hunger, from diseases—whooping cough, diphtheria, dysentery, pneumonia, typhus, and typhoid fever, to name a few. They did not award mothers for saving their children's lives.

All she still hopes for is that they will award me a silver medal at least. If the math question is debatable and challenging to solve, all her faith now lies in the essay. Two commas, ha! It is as if Mom is weighing whether there is enough of the old dogfight in her for *both* revisions. I need to have an A in composition; otherwise, there would not be any medals. She glances at me. I think, for a moment, she harbors doubt and her eyes flash reproach. *How did you manage! A solid-A student, ten letters of commendation, and here you are. . . . Did you have to screw up in the most crucial of moments?*

However, she takes control of herself and decides there is no reason to dwell on this. She must act, and she must do it now.

"That cannot be!" She shakes her head, sweeping away any doubts.

She rushes to the office of the district department of public education, determined to see her son's essay. She wants to see it with her own eyes.

The sun had already begun its descent. Bars of light blaze on the far corner of the reception room's ceiling. Then they thicken, redden, and disappear. As happens all the time in many Soviet institutions, by the end of the day, the regional officials have slipped away from work under various pretexts. In the office, only a young secretary stays behind to answer the phone. Mom demands that the secretary hands over my exam.

The secretary is about to get rid of her with the bureaucratic phrase, "It's not allowed," but it won't fly with my mom. She is not your typical Soviet petitioner who, at the first rebuff, recedes into the hall, apologizing for any inconveniences caused. No way! Mom is not easily tamed.

Unable to withstand the pressure, the secretary concedes. She allows my mother to look over my writing. She pulls a yellow school notebook with my name on it from a drawer.

Mom devours the cover with her eyes. On it, in ink, thick and dark-red as if it were devil's blood, she sees the "B" mark with "0/2" next to it, which means the examiner found zero grammatical errors and two syntactic. The letter is so large she thinks those who had drawn it gloated in delight as if extending the middle finger, saying, "Fat chance! No gold or silver medal to you, Jewboy!"

That only enrages my mom. She still does not believe it. She wants to see the proof of why I received the downgrade. She leafs through the notebook. Yes, there are two syntax errors. Both extra commas. Both are crossed out as superfluous.

She peers at the insolent commas that have snuck into her son's essay. Not for a second does she believe her son made these mistakes. He couldn't have! Her son couldn't have put commas where they shouldn't have been. He couldn't, that's that! She was convinced that somebody else's hand, the hand of an enemy, a vicious perpetrator, had written them in.

She brings the notebook to the window first. But it is already getting dark, and she sticks it under the light of a desk lamp, which the secretary turns on for her. Mom devours the damned commas with her eyes with no less fury than Louis Pasteur felt when spotting malicious organisms under a microscope. Her case is far more worthy than rendering milk harmless. She need not save humanity in all its abstraction. She must save her son.

That's it! That's what she suspected all along! It's fake! To fail her son, they've stooped to forgery. The ink of both unnecessary commas is not purplish-blue like the rest of the essay but blue-black, the color of the sky before a thunderstorm. Suffused with the anger, mom's eyes are also getting dark.

Mom rolls the notebook into a tube, determined to take it wherever necessary for expert analysis. Even to the office of the Minister of Education or the Prosecutor General of the Ukrainian Soviet Socialist Republic.

The secretary, a young girl who perhaps graduated from high school the year before, kneads a handkerchief in her hands and, realizing that she cannot stop my mother, blows her nose into it. *Please, please give the notebook back, Miss. They'll fire me. . . . They'll sue me for disclosing official secrets. . . . My mom won't be able to bear it. . . . My father perished in the war.*

After a long internal struggle, my mom backs down. Even in a moment of grave danger to her son, she cannot overcome herself. She is incapable of punishing the secretary for the sins of other people.

All too clear! They have committed a crime. Of this Mom has no doubt. But how to prove it! How to make the local board hand over the essay for forensic analysis? And who would be willing to investigate it? Sherlock Holmes?

She returns home, tells of her discovery, and says, "Now you see the country you live in!" She is sure of one thing. They have rigged my exam for one reason: I am a Jew.

That day, she sits down on the couch next to me, hugs me and weeps. Affected by her sobbing, my eyes also moisten. I do not feel as sorry for myself as I feel for her. She had hoped so much!

I try to understand why she is so upset. At first, I believe it is a matter of pride. For all ten years of my schooling, she has supervised my studies to ensure that I am an excellent student. She has taken any B mark I earned as a personal offense, as a sign of disrespect for her feelings. For ten years, her efforts have been rewarded: at the end of each school year, I have received a sheet of yellow paper with portraits of Lenin and Stalin on it, stamped and signed by the school principal, "For excellent academic achievement and good behavior." And now this disaster!

My mom, however, is mistaken in believing the episode with the exams has opened my eyes to the injustice. Somehow, I am not surprised the medal, neither gold nor silver, didn't come my way. Unlike my mom, I believe I alone am to blame. By this time, I am accustomed already to blaming myself for everything. I brush aside her suspicions of foul play and decide that not receiving a medal is all my fault. I did not check over my work well enough. I made this mess, and I deserve to suffer the consequences. Every day, newspapers, magazines, radio, and the teachers at the school assure me that every person is the "blacksmith of his or her happiness" in my country.

I keep telling myself that my grade is correct, that I am not worthy of any medal. However, at night, visions of the two fateful commas come to me, bringing with them the third one. They come as the Russian epic heroes Ilya Muromets, Dobrynya Nikitich, and Alyosha Popovich, prancing on their horses and complimenting one another on the fact they have not blundered, that they have defended the honor of Russian land. They prevailed over their nemesis, the Jewish youngster who took it into his head to go not to any school—get a load of this!—but to a school of his choice. What nerve he had, the insolent fellow!

~

Half a century later, the mystery of my failure was dispelled by chance. I was not aware that in those days there were distribution lists for medals. They decided in advance how many gold and silver medals would go to each school. The decoration in my class went to my fellow student Peter Orlenko. In my memory, he is a lanky boy with a flexible body and a handsome, gentle face studded with brown Ukrainian eyes and full lips. He looked very much like his mother.

A bright student, he learned easily. At the blackboard to give a report in front of the class, he would place his hands behind his back and recite the assigned poems by heart, rolling his eyes in boredom, or solve a geometry problem with a lazy disposition. After writing the solution on the board, he would lick his chalk-stained fingers (it looked like he lacked calcium intake). We had a civil, respectful relationship. From afar, we would glance at each other like runners sizing up their next-lane neighbor before the start of a race: we both had to fight for a medal. Everyone in our class knew it.

But my chances of success were not the same as Peter's. His father belonged to the elite ruling subclass, called the *nomenklatura*. He was a prominent official at the port of Odessa and, before that, had been the head of the important northern port of Murmansk; he was an Order bearer. Peter's mother worked as a secretary for the rector of the Institute of Civil Engineering and had close connections to City Hall. That I was of humble origins (my father was a housepainter) and Jewish, no less, made it easy for those deciding who would get the medals in my school. There was no shred of doubt whom they would cross off the list of candidates.

In the early twentieth century, the famous Odessa journalist Vlas Doroshevich reported how the question of whom to accept to Odessa University had been resolved in his time. When they exhausted every conceivable way to reduce the number of competitors, they checked out each potential student's ethnicity. The chair of the admission committee would be overjoyed: "What luck! When you have to strike someone from the list of prospects, you won't find anyone better than a Jew."

That is how it was half a century earlier. Since then, Russia has undergone two revolutions, and two world wars have cast their thunder. With all that, nothing had changed by the time I am a teenager living in Russia. . . .

~

In that blazing summer of 1955, it will fall to me to take part in an even greater drama: getting into college.

3

A Fortress Named College

"Let me tell you, Sonya. It's ugly out there," Big Abram says.

July in Odessa is the hottest time of the year in all senses of the word. At night, two kinds of people cannot fall asleep: the sunburned vacationers from the north and the Jewish parents whose offspring have applied to one of the local temples of higher education.

When the fact of my medal fiasco sinks into my mother's consciousness, she mourns the way one does after a family member who, while expected to live a long and prosperous life, suddenly expires. From the corner of my eye, I see my mother sitting on a chair turned to the wall, moving her body back and forth the way Orthodox Jews do while praying. It seems odd: she is only borderline religious.

Coming from an observant Jewish family, she had adjusted her religiosity to the Soviet reality of the time. Short of forbidding religion altogether, the powers that be strongly discouraged it. So, my mom keeps her religion on a strict diet. She observes only the Yom Kippur (the Day of Atonement) rituals to the letter. Together with my father, she spends the day fasting and visiting the temple, the only one in all of Odessa. All other religious holidays, be it Rosh Hashanah or Hanukkah, Purim or Passover, she celebrates by cooking and baking her signature dishes— gefilte fish and strudel—and bringing our whole extended family (*mishpocha*) over to dinner. That is about all. In practical matters, she never counts on God's helping hand, thus doubting the veracity of his other name—the Almighty.

As soon as she regains the senses she lost after my failure to receive the medal for school performance, she decides to fight the momentous battle she has hoped to avoid. She has resolved to do whatever it takes for me to succeed. After all, she had fought bigger and more dangerous battles for her son's sake. She had saved me many times during the not-so-distant war. She rushed me to the bomb shelters at the first sound of the German bombers roaring in the sky. When on the run from the advancing Nazis, she pulled me from makeshift hospital wards where I lay bedridden, struck down with about a dozen ailments, one after another. When there was nowhere else to run, she turned the starving city of Tashkent upside down to find scraps of food for her famished child.

As the season of filing college applications starts, mom's first move is to seek our extended family's council. She calls it a *consilium. Con-si-li-um* . . . they revere this Latin word in Odessa. It has a serious, life-or-death ring to it. It smells of medicine and evokes an image of a quiet hospital ward where gray-haired luminaries of medical science gather for a conference. Smoothing their beards and scratching their heads in thought, they decide the fate of a terminally ill patient. What can they do to save him? Does he have a fighting chance to make it?

For my mom, the case at hand is no less fateful than the threat of some fatal disease. Saturday night comes, and, at the doorway of our apartment, my relatives appear one by one. Their faces are unsmiling, even somber, as if they must observe another, out of the yearly schedule, Yom Kippur. The difference is that, instead of fasting, as soon as they step into our apartment, they take seats around the dinner table crammed with Mama's cooking and baking.

They eat, their eyes downcast. They feel awkward. They walk a fine line. Of course, they want to let the hostess know how upset they are by the unfortunate turn in the life of her Milya (they use my domestic name) and her own life. They know how much she was counting on him earning that darn medal. At the same time, they do not want her to think they are not delighted, as usual, by her culinary art. She has an unshakable reputation for being the great cook in the family.

Two of my uncles are both named Abram in their Soviet passports. However, while everyone calls one by his diminutive, Abrasha, the other one goes by the name Big Abram. He is married to my mother's sister, Clara, a brunette of biblical beauty with her big dark eyes reflecting her every emotion. Similarities between the two men stop with their given name. While Abrasha is of average height and soft-mannered, Big Abram is tall and wide-shouldered with large facial features. He always wears his steel-framed glasses, and he speaks loudly and authoritatively. During the war, Big Abram served in the artillery unit as a gun layer. Maybe this is why he delivers his thoughts in the same way he shot open-fire rounds on the battlefields.

It is at this point he cleanses his palette with a shot of vodka and says: "Let me tell you, Sonya, it's bad out there. . . . It's ugly. . . . It's almost as bad for us Jews now as it was back when Yoska was still alive and kicking."

It takes me some time to realize that he uses the off-hand diminutive Yoska, having only the larger-than-life Joseph Stalin, the deceased Soviet leader, in mind.

"Don't even waste your time breaking your head over where your Milya has to apply," he continues. "We all know he's a capable *boychik*."

He gives me an approving look but looks away, as if to say whether I have the smarts is beside the point. It does not matter in the current political climate.

"A law school?" he keeps on. "Forget it! Everybody knows they reserve it for future police officers and the KGB cadres. They don't want us Yids in their ranks. . . . The Moscow Institute of Eastern Languages? Or the Foreign Commerce Institute? Forget it. Both colleges prepare future diplomats. Have you ever heard about any Jewish Soviet diplomat?"

Big Abram pauses for dramatic effect. Then, shaking his head in disapproval, he continues: "Don't even strain your brain! It's been ages. Over fifteen years ago . . . before the war broke out. . . . The man's name was Maxim Litvinov. . . . Meir Wallach-Finkelstein was his real name. People's Commissar of Foreign Affairs! He represented the Soviet Union in the League of Nations! And what happened to him? Back in March 1939, Yoska decided to cozy up to Adolf Hitler, to soften the monster up before signing the hideous Molotov-Ribbentrop Pact a few months down the road. He dismissed Litvinov from his position to please the Fuhrer. So, do you know what those bastards at the admission committees in there, in the Eastern Languages or Foreign Commerce institutes, do when they get an application from a Jewish kid?"

Now he pauses, peering into my mother's face with a scrutinizing look, as if his question were not merely rhetorical.

"I'll tell you what they do with that application over there," he announces to the hushed room.

By now, my uncle's omniscience overwhelms everyone around the table. They try not to miss a word of his insight into the mysterious world of the institutions of higher education.

"As soon as they see the sender's surname on the envelope, be it Gold-berg, Silberman, or . . . Draitser," Uncle Abram shoots me a quick dis-approving look, confirming that yes, he suspects I may have such a stupid idea in my head, to apply for one of those highbrow schools, "they take that envelope, and, without even opening it, they toss it into the nearest wastebasket."

As if his words were not enough to illustrate his point, Uncle Abram grabs the paper napkin next to his plate, and, after scanning the room for a wastebasket and not finding one, he throws the crumpled-up napkin into the farthest corner.

"Do you know why they are doing it?"

He holds a long theatrical pause before he continues: "Because, in their minds, it's bad enough that the applicant is a Jew. He also must be feeble-minded if he wastes his time and money sending his documents to their institute. Over there, they hardly consider *any* Aryan [that is, Russian] boy worthy of their attention. For that, be a scion of a member of the Russian elite—a son of a general or a diplomat. Don't you know our Soviet elite replenishes its ranks through reproducing its kind? Like an amoeba, it multiplies through simple division."

Everyone around the table is silent for a while, overwhelmed by Big Abram's rhetoric and hypnotized by his graphic demonstration of the fate awaiting a Jewish applicant who dares to apply to an institution where he is not welcome.

Getting it all off his chest, Big Abram has exhausted all his energy, which he must restore right away. From a plate in the table's center, he grabs a piece of my mother's other signature dish, chicken cutlets. He gobbles it up as if in a cannibalistic fit meant not only to obliterate the enemy but to discourage other foes from attacking.

Though she does not totally buy whatever Big Abram says, my mom still gets nervous listening to him talk. She expects to hear something con-structive from her guests, not have another pail of freezing water poured all over her.

My father does not take part in the debates. He eats, pausing with his fork in midair to ponder something. No one expects any input from him. Everyone in my extended family knows well that my mother is the one who wears the pants in our family.

Everyone in the neighborhood, including the district police officer, knows well her resolute character, her ability to stand up for herself. As his job stipulates, the officer has to be in contact with the public representatives. My mom serves as one. She is a spokesperson for our building tenants, even though everyone knows the authorities care little about what the tenants have to say.

From an open window, the sound of a recent smash hit breaks into the room:

Mishka, Mishka, where's your smile,
Full of grit and fire?
How silly of you
Dumping one who loves you.

As if prompted by the jolly tune, my other uncle Abrasha (little Abram) tries to cheer everyone up. To soften the effect of Big Abram's heavy-artillery speech, he chuckles and takes a conciliatory tone.

"Look, we all know how bad it is out there," he says. "But let's be realistic. Why worry about some elite foreign language institute for no reason? Has our Milya ever even contemplated a diplomatic career? I don't think so."

He gives me a quick warm look, designed to assure me he does not doubt my intellectual potentials, but he counts on my common sense. A Soviet Jewish diplomat? There were some of them, even prominent, before the Hitler-Ribbentrop pact. But nowadays?

"Yes, it's true," he continues, "that, most likely, they won't take him at either of our nautical schools in Odessa—the Maritime School of Commerce or the Naval Academy. Is it a secret why? You know when you graduate, they have to send you overseas. And they know, given an opportunity, any of us Yids will skip the country forever. . . . And they're right!" he chuckles. "*Halevai!*" he adds in Yiddish, which I know already means *It should only be so.*

"Then why get upset about the fact they discriminate against Jews over there? Besides, let's be frank, is our Milya sailor material? He's an intellectual, for God's sake. And such boys are always in demand at the Odessan Credit and Finance College. Let him apply there. Why not capitalize on their belief that all Jews are born Rothschilds? Not regarding being filthy rich, mind you, but regarding them knowing how to count money."

Abrasha talks with authority because he practices what he preaches: he works as a bookkeeper at one of Odessa's small factories.

One of my father's close friends and colleagues, Adolf Marshak, also attends the *consilium*. Marshak is a former actor of the Jewish theater in Odessa. With the onslaught of German armies, they moved the theater to Central Asia. With the war over, in the wake of Stalin's campaigns against the "rootless cosmopolitans," they disbanded the theater and let all the actors go. Marshak hurry-scurry learned the wallpaper-hanging business. Now and then, he turns to his beloved profession when visiting close friends and entertaining them.

Marshak understands that, at today's meeting, his comedic skills will be uncalled for. The conversations around the table make him shake his head. Judging by the sad smile on his face, it is clear he does not have much enthusiasm regarding what, after all their deliberation, my relatives will recommend for my future profession. Although he does not know about my secret literary ambitions, he guesses that my fate will resemble his. I will be forced to make a living by doing who-the-hell-knows-what for the sake of sustenance—whether it be accounting, or some technical stuff, or, maybe, just like him, hanging wallpaper—and only on the side in my spare time doing what I love most.

My father's younger brother, my Uncle Misha, joins the party. For several years after being discharged from the army, he has worked with my father painting houses. He is the business's powerhouse. He uses his muscles to pump up the pressure of the compressed air my father needs for his air gun. Besides whitening ceilings, painting doors and window frames, and hanging wallpaper, my father, with his help, does stenciling. He spray-paints blue and white pairs of circles at equal distances from one another.

My uncle is a former tank commander. He served as a master sergeant of his company. He is more used to giving orders than following them. Now, he has to swallow his pride and do what his older brother asks him to do.

Now he takes his seat, pours himself a shot of vodka, and, grasping the bone of contention of the roundtable talk, turns toward me. He raises his glass and says loud enough for everyone to hear him: "Little Milya, dear boy! Don't listen to anyone here. Trust me, it's all blah-blah-blah. . . . Bullshit, no more than that. When you decide what school you will apply to, let me know just one thing—the name of the school's dean. That's all! Let me worry about the rest. So, *khaverim*, let's cheer up. May you have your health and *parnuse! L'haim!*" he finishes, without bothering to explain himself.

I know by now what the Yiddish words he uses mean. *Khaverim* is comrades, *parnuse* is income, and *l'haim* is "to life." But his request that I give him the name of the purported dean of the school will remain a mystery for at least two years down the road.

~

In the meantime, as the Odessan summer rolls in, I learn bit by bit what it takes to be a Jewish applicant seeking higher education. The whole picture of how the college admission committees operate in Odessa finally sinks in. As a history buff, I imagine such a committee as a defense squad perched atop a medieval fortress. They do whatever they can to stop the advancing enemy—Jewish boys and girls trying to get into a college.

In the good old days, there were plenty of simple and effective means, sanctified by ancient tradition, at the disposal of the fortress defenders. They cast arrows. They hurled stones. They poured molten pitch on the heads of the climbers. Spiked clubs in hand, they split the skulls of the rascals who had reached the top of the fortress.

So much for ancient history. Nowadays, the college admission committee members envy their predecessors of the tsarist times. Back then, there was no headache over how to stop a Jew from getting a higher education. Official stipulations were crystal clear. Within the Pale of Settlement, the prescribed area in which Jews were allowed to live, the population of Jewish college students could not exceed 10 percent; outside the Pale, no more than 5. End of story.

Alas, in postwar Odessa, none of these things would work. The country's constitution states that all hundred-odd ethnic groups populating the country are to be treated equally. What a drag! The heads of college admission boards have to rack their brains over how to make sure no Jewish kid makes it into their temple of higher learning, all the while leaving no trace of discrimination.

For starters, even detecting a Jew is not always that easy. It is a no-brainer if the applicant is marked as Jewish in his papers. Everyone must carry an internal passport in which its owner's ethnicity is specified. But what if he or she is *mixed grains*, a half-Jew? How do you fish these people out? If one parent is Jewish and the other is Russian or Ukrainian, you can bet, if they are sane, of course, they had marked their offspring as Russian or Ukrainian. Go figure what to do under such murky circumstances!

Letting in a half-Jew could still get you into hot water for "contaminating the national cadres," as the secret instructions sent from the government of the Ukrainian Socialist Republic in Kiev have it. Odessa is part of Ukraine, so the professional cadres *should* be composed primarily of Ukrainians.

When, with God's help, they finally discover people of a "nonindigenous nationality," as they call Jews in the Soviet press, the only thing left to do is to make sure they fail the entrance exams.

It is easier said than done. The Jewish entrant knows he or she has to prepare for the exams no less vigorously than Rocky Balboa for his world championship fight.

To fail an entrant on written examinations is a nuisance. *Show me where the error is. Why was I given a C or even an F?* Now you go and prove it. Admission counselors across the country prefer oral exams. That way, they can do so much more to derail the Jewish entrant. For starters, they give him a hard math problem with only a few minutes to solve it. When you press the examinee with time, there are plenty of opportunities to distract, badger, interrupt, or confuse him or her. In those rare cases when, despite all efforts, the entrant solves the problem, it is still possible for the proctor to announce that the exam is over and fail him or her. Try proving otherwise! As a Russian proverb has it, "A word is not a sparrow: once it's out, you won't catch it."

Here in Odessa, in the provinces, they fail Jewish applicants right and left by throwing them one curveball after another, often from the outfield, from beyond the high school program. One day, my cousin Eva, the daughter of my mother's sister Clara, stops by to share her sad news. She has applied to the pharmacy school. During her chemistry exam—her last one, which meant that if they did not fail her, they would have to accept her—the examiner asked, raising his brow into a Mephistophelean arc, "What is the Zinin reaction?"

There had not ever been a single word about this reaction in the school textbook. To the examiner's dismay, Eva had read everything she could find about pharmaceuticals. She had been dreaming of becoming a druggist since childhood.

She answered, "It's a reaction between aniline and hydrogen."

The examiner's heart sank: the accursed Jewess knew that too. What to do now, for Christ's sake! How to stop this villain of a girl!

He threw another curveball: "A reaction with hydrogen of what kind?"

"Atomic hydrogen," she replied.

"And what is the name of the 'moment' of this reaction?" the examiner uttered desperately.

Here, no matter how hard Eva jogged her memory for the name of the "moment," she could not recall.

The examiner could hardly hide his triumph, taking his time to draw an "F" against Eva's surname in the grade roster. He saved the citadel of enlightenment from Jewish dominance.

In tears, Eva went to the drugstore where she worked and asked the pharmacist, a specialist with many years of experience, about the "moment of the Zinin reaction," but neither he nor any of his colleagues at other pharmacies could remember the name of that faithful "moment" when aniline grappled in mortal combat with atomic hydrogen.

Things went no better for Eva's newlywed husband, Yefim Ingerman. During the physics exam at Odessa University, while hardly listening to him, the examiner kept uttering, "A wrong aria from a wrong opera."

Rigged entrance exams have become so widespread that Jews all over the country shake their heads, telling each other the same bitter joke:

"What's a Purim miracle?"
"A Jewish boy getting into Moscow University."

In Odessa, the birthplace of go-getters, Jewish applicants' parents have come up with ways to deal with this desperate situation. They have honed their technique to perfection. First, they present a secretary of college admissions with a box of chocolates and a vial of "Red Moscow" perfume. In return, they ask for a trifle or favor—the list of the college's examining professors. Then, through the same secretary, they offer the professors a moonlighting opportunity—tutoring a high-school student readying himself to apply to college. They pay the tutor well if he teaches his pupil everything one should know to pass the entry exam with flying colors.

In time, a black market of these private tutors evolved in Odessa. Not every Jewish family could cough up so much cash. Not my family, for sure. That is why I am surprised that I pass the entrance exams with little trouble, and they accept me as a first-year student in the Department of Electrical Engineering at the Odessa Polytechnic Institute. It is true that, an all-around A student in my secondary school, I have been well prepared for the exams. However, the way they conducted them was odd. They hardly gave me much opportunity to show my knowledge. Soon after I began answering the questions, my examiners consulted some list and, apparently discovering they should not fail me, stopped me and gave me a good grade.

The mystery was cleared up for me two years down the road. It happened by sheer accident. One day, while passing my department dean's office, his secretary stopped me and asked if I would not mind delivering a package to the dean's house after my classes. It turned out he lived nearby. I agreed.

The woman of the house answered the door. While I handed over the package, the sight of the living room wall startled me. I did not believe my own eyes. Blue and white pairs of circles, spray-painted. . . . Little cherry branches strewn with white flowers and green leaves. . . . This was my father's and my Uncle Misha's signature work.

I was shocked and staggered at this revelation. My heart sank. So, that is why my examiners had stopped me way before I had finished answering my questions! It looked like my father and my uncle had not played dice with my chance of getting into a college just on the strength of my knowledge. To be on the safe side, they had resorted to softening up the dean with their services, free of charge.

PART II

Serendipity, 1964

4

The Sudden Offer

"Where are you from? From Odessa? Oh, then why don't you write satire for us?" the editor says.

It is the beginning of May 1964. Four years have elapsed since I graduated from the Odessa Polytechnic Institute with a BS in electrical engineering. First, I worked as an assembly unit supervisor at the Kiev Assembly Directorate #3 in the gas industry. After that, they transferred me to one of the research labs near Moscow. Having been denied a chance to receive an education in the humanities, I have accepted that to do what you *have* to, not what you *want* to, is part and parcel of being an adult.

My work in the lab is no sweat. There is not much to do there, not just for me but also for most of the people employed there. Overstaffing is a measure taken to ensure that there is no unemployment in the country. To kill time at lunch we organize chess tournaments, which, if no bosses are around, stretch out until the end of the working day. Out of boredom, I have even come up with some technical innovations for the gas-pumping stations. To implement them, I have made several trips to one of these stations in the town of Klin, near Moscow. As in other small Russian towns, brutal, horrific boredom creeps over the local citizens in the evenings, drying out their brains; they fight it off with moonshine.

Fed up with my job, I find refuge in writing. The scribbler's bug that bit me in my teens has not let me go. I jot down whatever I feel like writing—some diary entries, some sketches. I am not sure whether any of my work is good. If only they would publish at least some of my scrawling! Just that would prove I am not fooling myself, that I have at least a shred of what it takes to make a real writer. A writer! It is something I can only dream about. The term is highly revered in Russian culture; it is not to be used in vain.

Scriptwriter Boris Lobkov

On one of my days off, I decide to visit Boris Lobkov, my old Odessan friend. Like me, Boris received an engineering degree, in his case from the Odessa Institute of Marine Engineers, even though he has always been drawn to the cinema. A few years older than me, he also could not pursue the higher education he wished. For him, times were even more trying than in my case: in 1952, Stalin was still alive.

Boris is one of the most jovial people I have ever met. Round-eyed, corpulent, puffy-cheeked, he is one big cuddly panda of a man. Enchanted by his extraordinary zest for life, women cling to him. He likes it all, whether it is good food, good music, or a good joke. His whole being makes you ask, "How can anyone be in a bad mood when life is so full of joy?" Just being in his company makes me feel better about myself, and my most sour mood dissipates.

Eventually, Boris migrated to Moscow, and, thanks to his charm and talent, he broke into scriptwriting. He writes scripts for both feature films and documentaries.

Boris lives with his wife, Tanya, in the Mariina Roshcha district, on the other end of town. On my way to visit him, I decide to make a stop in the downtown area and visit the editorial offices of the newspaper

Moscow Komsomol Member (Moskovskij komsomolets). It is one of Moscow's well-regarded papers of the time. Under the rubric "The Creative Work of Our Readers," they publish short pieces written not by professional writers but by ordinary folks. Well, I have decided I qualify for that as I *am* one of the paper's readers.

I take along a few of my literary sketches that seem more polished than others. My feeling is a disproportionate mixture of hope and fear. I have some confidence, but I am petrified at the prospect of rejection. What if my scribbling is not good enough to be published even as amateur writing?

I exit the Clear-Water Ponds (*Chistye Prudy*) subway station and walk around for a while until I find the paper's editorial offices a block away. A few pages of my sketches in hand, I wander along the corridors, passing by many doors, typewriters rattling and telephones ringing beyond them. It smells of paper glue and used coffee grounds. Some parts of the halls are poorly lit. Here and there, floorboards creak under my feet, as they do in a typical Soviet public office.

I stop at one door with the cutout of the headline "Our Readers' Creative Corner" pasted on it. There is a sign with the "Corner" editor's name—Yan Vishnevetsky.

I tap on the door and, since nobody answers, I enter the room. A tall man in his early forties, his head full of curly dark hair graying at the temples, his bulging eyes red from smoking, keeps on typing without raising his head.

He finally sees I do not know how to introduce myself and where to start. He tears himself away from his typewriter and, without saying a word, pulls the pages from my clenched fingers and does something I did not expect him to do: he reads my sketch right then and there.

First, out of surprise, I freeze. Then my heart pounds faster. Here is the moment of truth. My throat dries up. I try to swallow, but there is no saliva in my mouth. Why does it take the man so long? It is just three pages, for God's sake!

Well, now he has made it to the second page. He knits his brow in one place. Is it that bad? . . . Now it looks like he is grinning. What the hell! Can he stop dragging it out and deliver his verdict, so it can be over and done?

At last, the man puts my papers down on his desk. Before saying anything, he draws back his shoulders, works the muscles, and tries to smooth his unruly curls.

"Well," he says, scratching behind his ear with his pencil. "It's written well, all right. But . . ."

Oh hell, there is some "but" there, after all.

"But," he continues, "we're a newspaper here. We need something topical . . . something with a fighting spirit."

I feel both relieved and disappointed. Gosh, the editor likes my piece, but it seems he is not too eager to publish it.

I hardly tune in to what he is talking about now. The man asks me some questions, trying to find out who I am. Self-conscious, I force myself to mumble in response that my day job is engineering, but I am keen on penning literary sketches, the kind I have brought to show him.

"You speak with some accent," Vishnevetsky says. "Where are you from? Oh, you're from Odessa? Well, why didn't you tell me that in the first place? You should write a satirical piece for us."

He sorts through the pile of papers on his desk, pulls out an unsealed, stamped envelope and extends it to me.

"There isn't enough material for a full-length satirical article here," he says. "For starters, write us a short piece. Call whoever you think you need to check it out and give us, say, a hundred lines."

I take the letter. The telephone on the editor's desk rings; he grabs it and engrosses in conversation.

I flip over the envelope the editor has handed me. I scan the letter. It is something about the poor quality of baby rompers.

My first reaction is that of disappointment. What should I do with such boring stuff? Can't the editor give me something more fun to write about?

I wait for a while, shifting from foot to foot, hoping to talk to him. Then, I realize he will be busy for a long time, and I leave.

I head back to the subway station, mulling over what has just happened. The sudden offer to write for the paper catches me off guard. It baffles me. A whole gamut of emotions runs through me at this moment in my life. On one hand, I am disappointed that he did not take my lyric sketch, though he seemed to like it. On the other, he gave me some boring letter and asked me to write a satirical piece based on it. If I am good at doing a short one, then, perhaps, they may commission me to write a full-length lampoon, called a feuilleton. What should I do? Am I cut out for writing such stuff?

I know what a feuilleton is. I have read lots of them. I have always been in love with the printed word. While wandering along Odessa streets as a youth, I would rush to newsstands along the way. There, in the glass-covered showcases, they displayed not only our local Odessa-based papers both in Russian, *The Bolshevik Banner* (Bol'shevistkoe znamya), and Ukrainian, *The Black-Sea Commune* (Chernomor'ska Komuna), but also the papers published in Kiev (*Pravda Ukrainy*) and Moscow—*Pravda, Izvestiya, Literary Gazette*, and several others. I rushed to read them, hoping to find a new feuilleton. This satirical format combined journalistic and novelistic elements; its language was much livelier than that of the rest of the newspaper. Feuilletons addressed people's wrongdoings but did so playfully, using the whole bag of comic tricks—sarcasm, irony, puns, you name it.

That was the only part of a Soviet newspaper that did not bore me to death. They filled the rest of the printed space with bombastic reports about the great victories of socialism, be it an opening of an electrical power plant ahead of schedule or a successful harvesting campaign. None of this news excited me.

Now that I have an offer to contribute to this favorite Moscow paper, I am confused. It is one thing to enjoy reading feuilletons and quite another to write one. On the logo of the main satirical magazine in the country, *Crocodile*, the aquatic reptile has a pipe in its oversized teeth, the pipe some old salt smokes. Give me a break! Me, an old salt? Though I was born and raised in a seaside city, I am hardly made of nautical fabric.

The crocodile mascot implies that a satirist should be sharp-toothed, bloodthirsty, and aggressive. By nature, I hardly qualify. I am too shy. As a student, I tried to get rid of this defect of character by joining the theater club at my Odessa Polytechnic Institute. Stepping on the stage not as yourself but as some character in a play helps you overcome your inborn timidity. The moment I did it for the first time I was no longer myself but a student named Misha in the play *The Immortals* (Vechno zhivye) by Victor Rozov. That year, back at the Mosfilm Studios, they were busy making the movie based on this play. *The Cranes Are Flying* won the Palme d'Or at the Cannes Film Festival. Together with his girlfriend, Misha arrives at a birthday party for the mistress of Mark, the husband of Veronica, the film's heroine. (This episode didn't make it to the screen.)

The part did not demand much transformation. Like the character I played, I was also a student. Like Misha, I was a romantic; I considered only matters of a higher order worthy in life. I also believed that all people are good by nature.

With my legs made of cotton, I stepped onto the stage of our Odessa Ukrainian Drama Theater rented for the evening by the college. The floor beneath me careened the way a ship's deck does in stormy weather. In the darkness of the crowded auditorium, there were only pinkish spots, the spectators' faces. From below my chest, as if from a loudspeaker, someone's hoarse voice blurted out the first line of my part. I was not supposed to be funny, but the dark hall roared with good-natured laughter.

After my first stage appearance, they typecast me as a romantic and shy college student. Next summer in Odessa, they invited me to play a similar part in *The Course Is Set on the Spring* (Kurs na vesnu), a play written by the same Boris Lobkov whom I am on my way to visit now. The citywide student theater called Parnassus-2 staged it. This Soviet equivalent of Chicago's Second City improvisational theater also became an incubator for future celebrities—comedians, actors, and writers. There, at Parnassus-2, the famous standup comedian and writer Mikhail Zhvanetsky, actors Victor Ilchenko, Roman Kartsev (né Kats), and Nikolai Gubenko, who later would become the last Soviet minister of culture, launched their careers.

～

Looking back at myself, the eighteen-year-old, I realize where the needle of my destiny moved in a direction my parents were not too happy about. As is often the case, His Majesty Happenstance played a role. One day, during a break between lectures on the resistance of materials and the theoretical fundamentals of electrical engineering (both of which bored me to death), this monarch arranged for me to stumble upon a handwritten playbill in my college lobby. It announced that the drama club was seeking recruits. To catch a glimpse of the club, I stepped into the half-dark assembly hall and, right there and then, became infected with the theatrical bacillus. From a distance of over half a century, I realize that the drama club served not only as a welcome diversion from lectures about electrical motor windings but it was also my first attempt at artistic self-expression and a safe way of doing it. I hid my true self under the guise of a character in a play.

～

Now back to the day I visited the paper. I arrive at the Prospekt Mira subway station. Once I reach the street, I board a local bus that takes me to the Mariina Roshcha district. With some effort, I find the building where Boris and his wife, Tanya, live among all the similar, newly built structures. Tanya is a native Muscovite, an energetic and pretty woman in her late twenties. She works as a splicing girl at the Mosfilm Studios. Tanya radiates happiness. It seems her whole being is thrilled that she has the good fortune to be Boris's wife and friend. Whenever his creative juices stop flowing and, as sand in an hourglass, his self-confidence bleeds out, Tanya rushes to his aid, saying, "Little Boris, honey, don't let it get to you. . . . Give it time. Trust me—it'll go away soon. Have some of this borscht you like so much; I've just cooked it for you."

Boris meets me on the threshold. His face melts into a smile. He gives me a big hug and says, "We'll feed you, Emil. Right now."

Whenever I visit him, he offers to feed me. Though I have hardly ever looked emaciated, he can't help it; hospitality is in his blood. Back in our student days, the moment I stepped into his Odessa apartment, he also greeted me the same way—offering to feed me at once.

Tanya greets me too and rushes to the kitchen.

Boris brings me there, sits me down at the table, and asks me about my life. I tell him about what happened about an hour ago at the paper's editorial offices.

"Congratulations!" he says, beaming at me in excitement.

"Well, I don't know," I mumble.

"What's not to know, Milya, dear boy?"

A few years older, Boris treats me with the loving care of an older brother.

"Don't be a fool!" He slaps me on the shoulder. "Get yourself published in the *Moscow Komsomol Member*. It's a great paper. Some of my friends published their pieces there. They've said good things about it. It's not as orthodox as many others. It gives voice to the young generation, a voice to us."

"It beats me why the editor decided I can write satire," I shrug. "Just because I was born and raised in Odessa? Is he serious? Is this alone enough? What, any Odessan is a born satirist? Like Ilya Ilf and Yevgeny Petrov?"

Published back in the late 1920s and early 1930s, Ilf and Petrov's picaresque novels *The Twelve Chairs* and *The Golden Calf* chronicle the adventures of the witty con artist Ostap Bender. The books have become Soviet cult classics; many of their best lines have long been part of Russian banter throughout the Russophone world.

"The business of saving the drowning is the business of the drowning themselves."

"You didn't evolve from monkeys like all the other citizens. You're so thick-headed you must have descended from the cows."

"I'm not a cherub, I don't have wings, but I respect the criminal code—that's my weakness."

"But of course!" Boris says. "Who else, for God's sake, can write satire? People from Minsk or Pinsk? It's us, the Odessans!" he adds. "It's in our blood."

"That's true, Milya," Tanya interjects as she bustles around her pots, a ladle in her hand. "Last summer, Boris and I visited his folks in Odessa, and he took me to your huge farmers' market over there. What's its name?"

"*Privoz*," Boris says with a chuckle, shaking his head, also recalling that visit. "It means 'Most fresh supply.'"

"Yes, *Privoz*," Tanya says, giggling. "Every minute I spent there I thought I'd die laughing! Some characters gather there, oh my God! We passed by the milk stall where a woman in a babushka hailed a passerby, a middle-aged man. 'Come over here, handsome! Taste my milk.' Guess what the man says in response?"

Tanya's eyes grow big. She is about to burst into laughter.

"'Taste your milk?' he says. 'Why should I? Am I a newborn baby?' And the seller shoots back right away, 'Don't be a smart aleck! Not my milk, my cow's milk. Trust me; it's one of a kind! Just take a sip.' The man sips some milk from her cup, and she asks, 'Well, what do you say now?' And the man replies, without batting an eyelid, mind you, 'I say—buy an umbrella for your cow.' 'What has an umbrella to do with it?' she asks. He says, 'Your cow's milk is too watery!'"

Tanya laughs, closing her eyes with her hand. Then she adds: "I've shopped in the Moscow farmers' markets since my teens, but I've never run into characters like that."

Boris takes over the conversation and, looking at Tanya as if inviting her to collaborate on his report, says: "Then, as we came to the stalls where they sell fish, we heard a customer ask the seller why one of his fish looked crooked. With a poker face, the seller uttered, 'Oh, I caught it as it was making a turn.'"

Tanya announces that the dinner is served, and we take our places at the table. Tanya's borscht is excellent. We lap up everything in the pot until the last drop is gone.

"Well, now," Boris says when we retire to the living room and sit on the sofa, "show me the letter the editor's given you."

I pull it out of my pocket. The envelope is worn out. This is understandable. It passed several hands before winding up at the desk of the department editor, who, upon rereading, decided it would be good material for a satirical piece.

I give it to Boris with little enthusiasm. The letter is about boring, everyday stuff, about the poor quality of consumer goods. What else is new!

But Boris's eyes sparkle with excitement.

"C'mon, Milya!" he says. "I'm sure you'll come up with something. Hey, you're an Odessan, aren't you? Mark my words, you'll do it."

I hem and haw for a while. Stammering and blushing, I say, "Well, you know, Boris . . . satire . . . I'm kind of in favor of serious prose writing."

I confide in Boris that, for a long time, I have been gearing myself up to become a *belles-lettres* writer. Satirists and humorists are second fiddles in the literary orchestra. My idols are not Ilf and Petrov, no matter how much I enjoy reading their books, but classic Russian authors— Ivan Turgenev, Anton Chekhov, Ivan Bunin, Alexander Kuprin, and, of my contemporaries, Yuri Kazakov and Konstantin Paustovsky. Like all beginners, in my scribblings, I have been trying to emulate these writers' work. I have strained myself to match their lyricism, the style of Russian literature their work represents. Paustovsky's *The Golden Rose*, a book about becoming a writer, I had read a few years ago. It impressed me so much that, when I finished reading it, blood rushed to my face, and I told myself, "That's what I want to do in my life."

"But you have to start somewhere, man!" Boris says. "Didn't your precious Chekhov write humorous pieces when he was in medical school? C'mon, Milya, you know that as well as everyone else. What about Yuri Olesha, the author of *Envy* and *Three Fat Men*? What about Mikhail Bulgakov, before he penned his masterpieces *The Heart of a Dog* and *Master and Margarita*?"

"What about them?"

"Don't you know, back in the twenties, they wrote satirical pieces? The same kind that the *Moscow Komsomol Member* wants you to do. And they wrote them for some industry paper, *The Whistle* (Gudok), a publication of the railroad workers' union. They made the paper famous; everybody bought it, not only switchmen and conductors."

I know about that part of these literary maestros' biographies. Simple folks wrote to the *Whistle* about trials and tribulations in their work, and these writers turned those semiliterate letters into satirical gems the whole country enjoyed reading.

"So, what's with you?" Boris slaps me on my shoulder again. "You should be flattered. The popular Moscow paper offers you to follow in the footsteps of the great masters."

We have some tea with marshmallow sticks. It is getting late. Boris sees me off to the bus stop, gives me a big hug again, and says, "Go for it, Milya. Break a leg! And don't you forget to get me a copy of the paper with your first piece."

I board the bus in an uplifted mood. Heartened by my friend's support, I am determined to start my writing career as soon as possible.

On my way home—I rent a small room in a communal apartment on Stoleshnikov Alley in the center of Moscow—I chastise myself. What the hell is wrong with me? Why, while being humble in every other aspect, am I so ridiculously snobbish in my literary preferences? Why am I not keen on writing in the comic style altogether? Both the paper's editor and Boris find it only natural to expect it from someone like me who was born and raised in Odessa. So, why, why don't I jump at the opportunity?

5

Funny People

"Give me the kind of stuff you know I want." I hear these words in my head.

I ride the bus to the subway station on my way home and think of my adolescent years in Odessa. I wandered the streets of the city then, a book of stories by one or another Russian writer pressed under my arm. Those tales were set in the gray, wintry landscapes of central Russia, its deserted snowy plains and the hoarfrost-powdered forests somewhere in the Orel or Kursk region. My heart belonged there. It seems like I was oblivious—even myopic, if not altogether blind—to life rushing around me as if on a merry-go-round. Life in my native city was by far more colorful and jazzier than that of the northern Russian towns. While I have no scientific method to prove it, I believe the Odessans are cheerful and have an optimistic world outlook and joyous predispositions because of the abundance of the sun in the Odessa skies. The crystal-blue water of the sea is warm year-round. Even the migrating fish in the Black Sea, all two hundred kinds, cannot help but jump out of the water and rejoice when they reach the Odessa shores.

Over there, in the country's north, under the gloomy skies, wrapped up in their overcoats, people grow into introverts. Odessan folks wear their emotions on their sleeves and have no qualms about making their thoughts public. By their temperament, they are tragicomic actors par excellence. Everything is for show in this town. Everyday life is exposed to the world's gaze.

(America and the world should be grateful to Odessan acting genes. Not only did the grandmothers of superstars Leonardo DiCaprio and Sylvester Stallone come from this city, but Stella Adler, a daughter of two

Odessa actors, taught acting to Marlon Brando, Robert De Niro, Eliza-
beth Taylor, Warren Beatty, and Judy Garland, to name a few.)

Sneak into any old Odessan courtyard. Overgrown with ivy and wild
vines that crawl over the cracked walls of the dilapidated buildings, the
yards are haunted by a ceaseless babble of voices. The courtyard air com-
bines the smells of freshly cooked borscht, roasted mackerel, and boiled
laundry. People live cheek by jowl in tight spaces here.

Privacy, you ask? Forget it! Everyone here knows everything about everyone else. No one bothers to hide anything from the rest of the courtyard's
inhabitants. In such close quarters, secrets are impossible to keep. No one
burdens himself with etiquette or propriety. People step out of their rooms
half-dressed or walk into a neighbor's apartment without knocking.

It is especially true of life on the second floor of the building, on the
circular gallery stretching around the courtyard. Over there, they expose
everything to the outer world. The people who live there hoist their ker-
osene stoves to cook their dinner. Afterward, they will consume it in that
same gallery, while discussing family matters. They will prop their toddlers on their potties. They will teach them good manners with the whole
courtyard population observing and giving their two cents. When the
yard is in a good mood, the gallery might fill with a song. From time to
time, the tenants also swear and shout at the neighbors for real or imagi-
nary transgressions.

It will not be too long before a woman wrapped in her bathrobe, her
hair in curlers, her face glistening with moisturizer, appears in the gallery.
She calls her unruly little son. Oblivious to everything, he runs around
the courtyard with his wild buddies. Instead of coming down to fetch
him, not unlike in the ancient Greek tragic story of Medea, the woman
turns her sight to the heavens. She addresses the gods and her courtyard
neighbors. Her voice trembling in outrage, she begs for sympathy in her
predicament: "Just look at that little scoundrel, good people!"

To have us witness the biblical proportions of her suffering, she does
not stop here. It is just the opening line of what promises to be a twenty-
minute monologue inviting the whole wide world to bear witness to her
suffering. She needs everyone to know what a miserable lot has befallen
her—to be the mother of that little rascal.

"You shouldn't give birth to children!" she cries out. "You would be
better off giving birth to stones!"

She also bemoans her lot being married to a useless man, a vagabond with no family responsibilities. God only knows where he is hanging out all day long, instead of watching over his madcap son! When he is at home, he is not of much use either. He spends the day reclining on the sofa or playing dominos with his buddies, instead of running to the store to get in line for Moroccan oranges, which are, as usual, in short supply.

Such modernist spectacles with no border between the stage and the spectators are an everyday occurrence in Odessa. They take place even in such mundane situations as food shopping.

As a teenager, I often accompanied my mother on her trips to the city markets. In her quixotic search for the best food our family budget could afford, I played the part of Sancho Panza. I carried the bags while she negotiated with the sellers. There were always shortages of the most basic goods back then. Buying a good piece of meat was especially hard. The seller of such a precious product kept it under the counter until the right customer came along, one willing to pay its real market value, not the ridiculously low price that is set by the state.

Laughter is especially at a premium in harsh times. "As soap is to the body, so laughter is to the soul," a Jewish proverb says. An innocent youth, I was not aware of all that. Thus, the dialogue between my mother and a butcher baffled me, as if it were a scene out of the theater of the absurd. Later, when I grew up and saw the works of Eugene Ionesco, Samuel Beckett, Jean Genet, and other masters of the absurd, I found that all of them measure up poorly to my mother.

She would walk into a butcher shop and, looking straight into the seller's eyes and say, "Give me the kind of stuff you know I want."

"How am I to know what you want, lady?" the man chuckled.

"You do, you do," Mama said. "I'm sure you do. Don't pretend you don't."

"Well, just look at her!" the butcher giggled. "Here she comes to my shop and asks me to guess what she wants to buy. What am I, a mind reader? Am I that circus magician—what's his name? Wolf Messing?"

"Messing-Schmessing," Mama waved her hand. "Don't make me laugh. My thoughts aren't that complicated. You don't need some Messing to read my mind. You can do it yourself."

My mother's behavior just appeared aggressive. Both she and the butcher carried on in good humor. They laughed at the idiocy of the situation where there was no use for her to utter a simple phrase, "I want a good piece of meat—no fat, no bones." She had to hint somehow that she is ready to pay the black-market price.

Further on, the dialogue kept developing along the same absurdist script.

"Well," the butcher said, "how much do you want of what you want?"

"Gimme about five pounds," Mama said. "If your conscience lets you do it."

The butcher laughed and, peeking out the window to ensure that a city financial inspector would not pay him an unexpected visit, pulled out a considerable chunk of prime-cut beef from under the counter, threw it on the slab, and swung his ax over his shoulder.

～

I recall all these scenes, and I cannot help but giggle to myself. So, what the hell is wrong with me? I come from a funny place. Why am I still not excited to try my hand at comic writing?

When my bus rolls up to the Prospekt Mira station, the real reason for my resistance to accepting the editor's offer shimmers in the back of my mind. It is so secretive I could not reveal it even to Boris, my old friend. I have a hard time putting my finger on it myself.

6

To Laugh or Not to Laugh

"Don't be such a *schmuck*!" . . . "Some *schlimazel* you are!" . . . "Look at that *schmendrick*!"

Burned into my psyche, these Odessan street jibes pop up in my head. I take the subway escalator down to the platform. The station interior is cold and austere. Its pylons tiled with white marble, its chessboard granite floor, its walls adorned with the yellowish ceramic tiles crisscrossed with black stripes project calculation and rationality. No warm colors of my native Odessa are in sight. I do not feel at home here, in this capital of Soviet power.

Little by little, it comes to me that I am reluctant to accept the editor's offer for a reason other than the discrepancy between my dream literary style and the one the editor expects me to use. This much weightier reason has to do not so much with the preferable genre itself as with my Odessan background.

The Moscow editor thinks I can use my Odessan roots to my advantage as a satirist, but, in my mind, these roots are my liability. Although I was brought up in a Jewish family, my schooling had Russified me through and through. For the literary language I use in my scribblings, I shy away from the Odessan vernacular. The Odessan variant of Russian "Yinglish" is sprinkled with dismissive epithets like *schmendrick* (a nincompoop), *schmuck* (a jerk), *schwitzer* (a braggart), *schlimazel* (a down-on-his-luck man), and *schlemiel* (a loser). Soaked with Yiddish, it seems the Odessan vernacular is only a shtetl lingo, a shtetl being a pre–World War II small Jewish town. Following through on the editor's offer would mean stepping back into that bygone world. The wretched and cheerless life in those towns depicted in Sholem Aleichem's stories published in Russian translation is brightened only by self-effacing humor. Therefore, I perceive writing in the comic mode as surrender, as an acceptance of the bitter Jewish lot. I want to flee such a predicament. My desire is as intense as that of the people of the valley trying to escape the coming glacial mud-flow, climbing the rocky cliffs, breaking their nails until they bleed.

I strive to move in the opposite direction—to reach for a larger world, which, in literary terms, I associate with serious prose writing. Fascinated by literature early in my life, I chose not Sholem Aleichem, the only Jewish writer I read, but Pushkin, Turgenev, and Chekhov. I devoured everything those classic Russian writers wrote that I could get hold of in the libraries and bookstores.

~

Although I was not aware of it then, my desire to break away from the stifling life of my parents and to become part of a larger world was my attempt at self-realization. In the long line of my family members, I was the first one who received a higher education, although not the kind I wanted. My father and my uncle, my grandfather and my great-grandfather, all had been housepainters and wallpaper hangers. On my mother's side, there were Jews well versed in the sacred books of Judaism but not in hard science or secular literature. My college degree in engineering confined me to the technical field. I longed for a literary life, which would help me part with the life conditioned by my birth and upbringing.

As a teenager I read one of Jack London's books, *Martin Eden*. In this novel, young Martin launches his writing career, hoping that it will help him conquer the heart of a girl from a privileged family. This book captivated and excited me. I wanted the same life for myself. I identified with the protagonist. Like Martin, I came from a working-class family and was full of the desire to succeed. Though I was too young at that time and had no particular girl in mind, I hoped the path Martin chooses in the book would also help me win over the girl of my dreams in my future life.

To walk in the steps of Jack London's hero has been the sheer fantasy of a homegrown dreamer. Jack London, my foot! There was nothing in my young biography that would even come close to Jack's life as a sailor and adventurer.

~

The subway car stops at the Kuznetsk station. I have to make a transfer here. I pass the sculpture depicting a group of revolutionary sailors.

Perhaps because of that, my thoughts run in a different direction. *Wait a minute*, I say to myself, *what are my options at the moment? Why shouldn't I try my hand in journalism?* Here I have at least a fighting chance to find my work in print. They publish *belle lettres* works by well-established writers in literary journals. Am I ready to take them on? What's gotten into me? To author stories or even novels, that is, in the genres in which the greats of Russian literature, such as Tolstoy, Turgenev, and Chekhov, excelled, is nothing short of chutzpah, bordering on impudence. Why would I, a Jew, meddle in matters above my cut! The cobbler should stick to his last. . . .

Besides, is there something I could write about that I know well? I could describe what it meant growing up as a Jewish boy amid the lingering anti-Semitism in Stalin's post–World War II Odessa. But who will publish it? Has anything appeared lately that even touches upon a Jewish theme? True, a few years ago, they issued a volume of selected prose by the great Isaac Babel; they restored his reputation postmortem. Part of the book comprises the "Odessa Stories" about Jewish gangsters of the prerevolutionary times, romantically rendered. I doubt that, had Babel survived to this day, any of his work on contemporary Jewish life would have seen the light of day.

So, don't be a fool, Emil, I say to myself. At least see whether you have what it takes in you to be a writer. See whether *anything* you produce can make it to the printed page, to begin with.

~

I am about to exit the Petrovka subway station, as I hear my mother's voice in my head saying in Yiddish, *A melukhe!* I stop in my tracks. Gosh! Why hadn't I seen it earlier? I have something much weightier than the genre preference I have to deal with. In all earnestness, I should have thought of it first. I stand still in the middle of the sidewalk. It is a warm late spring evening, and Petrovka Street is crowded. With a walking cane in hand, an old man behind me almost runs into me.

The Yiddish phrase "*A melukhe!*" means "Some authorities!" It is the perennial expression of Jewish skepticism toward the powers that be, which means something like *What else can you expect from those damn scoundrels!*

Right after that, I hear my father say, "Don't have any business with them." What he means to say is, "Don't mess with the authorities. Sooner or later, you get in trouble."

Both these voices in my head make me realize that, besides the literary considerations regarding the editor's offer, I am also facing a moral quandary. No matter how you cut it, writing for the state-run paper (they are *all* state-run) means giving Soviet authorities a helping hand. By doing so, I would step onto one side of the divide, even though my parents and other relatives, my uncles and aunts, all have long anchored themselves to the other side.

With their heads shrunk into their shoulders, my parents live their lives in the most inconspicuous way possible. There are enough reasons for that. My father hates the Soviet system because, despite being a blue-collar worker, that is, belonging to the proclaimed proletarian core of Soviet society, he risks arrest. He runs a private business, a deadly sin in the Soviet catechism. He deals with people who want to freshen up their apartments: whitewashing ceilings, changing the wallpaper, repainting the doors, the sills and frames of their windows. By law, he should work for some state-run construction firm. Instead, he prefers to work with his younger brother, my Uncle Misha. He does so not only because the state-run companies would pay a wage hardly sufficient to support his family. He knows he would often be forced to stay idle for long stretches of time. The mismanagement endemic to many Soviet enterprises. Either they do not deliver the paint on time or, if they do, it will be the wrong one. Or some other mess that Soviet workplaces were prone to would impair his work, which would frustrate him greatly.

My other relatives' reasons for disliking the authorities are no less compelling. They all live their lives scraping by—hardly anything more. They also prefer to keep as much distance from the authorities as is possible.

So what? I say to myself. Let them live as they please. I want a different life. To live among people who pull their heads into their shoulders out of fear is not for me. Dreaming of a literary career, I am eager to break away into the wide-open world. I am gasping for fresh air. A life without a dream is not a life worth living; it is just vegetating. How is a human being without a spiritual component any different from a potato sprout in a humid basement? It is also life, but it is only the growth of cells, followed by their gradual demise. A primitive existence of mere survival is a kind of death, and such a prospect scares me. I try to get away from such a future for myself, a future in which, it seems, nothing will ever change.

～

Now, strolling along the sidewalks of the capital of the vast country, the editor's letter in my pocket, I think I should go for it. I should take on journalism. It is my chance to join a much larger world than the world of my parents and my relatives, who just wanted to get by.

Immersed in my thoughts, I pass the entrance to the building where I live. I do not hurry to return to my room in the communal apartment. I am too excited. I know I would not fall asleep tonight. I make a few rounds of my neighborhood. At first, when I reach the corner, I turn left onto Big Dmitrovka Street. Then, at the next intersection, I turn left again, coming back to Petrovka Street, where I turn into my Stoleshnikov Alley.

~

The political tension between my parents and me is not new. It goes back to the time of Khrushchev's speech at the Twentieth Congress of the Party in February 1956, the one in which he denounced Stalin's personality cult and his crimes against humanity.

Years of experience taught my parents that outright lying was the authorities' modus operandi. They did not trust a single word from Khrushchev. While they harbored not a shred of sympathy for Joseph Stalin, they were sure the reasons the new leader had denounced his crimes must be self-serving.

What eighteen-year-old listens to what his parents have to say! By definition, their outlook is antiquated. No wonder that, in the youth slang of the time, one's parents were called "ancestors" (*predki*). Just a generation older, they were several generations behind the young minds, especially regarding politics.

For me, the spring of 1956 was a twofold metaphor. It was the spring of my life—I was only eighteen—and, as I and many of my contemporaries felt, there was a rejuvenation of the country's life. It was not by chance my friend Boris titled his play *Setting the Course to Spring*. Written for Parnassus-2, the student theater in Odessa, it was about the old rusty life holding on to its past. Boris wrote his play after the celebrated speech by Khrushchev, and he set the action in the springtime.

It was impossible not to see that, in recent years, the country had at last opened to the outside world. The French movie stars Yves Montand and Simone Signoret arrived in Moscow. Milan's La Scala opera company toured in the capital. The first-ever Picasso expo opened here too. There was the first show ever of impressionist paintings in the Manezh, the country's biggest exhibition hall. . . . Unheard of! They launched the *Foreign Literature* journal, and, for the first time, people were able to read the works of American (Ernest Hemingway, John Steinbeck, John Updike), German (Erich Maria Remarque, Herman Hesse, Thomas Mann), and other world-renowned writers.

Back in the summer of 1957, Moscow hosted the Sixth International Festival of Youth and Students. Tens of thousands of young people from all around the world moved around Moscow and mingled with us, the Soviet youth. I attended those Moscow festivities and returned to Odessa with a sense that I had seen the world.

Many uplifting things have been happening in the country lately. While Bob Dylan, Pete Seeger, and Joan Baez took to the public stage to support international disarmament and civil rights, our young Russian poets—Yevgeny Yevtushenko, Robert Rozhdestvensky, Bella Akhmadulina, and Andrei Voznesensky—filled the stadiums with people eager to hear their verses. The poets called people to live up to the high ideals of the October Revolution. For too long, the hands of bureaucrats and opportunists had soiled these ideals. How could I, a Jew, be against the revolution's call for internationalism, for the equality of all nationalities, for rejecting the Great Russian chauvinism?

Yes, there were setbacks. In 1958, a big scandal broke out after Boris Pasternak's novel *Doctor Zhivago*, which described the 1917 Revolution and its aftermath, was published in the West. When the author was awarded the Nobel Prize for literature, a vicious public campaign started against him. He was expelled from the Union of Soviet Writers and forced to decline the Nobel Prize. He died soon after, in May 1960.

However, two years down the road, the unthinkable happened. One of the much-read Soviet literary journals, *The New World*, published Alexander Solzhenitsyn's novel *One Day in the Life of Ivan Denisovich*. The work describes a prisoner's day in one of Stalin's hard-labor camps.

Soon after came another chilling episode. Outraged by the works he was not able to appreciate, Khrushchev attacked the avant-garde artists during his visit to the Moscow Central Exhibition Hall. He threatened to cut all the funding of the arts and throw the culprits out of the country.

A few months later, at the Meeting of Creative Intelligentsia with the Leaders of the Party and Government, Khrushchev condemned young poets and writers for their publications in the West. How dare they air the country's dirty linen—Stalinism and its legacy—in public in the West!

He also attacked the writer Ilya Ehrenburg. His memoir, titled *People, Years, Life*, revealed that the older generation knew about the Stalin's crimes against humanity but was afraid to protest. This revelation implied that all members of Stalin's government, including Khrushchev himself, were responsible for Stalin's abuses of power.

Yet, last year, that is, 1963, Tvardovsky's long-suppressed poem, "Terkin in the Other World," a scathing satire of Stalin's repressions and his personality cult, was published first in the All-Union paper, *Izvestiya*, then in *The New World* journal.

Everyone still remembers the movie *The Clear Sky*. A Soviet airman fought the Nazi invaders heroically, but they captured him. After the war, like many other Soviet POWs he is treated with mistrust and suspicion. Like many Soviet soldiers who had been captured by the enemy, he "stained the moral character of the Soviet man." He can find neither a job nor a place to live. Only after the death of Stalin do officials clear him of the blemish on his reputation and reward him for his wartime service to the country.

The movie title proved to be symbolic. Into that cleared-up sky of the country, on April 12, 1961, a Soviet-made rocket sent Yuri Gagarin, the first human being to fly around the planet Earth in space. Soon after, another cosmonaut, Gherman Titov, did it seventeen times all over again. Then, two men, Andrian Nikolaev and Pavel Popovich, spent four days up there, in space. And in the summer of 1963, two more Soviets, Valery Bykovsky and Valentina Tereshkova, made the world gasp again when they simultaneously circled the Earth aboard two spacecrafts.

Now, in early May 1964, when I step into the editorial offices of the Moscow paper, Khrushchev is still in power. Nothing foretells his coming demise. The papers have just covered his visit to Egypt. In contrast to Stalin, who had traveled abroad only to attend the wartime conferences in Tehran and Potsdam, Khrushchev has been a globetrotter. Before Egypt, he had also visited Hungary, Bulgaria, and the German Democratic Republic. In the United States, they greeted him like a Hollywood celebrity, complete with adoring crowds and toasts from movie stars.

People joke about Khrushchev. No one I know takes him seriously. "Khrushch," as he is nicknamed, seems to be born to be the butt of jokes. Short, portly, and bald, gesticulating when speaking in public, he has entered the pantheon of underground jokelore. According to it, back in 1960, the world misinterpreted his speech at the United Nations, during which he banged his shoe on the podium. What looked like a threat to world peace was nothing but an advertising stunt. "Khrushch" just wanted to promote Soviet-made shoes. He tried to show they would not fall apart no matter how much you hammered them.

People also chuckle over reports that, while in America, the Soviet leader took time to see for himself what popcorn, the cancan, and Disneyland were all about. He enjoyed popcorn so much that, upon his return, he ordered it to be planted everywhere in the Soviet Union, including the Arctic Circle. He did not approve of the cancan, however. He found it distracting for a Soviet man who should look not down at pretty women's legs but up toward the shiny summits of communism. As for Disneyland, the Americans did not allow him in under the pretext that they already had one Mickey Mouse. . . .

As one of the jokes goes, when questioned why there were meat shortages in the USSR, Nikita brushed off the idea that the Soviet system was at fault. He insisted that only the cattle were to blame. "We're moving toward Communism so fast," he said, "the poor animals have a hard time catching up with us." According to another popular quip, "Khrushch" found the American economy in terrible shape. While the stores were full of goods, the people were too poor to buy them. He had not seen a single line of customers.

I take all these jokes at the expense of the country's leader in stride. If a leader makes you laugh, it is far better than when he makes you cry. Since that fateful day in February 1956, the day of Khrushchev's speech exposing Stalin's crimes against humanity, despite sporadic setbacks, the air in the country has been full of hope of renewal and rejuvenation.

~

It is getting late already. I pass by a well-lit poster for a newly released movie. Titled *Walking the Streets of Moscow* (Ia shagaiu po Moskve), this light socialist-realist comedy, complete with virtuous working-class heroes, has become a hit. A young Siberian steeplejack who has made a debut in literature spends the day passing through Moscow. He pays a visit to a famous writer at his invitation, befriends a young Muscovite man, also a blue-collar worker, a subway builder, and makes a pretty salesgirl fall for him.

The film is popular because it expresses the spirit of the times as perceived by the country's youth. A refreshed way of life is set in the country

at last. . . . The main charm of the movie is the tender and cheerful signature song, which creates and sustains a bright and optimistic mood
throughout the film:

> Sometimes it happens everything is fine in the world,
> Right away, you hardly grasp the reason. . . .
> It just a warm summer rain's poured
> A regular summer rain.
> . . . .
> And as I go, walk across Moscow,
> I feel capable of walking over
> The whole salty Pacific Ocean,
> The entire tundra, and the vast taiga. . . .

A Soviet variant of the American "Singing in the Rain," if you will. . . .
The optimistic mood of the flick reflects my feelings well. I identify with
the movie characters. I am also young, full of hope and energy, and my
whole life is still ahead of me; the entire world is about to open for me.
And I also walk the Moscow streets the way the picture hero does, full of
vague hopes and nebulous dreams.

> Sometimes it happens everything is fine in the world,
> Right away, you hardly grasp the reason. . . .

Earlier in the day, the mood of hopefulness had brought me to the editorial offices of the Moscow paper. In fact, on my way there, while walking along the Chistye Prudy Boulevard, I recognized the place where they
shot one of the movie scenes. It made me feel as if I had walked in the
footsteps of the movie's young protagonists, optimistic and hopeful.

Right before stepping inside the lobby of the building where I live,
I decide to shake off all my misgivings and get started on the editor's
assignment as soon as I wake up. After all, as Mark Twain observed, "The
best way to cheer yourself is to cheer someone else up."

The only question I still have to find an answer to is, "Can I do it? Am
I cut out for writing satire?"

PART III

On a Roll,
1964–70

7

The First Targets

"Do you have onesies for newborn babies?"
"What's your baby's temperament?" the salesclerk asks.

These lines pop into my head as soon as I wake up. I am relieved thinking my parents would approve of my writing for the papers. I cannot see how they could object to making fun of what they scold themselves—the dismal quality of consumer goods produced in the country. My first lesson in penning satire: to successfully attack your target, be emotionally charged. Just like every other Soviet citizen, I have also had pent-up fury regarding the poor quality of almost everything sold in the stores.

Growing up in Odessa has, in part, been responsible for my outrage regarding clothing. Perhaps the southern predisposition for dressing up is the reason for our craving for a sartorial splendor. No Odessan has ever worn Soviet-made suits or dresses. Every single part of Odessans' attire has always been foreign made. All goods from abroad appeared in the city the natural way: the sailors brought them from overseas. The black market has flourished. From time to time, my mother also brought some stern-looking aunties with sizable imitation-leather shopping bags into our home. Out of precaution, she closed the shutters on the windows of our first-floor apartment. Out of their bags, the aunties pulled out men's English sweaters, women's Italian cashmere sweaters, French low-cut evening dresses, ladies' lace underwear, and many other foreign-made goodies. . . .

Now, waking up in my room, I realize that no matter how much I resent admitting it, the editor at the *Moscow Komsomol Member* was right. Whether or not I like it, whatever literary preferences I may have, growing up in Odessa has imbued me with the sarcastic spirit of the city's

folks. As soon as the opening lines pop into my head, even before having
my morning cup of coffee, I rush to my desk and scribble:

To the Question of Temperament

"What's your baby's temperament? Is it choleric or phlegmatic?
Sanguine or melancholic?"

The salesclerk's questions puzzled Citizen Starikova a great deal.

"What are you talking about?" she said. "My baby boy is just
three months old."

"Well, does he move around a lot? Does he jerk his little legs?
Yes? Well, I have bad news for you, comrade. You're out of luck.
You won't find any onesies for your cutie-pie anywhere."

"What about these?" The young mother pointed at the glass
case with pieces of clothing for toddlers.

"I'm afraid these ones are not good for your boy. Chkalov
Sewing Factory #15 of the Gorky region produced them for
melancholic babies only, for the phlegmatic ones. . . . One
energetic movement of your boy's little leg will ruin this garment."

The mother of the high-energy baby took a risk and bought it.
As predicted, no good came of it. Soon after she put it on her little
son, the onesie burst at the seams.

I type it out on my Olympia typewriter and send it to the paper. For
the next couple of days, I go about my work in the lab. All I think about
is whether they will publish my satirical note.

A few days pass, and Vishnevetsky calls. Business-like, he invites me to
stop by his office the next time I am in town.

"Yeah," he adds, "and bring along your passport."

My passport? Ahem, what could that mean? Any Soviet citizen gets
worried when anyone asks for your ID, your internal passport, which
you were expected to carry on you at all times. It has all the information
the state wants to know about you right away. Not only your name—
your given one, your patronymc, and your surname—but also your place
of birth, your ethnicity, and your social status (are you a blue- or white-
colar worker, a collective farmer or a dependent?). The passport also in-
dicates whether or not you are liable for military service. It records who
issued your passport and on the basis of what documents it was done.
Besides, your passport must also have a stamp of the police authority
certifying your current place of living. The whole enchilada. . . .

The next day, with a heavy heart, I step into the editor's office, wondering what it is all about—his phone call, my passport. . . . He is on the phone. I wait and wait.

Finally, he has finished. He is laconic: he tells me to take a seat at another desk and gives me a strip of paper with the galley proof of my piece about the baby onesies. I have to proofread it and sign.

After I am done, he tells me, if I have my passport on me, to go down the corridor to the cashier's office and receive my honorarium. Before I rise from the chair, he picks up from his desk a bundle of letters secured with a red rubber band and throws it my way. It lands in my lap.

"Get to work, Emil," he says. "Read them and pick what you think will work for you."

And he gets back to his phone.

I put the bundle into my briefcase and leave. I locate the cashier's office in a dimly lit corridor corner. A stern-looking, middle-aged woman squints, examining my face against my picture in the passport. She points where to sign the register and hands me a pinkish ten-ruble bill featuring Lenin's famous profile. For a split second, I see the great Soviet leader giving me an intimate wink.

Wow! Having fun and being paid for it? Ten rubles is not much, but it is about the amount of money the young engineers at our lab lend each other when we are broke, and there is still a few days left before our monthly payday.

The next morning, on my way to work, I rush to the newspaper stand around the corner on the Bolshaya Dmitrovka Street and buy two copies of the *Moscow Komsomol Member*—one for myself and one for Boris. A promise is a promise. . . .

For the next few days, I feel as if I have beaten Jesus Christ himself: the man had reportedly walked on water, and here I was walking on air. . . . I reread the tiny item of mine again and again. Yay! I have made it to the printed page. . . .

With renewed enthusiasm, I read the letters Vishnevetsky has given me for my perusal. My heart doubles its beating. Then, as if in afterthought, it triples. I sense I am on the threshold of a new chapter of my life.

Most of the time, the things people write about to the paper are hardly funny. They are often mundane, even dull, if not outright dreary. I am challenged to make them a fun read. Using irony is my best bet. I look for a way to present the otherwise upsetting state of affairs as an achievement worthy of congratulations.

For example, writing about the poor city-run maintenance of people's living quarters, I state that, while discomforts in life are a nuisance, there is a bright side to them. They adorn our daily existence. They make it romantic, interesting. With inconveniences, your life is never boring. Thus, frustrated Moscow dwellers complain to the paper that water has flooded the basement of their apartment building, the electrical lines are short-circuiting, but the city officials are in no hurry to fix the busted pipelines and replace the wiring. I call on these dwellers to look at the comforting side of their situation. They should consider themselves lucky, being able to save a lot of time and money. Now there is no need to travel all the way to Venice. The flooding and the short-circuiting in their basement give them the same effect as visiting the famed city. They should just squint their eyes and imagine themselves being there, in Venice, reclining in a gondola. Hear the gentle swish of the water! Enjoy the fireworks!

Employees of the Sosnovka state farm in the Kolomna district write to the editor that someone cut off their homes from the local electrical circuit. All that has to be done to fix the problem is replace a wire hardly two hundred yards long. No matter how many times they have asked, begged, or cajoled the local authorities to do something about it, until this day, they remain in the dark—literally (in their homes) and figuratively (about when the line will be fixed).

Ah, dear comrades, don't be so rushed in your judgment. Is your situation really a good cause for concern? For angry letters to the paper? On the contrary! Your after-work hours at home should bring peace and tranquility into your hearts. The lack of electricity should put you in a contemplative mood. Think about it! Now, you can observe the starry skies in all their majestic beauty. And one day (or, rather, one night), one of you may discover a new star or, with good luck, even a brand-new constellation. . . .

Discomforts can turn regular folks not only into armchair travelers or home-bred astronomers. There are reasons to assume that soon the residents of Pavlov Street in Khimki are well on their way to becoming outstanding track-and-field athletes. Recently, the dispatchers redirected two bus routes, #222 from Moscow and the #2 local, into their narrow street with no sidewalks. So, as soon as people who live on that street push open their exit doors, they often face a rapidly approaching bus. This situation prompts them to reach the nearest street corner at high speed. A year or two of such daily practice—and, hold on, Olympic sprint records!

When a report comes to the paper of some fruit compote packaged so poorly that thousands of jars of it have blown up into pieces, I render it as a celebratory news item:

FRUIT COMPOTE EXPLOSIVES

A new explosive will assist the tunnel builders and the explorers of the earth's entrails. Now, they can say goodbye to nitroglycerine or dynamite, both being hazardous to handle and quite pricey. At the Heroes of Revolution Factory in the city of Bravegrad, they have invented new cheap and safe-to-handle explosives. The idea came about when workers discovered that if you add excess yeast to a jar of plum compote, even a small rise in temperature makes the glass explode.

Last month, at the Ust'-Telmen Station of the West Siberian Railroad, the Edisons of the factory tested the first batch of the new explosives. Fifteen thousand jars of plum compote blew up.

This test has cost the plant ten thousand rubles plus freight expenses, which is peanuts when compared to the cost of dynamite. The inventors plan to diversify the ingredients of their newly found explosive. Now, we can expect them to produce it from pear, cherry, and other fruit compotes.

A reader complains that it took a whole month for the local shoe-repair shop to fix the soles of his old boots. His frustration is the result of being clueless about the way the shop operates. First, they told him to come back in a week. When he did, they asked for another weeklong extension. After his next trip, there was another week to wait. It happened a few times more. By forcing the customer to walk to the shop many times, the management wanted to be sure that the soles of his loafers would wear out enough to warrant their fixing. Thus, the shop will never run out of work orders.

Shoe repair is not the only thing people complain about in their letters to the editor. The quality of many other public services, be it dry cleaning, taxi service, or eating places, is crappy. It is so poor that a slight exaggeration drives the point home.

KEEPING IT STRONG

I was about to bring a spoonful of soup to my mouth, but I forgot to shut off my sense of smell. As a result, my brain snapped into action and the spoon clanked against my clenched teeth.

The taste and texture of the main entrée made me feel I was trying to consume an undercooked rubber shoe.

I motioned to the waiter. He took his time. First, he showed a keen interest in the shapes of several female passersby's backs. Then he pulled a paperback out of his pocket and engrossed himself in it. After a while, apparently finding his book too dull, reluctantly, as if he does not have anything better to do anyway, he responded to my call.

On his way to my table, he made a side trip to a counter with dirty dishes and picked up some piece of worn-out cloth which was supposed to serve as a napkin. He took it to my table and shook its contents out onto my knees.

"Hey, what are you doing?" I cried out.

"Shut up!" the man hissed at me. "Don't raise a ruckus! Things will only get worse for you. I promise."

"Worse?"

"That's right. Understood?"

"What's going on?" I said. "Call the manager!"

I had to repeat it three times before, after also taking his time, the manager appeared.

He was all smiles. It looked like all of these goings-on cheered him up.

"What the hell do you call this place?" I sputtered, blanching from anger.

"Family Happiness Café, dear comrade," the manager said.

"What?" I thought I must have been hearing things. "You call this stinking joint of yours 'happiness'?"

"*Family* Happiness," the man said. Then he sighed and sat down next to me, "Do you know, young man, how a typical domestic quarrel ends?"

"What is this, a joke setup?" I roared.

"As a rule," the manager continued, "the action takes place along the following scenario. The angry husband shouts something like 'I'm through with you!' He grabs his coat and leaves, slamming the door of his apartment with a force capable of killing a bull. Now, when he's parted with the source of his irritation, he wants to recover his self-respect. His sense of identity, if you will. . . . And he heads for a nearby café. He wants to have a nice and quiet dinner. And here, in our place, we, my young man, champion family bliss. That's the frontier we want no one to cross. Doesn't a happy family make up the fabric of our society? Here, at our café, we do whatever we can to provide a public service of true value. We do everything in our power to ensure that, after visiting us, the distraught husband comes back to his senses. Eventually, he howls like a wolf and rushes headlong back to his dear, his kind angel of a wife who prepares his delicious breakfasts, lunches, and dinners so selflessly. On his way back, he curses himself for his unwarranted hubris and his misguided male pride. . . . Alas, we're deprived of witnessing the heartwarming finale," he sighed. "It takes place behind closed doors, in the sweet sobs of the loving couple."

I gathered my things.

"Um," the manager said. "I'd like to warn you. When you're on your way out, our doorman downstairs might give you a good one on the back of your neck."

"For what?"

"I don't know," the manager shrugged. "He'll find some reason. We don't restrain the creative initiatives of our employees." . . .

That same evening my legs carried me back to my wife, to whom, three hours earlier, I had resolved never to return.

As irony has it, unbeknownst to the editor, another of my write-ups for the paper turns out to be an unacknowledged vindication of my father's way of making a living for our family. That letter to the editor describes what its author had to go through when he hired a city-run repair shop to fix his apartment. The customer lived to regret the day such a weird idea entered his mind—to use officially available services.

Every single aspect of what he had to go through after he agreed to do business with the local home-repair shop drove him nuts. First, they tried to cheat him, jacking up their estimate to twice the amount on their price list. Then, though it was part of the shop's job, they made the customer and his wife spend the night before the appointment stripping off the old wallpaper. With their furniture moved into the corridor and their walls now bare, the couple waited all morning for the housepainters to show up—to no avail. They waited well into the evening, but nobody knocked on their door.

The next day, the customer ran to the home repair shop and begged the workmen to come and do the job. Desperate, he vowed not to leave the premises without them.

When they finally appeared, the foreman took his time. He walked around the empty rooms and spat on the floor in disgust, telling his work-force, oblivious to the likelihood of the customers hearing him: "Take a good look, fellows, at this man. Because of his stinginess, you'll be sober all week long, like some schmucks. Don't be shy to let him know what you think about him."

He examined first the walls of the apartment, then the faces of its dwellers. He scratched his head with gusto and uttered: "Hey, people! Before calling us, you should have done a major repair of your lousy place first. The way it is, it isn't worth our trouble."

In the end, at the risk of having a heart attack, the customer was able to get his money back.

I enjoy mocking those city-employed housepainters on the pages of the Moscow paper. It makes me proud of my father's work in compari-son. He is much sought after by his customers. They treat him as if he is not a mere housepainter but a famous surgeon whose patients' lives are in his hands. I try not to think about the oddity of his situation: if any-one reported him to the financial police, he would be in a lot of trouble.

~

My newfound trade excites me. When the editor calls me from his office to come over to proofread the galleys, I rush to the paper. As soon as I get there, I sit down at the desk of one of the staff members and, trem-bling from excitement, lean over still-damp, freshly printed proofs. They give off a sharp odor of printing ink. It is hardly a pleasant odor, but to me it is the best aroma in the world. All I do is proofread my short satirical quips about some small-time bureaucrat or a poorly run diner. But I have finally realized my teenage dream of becoming privy to the sacred mystery of the printed word. Is it not true magic that a mere string of letters in a certain fashion can stir human emotions, can make readers smile or frown?

I am just a neophyte; I am still learning the ropes. A beggar sitting on a sidewalk rejoices when he spots a ruble bill in a pile of change. I feel the same way when I reread my lines and see that at least some devices of *belles-lettres* have survived the editorial pen. Gee, I say to myself, my editor, a professional writer, has not corrected them, let it go. It looks like I have done okay!

Then, when the editor lets me know when my piece is to appear in the paper, the morning of that day seems especially bright. I revel in seeing the lines I have composed on the pages of a metropolitan paper. At the first opportunity, I rush to a newsstand and buy a copy. I search for my item on the last page where they place all the satirical material. I reread my work, now with fresh eyes. For the first time, I see it not as a stand-alone but surrounded by the usual newspaper articles written in the clichéd language of Soviet newspapers. I feel that the entire world reads my little note, though I am perfectly aware of the fact that not too many people are all that interested in what the Soviet papers write about. Somehow, at least for a short time, this fact evaporates from my consciousness. Most people grab a copy on the go only to see what is on TV tonight or in the movies. Because of the shortage of paper in the country, many people use newspapers to wrap their lunch sandwiches.

Sometimes, to my distress, my piece does not appear on the target day. An unscheduled speech by Leonid Brezhnev, the country's leader, or a new government decree, or some other important material takes over the allotted printing space. At first, I am disappointed not seeing my work in the paper. Then I worry. What if, for whatever reason, at the last moment, the editor-in-chief has had a change of heart regarding my work and killed it?

However, this happens rarely. Any editor knows people would rather read a satirical piece than any other newspaper stuff. Usually, my note appears a few days later.

~

Soon I learn that other Moscow papers need writers capable of, as the journalistic slang has it, "making candy out of crap." It means taking a boring letter to the editor and making it fun to read. At the editorial offices of the *Moscow Komsomol Member*, I am introduced to Vitaly Reznikov, a lanky blond man with a thinning hairline and bulging gray eyes. As the journalist rumors have it, he has worked as a waiter at one of the Kremlin dining rooms. You would never guess it. He is one of the wittiest people I have ever met. In time, he becomes my satirical godfather. When the all-union paper *Komsomol Pravda* hires him to manage the department of feuilletons, he invites me to contribute to that paper.

Soon, the man recommends me to Vladimir Nadein, the editor of *Crocodile*'s economics department. This magazine, an instrument of the Central Committee of the Communist Party, is the most prestigious satirical publication in the country. It has existed for more than forty years. Satirical works by the biggest literary names of bygone eras, now legendary—Ilya Ilf and Evgeny Petrov, Mikhail Zoshchenko, Yuri Olesha, Valentin Kataev, Mikhail Koltsov, to name a few—have graced its pages.

Everything related to my new undertaking excites me. From the readers' letters, I learn so much more about the true life of the country than I would ever have known if I would have stuck to my engineering job. My network of acquaintances in the journalistic world grows fast. My writing appears on the pages of a growing number of newspapers and magazines.

However, I soon learn that this new, exciting life of mine comes with a certain caveat. . . .

My *Crocodile* correspondent ID

8

My Pen Name

"Your surname isn't quite for the newspapers, Emil."
I wish I had never heard this declaration. It stunted my enthusiasm for my new occupation.

By the time I contributed to *Crocodile*, I had already signed my work not with my real name but my pen name. When I brought my first satirical piece signed "Emil Draitser" to the editorial offices of *Soviet Russia*, the central paper of the Russian Federation, the head of its feuilleton department, a well-known journalist named Boris Protopopov, read it, nodded in satisfaction, and raised his pen to sign it off for typesetting. But then his pen froze in midair.

The man thought for a minute, chewing his lips and adjusting his thinning gray hair, and said: "Listen, Emil." He chewed his lips some more. "Your surname . . . well, you know . . . it's not quite for the newspapers. Change your byline."

He lowered his face and looked over the rim of his glasses at me.

I understood that his suggestion was the condition for publication, not only of the article in hand but also of my future contributions to the paper. It was not too hard to guess that a surname "not quite for the newspapers" was his way of saying it was Jewish.

As a rule, my earlier publications rarely had my name in the byline. They amounted to short satirical notes based on readers' letters to the editor. The notes were signed either with the name of the person who wrote the letter or with some made-up name, like Samoletov, which means "Son of an Airplane."

I figured that Protopopov did not mind my first name. It did not sound outright Jewish, like Isaac, Haim, or Baruch. The man was not aware "Emil" was not my actual given name.

I grew up at the time of Stalin-inspired anti-Semitic campaigns. My given name, Samuil, unmistakably Jewish, tormented me. By the time I was eighteen, I had been introducing myself as "Emil" in social interactions. It seemed to be an ennobling, European-sounding variant of my given name, of which I preserved half the letters. The name had a positive aura in the country's cultural firmament of the time. Soviet literary critics praised the French writer Emile Zola for his "uncompromising criticism of bourgeois mores" in his novel *Nana*, about a high-class prostitute. He also "truthfully depicted the sufferings and struggles of the working class" in his book *Germinal*. Emil Zátopek was an Olympic champion in long-distance running, a Czech by nationality. The Soviet newspapers wrote about his victories with much adulation. Though he was not a Soviet athlete, he represented a "brotherly socialist state," in which (as in the USSR) sports were a matter of his "country's honor and glory," not a "means of personal gain and profit," as it was for capitalist countries' athletes.

(I was so used to hiding my Jewish name that, even after immigrating to America, when getting my naturalization papers, I changed my given name "Samuil" to "Emil.")

To add insult to injury, both my patronymic "Abramovich" and my surname gave me away as a Jew. Unlike in America where a Jewish person is someone who practices Judaism, in both the Soviet Union and Nazi Germany, Jewishness was a matter of race or ethnicity, regardless of religion.

By the time Boris Protopopov found my surname "not quite for the newspapers," I knew already how to make it "kosher." I had to Russify it. Plenty of articles written by Shapiros, Levins, Katzes, and other Jewish journalists appeared in the Soviet press, but you would not know it by reading their bylines. The alteration was a rather simple procedure. The Jewish-sounding surname of the author had to be eradicated without a trace. What was there to salvage from a surname like "Rabinowitz," where each syllable screams your Jewish origin? Instead, you had to prune down your patronymic (Borisovich, Efimovich, Markovich), by discarding the possessive suffix -*ovich*, and your pen name was ready. Soviet publications of all kinds were replete with pen names "Borisov," "Efimov," and "Markov."

Some Jewish journalists also tried to hide behind their wives' names, a move that flattered their spouses and thus strengthened the writer's marriage. This way, bylines such as Sonin (from Sonia), Svetlanin (from

Svetlana), and Natashin (from Natasha) appeared in print. (Only authors with wives named "Lena" were out of luck; they could not sign their work as "Lenin" without raising readers' eyebrows.)

I guess the authors of these pen names may not have suspected they were following an old Jewish tradition. They formed the surnames the way, in the past, the surnames were given to the Jewish children raised without fathers—from their mothers' names. That was how surnames such as Khaikin (from Khaika, a diminutive of Khaia), Sorkin (from Sorka, a diminutive of Sora), and Khanin (from Khana) had appeared.

I followed the custom. I shortened my patronymic "Abramovich" and signed my article "Emil Abramov." I thought the editor would nix my idea. Abramov! Who could the bearer of such a surname be if not a Jew!

However, Protopopov did not mind. My article appeared in the paper the next day. Only then did I realize that there were ethnic Russian Abramovs, such as Fyodor Abramov, a well-known writer. He belonged to the new generation of Russian village prose writers; they called for the rejection of the corrupt ways of city life and a return to the moral purity of country folks.

There were also ethnic Russians with surnames like "Moiseev" and "Davydov." In fact, Denis Davydov was a famous military commander during the 1812 war with Napoleon and a notable poet of Pushkin's circle. These surnames were that of the Christian Old Believers' families; they drew the names for their children from the Old Testament.

Yet, I think no reader had any doubts about the ethnicity of "Emil Abramov." In the Russian consciousness, the European name "Emil" denotes a foreigner. Thus, it was clear even to a fool that "Emil Abramov" was a made-up name that belonged to "our foreigner," that is, to a Jew.

However, the formalities had been observed. The Party-controlled press probably had grown tired of obliterating all Jewish names from its many publications. They needed me and my Jewish comrades-in-pen to carry out an important function: as Alexander Pushkin put it, "to burn human hearts with words." We journalists were not Pushkins, of course. But, apparently, there were not enough ethnic Russian "non-Pushkins" for such a labor-intensive task.

~

One day, a curious incident occurred. Sasha Shcherbakov, head of the feuilleton department at *Komsomol Pravda*, who had replaced Reznikov in this position, told me, grinning: "Well, Emil, the other day I got a call from one Eduard Abramov. He was asking for you."

I mentally scanned my recent publications, but I recalled no one by this name.

"Who is he?"

"He's introduced himself as a Moscow police officer in the rank of major."

I pricked up my ears. Ha, why is a police officer interested in me? A major to boot. . . . Like many Soviet citizens, to be on the safe side, I tried to keep a distance from any policeman, even if he was just a traffic cop.

"What was it all about?"

"Well, he wants to meet with you."

"What does Major Abramov want from me?" I asked.

"Have you written anything about him?"

"Nope," I said.

"Well," Sasha says, "if you wrote about him, and he didn't like your criticism, he'd want to talk to the editor, to me. It looks like he wants to have a private meeting with you."

"Huh! What in the world does he want from me?"

We put our heads together and guessed what had taken place. Some poetic miniatures under the same pen name as mine, "E. Abramov," have appeared in the Moscow press. Seemingly, in his free-from-police-business time, Major Abramov dabbled in writing. From time to time, in my satirical pieces, employees of the local law enforcement agencies had appeared. So it was only logical to assume that, offended by the criticism in the central press, the police chiefs had suspected Major Abramov of defaming their line of work and had called him on the carpet for an explanation. Where did he find the nerve to air dirty police laundry in public?! It was possible that, to avoid further embarrassment, Major Abramov wanted to ask me to change my pen name.

Upon reflection, I decided not to respond to the cop's call. If he was so concerned with his unfortunate byline, let him change it. I had nowhere to retreat. By signing my work the way I did, by truncating my patronymic, I preserved my father's name at least. I was thankful for that.

~

I appreciated how lucky I was with my pen name when, one day, at the editorial offices of the trade union paper *Labor* (Trud), I met another

Jewish freelancer. The head of the feuilleton department, Yuri Zolotarev, a tall middle-aged man, bug-eyed, with bags under the eyes, introduced me to him. A thin young man of medium height, trim, agile, with a quick, inquisitive look, he listened to every word of his interlocutor. Despite the liveliness of his nature, he did not seem to be an easygoing fellow. Melancholy was frozen in his big, dark-brown eyes. His name was Grigory Kremer.

His was the Muscovite version of my biography. He had also graduated from a technical college (in his case, Moscow Civil Engineering Institute) and, while maintaining his job as a civil design engineer, he had also contributed satirical pieces to the Moscow press. Just as I had been doing, he used his weekends, holidays, and vacation days to travel for his journalistic assignments. Sometimes, he took days off at his own expense, and, just like me, in his spare time during his engineering business trips, he would manage to fact-check a letter to the paper sent from the same locality.

The man both looked Jewish and had a Jewish surname, Kremer. So, it puzzled me that his pen name, "Grigory Kroshin," was not created the way most Jewish journalists made their pen names. I asked him about it.

Satirist Grigory Kroshin, c. 1970 (courtesy of Grigory Kroshin)

"Well, my friend," Grigory said with a sad grin, "you're just plain lucky with your father's name. Everybody knows Fyodor Abramov, our remarkable village prose author. But what could I do since my father's name is Max and my patronymic is Maxovich? If I were to go your way of creating my pen name, circumcising my patronymic, what would we have? That's right—Maxov. Have you ever heard of such a Russian surname? I bet you haven't. There are no biblical characters in either the Old or the New Testament named Max, and that's that! So, there are no ethnic Russian Maxovs, period. In my case, the fig leaf of the possessive suffix -*ov* wouldn't fool anyone. What could I do?"

"I had to be inventive," Grigory continued. His eyes sparkled with mischief. "I came up with a Russian pen name, 'G. Kroshin.' At least, it allows me to keep the first two letters of my Jewish surname. It's better than nothing, buddy, isn't it?"

I agreed.

"Well, to add insult to injury," Grigory said, "I had to change my surname legally from 'Kremer' to 'Kroshin.' The payroll departments at various papers I'm writing for kept mixing up my true surname with my pen name."

The man produced a strained smile: "My fictitious pen name suits a satirist. The root of it comes from the verb *kroshit'*, 'to shred.' Aren't we, Soviet satirists," he grinned sardonically, "supposed to have crocodile-sized teeth to shred those 'isolated shortcomings that slow down our moving to the shining heights of communism'?"

We stepped outside, onto the sidewalk of Gorky Street, and, narrowing his eyes as people do when they know their interlocutor would not be able to answer their next question, he asked, "Guess where and when it all started—forcing all Soviet journalists with Jewish surnames to use Russian-sounding pen names?"

I shrugged. It had always been out there in my lifetime—the need to hide your Jewishness.

"Well, I'll tell you what prompted it. I bet you won't believe it."

He lowered his voice and almost whispered it into my ear: "It was all because of . . . Adolf Hitler. Ye, ye, the Fuhrer of the Third Reich himself!"

I stopped in the middle of the sidewalk in surprise.

"Don't pull my leg, Grisha!" I said, using his nickname.

"I knew it," he laughed, satisfied by the effect he had produced. Then he continued, this time in a serious tone: "I learned about it at the *Pravda* editorial office one day. They were running my piece in the paper. So, I stopped by to proofread the galleys. After that, I popped by their buffet to get a bite; it was lunchtime. I sat down at a table next to a typesetter. A puny old man, his small body thin and light as a dried mushroom. We chatted for a while. I asked him whether he had ever typeset any of my pieces. Curiosity got the best of me. You, of all people, know well it's not every day you meet a person who composes your story by hand, line by line. So, I told him my pen name—'Kroshin.' He stared at me and snorted. 'Don't pull my leg, man,' he said. 'Judging by your face, you are as much Kroshin, as I am Finkelstein.' Well, I told him he was right, my family name was Kremer. 'That's better,' he blabbed out. 'And you're telling me—Kroshin, Kroshin . . . ha!' He waved his hand in my direction in such a slow motion that I realized that, despite being on the clock, he was tipsy. As I bet you know, in any printing shop, there's alcohol on hand. To dilute printing ink if needed . . .

"And here he asks me whether I know when and where it all started in our Soviet land—the tradition of substituting Russian-sounding pen names for the Jewish names of Soviet journalists. He remembered it, he said, as if it were yesterday, although it had all started almost thirty years ago. He couldn't remember the exact day, but he believed it was in September 1937. Speaking in the Reichstag, the Fuhrer waved a copy of *Pravda* at the podium. 'Here,' he shouted, 'see who leads the Bolshevik propaganda, dear comrades-in-arms! All the articles, one after another, are written by damn Jews!'

"'Well, the very next day, up there,' the typesetter said, while pointing to the ceiling, 'they dispatched a circular directive to all editorial offices around the country. The order was to replace all Jewish bylines with Russian-sounding pen names. I remember it well because I was young then, just married, and I couldn't wait for when my shift ended so I could run home and hop into bed with my young wife. Here our printing shop manager runs into the shop and cries out, "Stop the presses! Stop the presses!" He didn't allow us to leave the premises before we went through the whole typeset of the morning issue, picked out all the Jewish pen names, replaced them with Russian-sounding ones, and reset the pages.'

"So, Emil," Grigory said before we were about to part ways, "it looks like we both are part of a historical process, aren't we?"

9

How to Win Them Over

Time passes by. Comes June, my vacation time. I go home, to Odessa. To see my family, to jump into the warm waves of the Black Sea, to catch up with my old high school and college friends.

This time, I have decided not to fly home, as I usually do, but to take a train. It is a thousand-mile ride, which takes a full twenty-four hours, but I need time to collect my thoughts. There is a lot of stuff on my plate I have to digest. I want to be prepared to face my loved ones now that I have ventured on a new path in my life.

After I arrive, there will be Mama's birthday. As usual, she will throw a party, and I will be facing all the members of our extended family. My father's friend and colleague, Adolf Marshak, the former actor at the Odessa Yiddish theater, will also be there. He will come with his wife, Lia, and his son, Mark, a teenager.

Guests will pack our living room, which at night serves as my parents' bedroom. They all will take their seats around our dinner table, which Mama will expand with a smaller one, from the kitchen. We do not have enough chairs for everybody. So, from a small lumber-room, Papa and Uncle Misha will bring a few planed and oil-painted boards prepared for such occasions.

As usual, Mama will cook all her delicious dishes and bake her irresistible pastries; she is famous in the family for that.

The reason for my anxiety is as follows. I am not ashamed of my press work. Though I write for the press, I do not sing *Alleluia* to the authorities. I criticize whatever wrongdoings people write about in their letters to the editors. Besides bureaucracy and red tape, I write about the so-called "vestiges of the past, birthmarks of capitalism in the people's consciousness," such as envy, selfishness, greed, sycophancy, careerism, rudeness, bad manners, and the like. . . .

However, my family cares little for the Soviet media. From where my parents and other relatives stand, I am a sheep that has strayed from the flock.

I have informed no one about the journalistic part of my Moscow life. During my previous visit, I confided this to one person only—my younger brother, Vladimir. I guessed that he, a teenager, would hardly find anything wrong with what I do. He might even be a bit proud of the fact that his older brother writes for Moscow papers. I told him about it as a big secret, as one brother to another. It is unlikely he would spill the beans to our parents. However, he could have blurted it out to our cousins, his peers. So, it is possible my secret is already no longer a secret to some members of our extended family.

Therefore, if, during the birthday party, someone asks me what I write about over there, in Moscow, I want to be ready for that. I have to think through how I will convince them I write for the papers not only for the sake of beefing up my rather meager wages at the engineering lab but also because I take my writing seriously as a job that has to be done.

So, here I lie on the upper berth of the train compartment and stare into the darkness of the night. If they were to ask me, which of my pieces should I talk about? Well, let me see what I have published over the last year.

For starters, my safest bet is the subject of bureaucracy; everyone hates it. Why not tell them that mind-boggling story I published in the *Soviet Russia* paper last fall? The Western Siberian Rail-Road Management did not clean car wagons thoroughly after emptying them of coal. Why? Because the state regulations did not list every single part of the cars subject to cleaning. They named a few of them but they did not add "etc." It looks like the absence of these three letters made a difference between clean and dirty wagons.

It does not take me long to skip this story. I see my Uncle Misha rolling his eyes. Who cares about the coal-carrying wagons! So they don't clean them. *Big deal! I wish I had their problems!*

Well, maybe I should choose something everyone can identify with. What about that story of mine published in *Crocodile* a few months ago? It is about the misadventures of a young fellow trying to get his first passport in the town of Nalchik of the Northern Caucasus. The story should make them smile. In the Soviet Union, receiving your first passport is a rite of passage to adulthood, like getting a driver's license in the United States. Waiting for that solemn event for days, the boy tried to speak only

in a deep voice. He saw to it that his handshake was as firm as that of a
grown man. On the morning of his birthday, trembling with excitement,
he shaved his cheeks squeaky clean, though there was not much to worry
about. He sprinkled his underarms with cologne. He ironed his best suit.
As he made his way to the local Passport Bureau office, his shoeshine
made the passersby squint.

However, the office doors were closed that day. And the next day.
When, several days later, they opened, the young fellow had to stand for
hours in a mile-long line. By the time his turn came up, they had closed
the doors again. And no one had any clue when they were to reopen. It
seemed to be tied to the mood of the Passport Bureau officials. Several
vagaries may have also affected it—the air humidity level . . . the seis-
mographic prognosis for the nearby Caucasian ridge . . . the current
standing of the local soccer team in the All-Union tournament. . . . You
name it!

It had taken the youngster a month to get his hands on that coveted
proof of his adulthood. Besides certifying his age, the document also
proved that he had adult-strength stamina when dealing with the local
officials.

Here a sobering thought visits me again. I realize I should scrap this
story from my repertoire as well. But for a different reason.

"What a young schmuck!" Big Abram would say, removing his glasses
and cleaning them with his handkerchief as he always does when agitated. "What was his hurry? Did he want to get married or something?
At sixteen, he's too young for that. Otherwise, why help the police track
you down?"

He is right. Every Soviet passport has to show the residence registration.

"Is your young yo-yo Jewish?" my uncle would ask. "If he is, then he's
a double schmuck. Why hurry to let everyone out there know you're a
Jew?"

~

My train is approaching the city of Tula, a hundred miles from Moscow,
and I still have nothing to show for myself. I keep jogging my memory.
What else could pique my loved ones' interest? Ahem, what about my
other piece published in *Komsomol Pravda*, the one that also makes fun
of bureaucracy?

Victims of Allotment

"Ninety-eight . . . ninety-nine . . ." the school custodian said. "A hundred percent! . . . Hold it right there!"

"What about us?"

"Back off!"

"We also want to go to school!"

"Get lost!"

The custodian shut the door and exhaled into the keyhole: "You're unplanned!"

Outraged fathers rushed to the school principal. The man, however, was in a peaceful mood: "No need to get excited, dear comrades! Cool it down. Not a chance I'll let your children into our school."

"Why? Are our kids worse than others?"

"They aren't. They're lovely youngsters. But we're only allowed to accept a certain number of pupils into our school."

"What should we do now?" The fathers were at a loss.

"I won't accept them, that's all!"

"We'll complain!"

"Be my guest!"

And the hapless fathers of the village of Marfino in the Vologda region turned to the province's board of education.

It did them no good doing it either. Because, on the occasion of the plan fulfillment, the board was in a blissful state of mind. Straight from the lips of the deputy head of the board, the fathers received a reply, whose tenderness grabs your heart and does not let it go: "In response to your letter, we clarify hereby that the number of students accepted to the ninth grade of secondary schools is determined by the national economic plan. We deny your sons access to the school for a good reason. At the time of your application, the ninth-grade classes of secondary school #6 of the settlement Molochnoe were filled in full accordance with the plan."

Plan fulfillment is a beautiful and solemn occasion. But what is there to do for the young fellows whose unthinking parents hadn't coordinated their appearance in this world with the national economic plan?

I hardly finish running this story in my head when I see my uncles and aunties rolling their eyes again. *Give us a break! The state is trying to plan every unpredictable thing in life! What else is new?!*

It is already nightfall. The locomotive puffs along into the darkness of the night. I cannot fall asleep. I take a sleeping pill, hoping that, in the morning, I will come up with a winning idea. Finally, I doze off to the rhythmic rumble of the wheels.

~

I wake up in the morning when the car conductor knocks on my compartment door. He brings in tea in a faceted glass placed in a metal holder with small pellets of sugar in blue wrappings.

I sip my tea, and, as I overcome my morning drowsiness, a new idea enters my mind. Red tape! That's it! I recall the most bizarre case of it I have ever encountered in my life. When I examined the folder that Boris Protopopov of *Soviet Russia* handed me, I was astonished. Permission to produce such a simple thing as a new tablecloth had to jump through so many hoops before it hits the store shelves!

That is how things are set up at the flax production plant in the town of Privolzhsk of the Upper Volga region. When the plant's Arts Council approves a new design, the drawing goes to the Flax Industry Management of the regional People's Economic Council in the city of Kostroma. From there, it travels to the city of Ivanovo. Over there, the Council's Administration has to okay it. Then, they mail the sketch to Moscow, to the All-Union Product Assortment Institute for Light Industry. However, the sanctification of the new tablecloth pattern has to wait until the local Arts Council meets. This happens only once every four months.

You may think that, four months later, when the Arts Council authorizes the pattern, the factory looms in Privolzhsk will start running at once.

Think again! First, they have to produce a prototype of the new tablecloth. Then, instead of flying it back to Moscow, to the same Product Assortment Institute for a quick approval—six months have passed already!—the tablecloth sample goes to Kostroma. Then again to Ivanovo. Only after all that do they send it to the Moscow Institute, where, I remind you, the Arts Council gathers once every four months.

It would be wrong again to assume a year is plenty of time to push the new tablecloth through the bureaucratic maze. Not so fast, comrades! Until now, they have cleared the production of a tablecloth pilot batch only. Now, like a magic carpet, the batch has to fly . . . or, more to the point, drag over the same route again: Flax Industry Management—Administration of the Linen Industry—Central Scientific Bast Research Institute. It is bound to make additional stops at the Ministry of Trade and the Russian Textile Trade Administration. . . .

Maybe now, finally, when all these bodies have endorsed the pilot batch, it is time to produce it?

Hold your horses! An order is an order, and subordination is subordination. What is the chairman of the Regional Economic Council for? First, he must approve a product sample.

"What is there to approve?" you may ask. "Haven't all experts in the field spoken already?"

So what? The regulations require it. Since the Council chairman had looked at that sample a while ago, you cannot expect him to recall whether he had authorized the pattern already. So, they send the tablecloth approval papers for the fourth time around. Now it is to okay the tablecloth pricing.

For a while, I feel good. Finally, I have something that will make my loved ones shake their heads in outrage.

However, it does not take too long before I hear my father uttering one word, "*NEP!*"

He does it with a mixture of wonder, triumph, and joy. There is his characteristic shy smile on his lips. He holds up his index finger in the air to underscore how significant that word is.

I remember that, as I was growing up, whenever the family discussed shortages of goods in the stores, often involving first necessities, my father always uttered this word in the same dramatic manner.

In time, I learned that the word is an acronym for the "New Economic Policy." Back in the early twenties, they had introduced it to help the country recover from the civil war, from widespread hunger and deprivation. Under the NEP, they allowed private ownership of small and medium-sized companies and some other elements of the free market. Dad was a teenager then. He had arrived in Moscow from his hometown, the hunger-stricken Minsk, to work as a bottle washer for a compatriot who owned a paint store.

"*Ah!*" Dad used to exclaim. "I couldn't believe my eyes! Almost overnight they packed all the Moscow stores with goods of all kinds. That's what private initiative can do! If you give it a chance."

They abolished the policy in 1928, after Joseph Stalin came to power.

Now, when I imagine Dad's most likely reaction to my tablecloth story, I hear him repeat it, "NEP!" That is, "What else could you expect from the dreadful command economy?"

Well, what now? . . . I pace along the car wagon corridor until I think of another satirical piece of mine published in *Crocodile*. In it, I describe a disaster that befell the Volgograd authorities last fall—a bumper crop. It caught the region utterly unprepared. There were no elevators or granaries to safeguard the grain from the coming season of rain and then snow. To liven up the story, I introduced a scene with some uninformed vacationer cruising down the Don River with his family. The father points his school-age son toward the mountain-high piles of corn on the horizon, "Look over there, little Sasha! That's what you've covered in your geography classes. Those are the spurs of the Central Russian Upland."

After thinking about it, however, I decide against citing this or any other of my pieces that make fun of mismanagement. When writing them, I felt good about bringing to light all those glitches in the state machine. But now, I realize that my father will only shrug it off. His cure for the economy hiccups will always be the same—"NEP!"

Well, it looks like I should abstain from mentioning any of my write-ups on the country's economic woes. If I cite any of them, I will hear the same thing in response all over again—"NEP!," "NEP!," and "NEP!"

I give up on finding any piece of mine about the country's problems that would give me a chance to win them over. Gosh! There must be other things I wrote about that they would accept. But what?

∼

There is a twenty-minute stop coming up at the Kiev station. To stretch my legs, I step down onto the platform. I push through the crowd of passengers. What, what can I bring up that would sway my most uncompromising relatives—my father and my Uncle Misha—to my side?

I stick to the themes close to home, those they are familiar with first-hand. Perhaps because, growing up, I saw how hard my father worked to make a living to support his family, I am incensed when writing about the bonus fraud. They throw bonuses left and right for the slightest reason and even when there is none. Save holidays, come early morning hours, his family still asleep, my father would wake up and get ready for work. Carefully, so as not to make the door creak, he would enter the kitchen. There, he would get the leftovers from yesterday's dinner out of the refrigerator, throw them into the frying pan, and pour in two eggs to scramble. As soon as he saw the teapot about to whistle, he jerked it off the gas range and made tea for himself.

After breakfast, he left for work. To ensure that the lock of our exit door did not click too loudly, he would close it with the utmost care.

He came home late sometimes. It was necessary to finish that day's job, to not leave until morning the mess in the apartment where he had been working. He smelled the way a man of his profession does—of oil paint, of the turpentine he used to dissolve the paint, of the sweat of a hardworking man. . . .

Uncle Misha's toil was no less intense. Often, in the morning, he stopped by to pick up my father or waited for him on the job, at the apartment they were going to spruce up together.

Those childhood memories of my hardworking father and uncle make me outraged when I write about the frivolous bonuses thrown around at the state-run enterprises. I hope my father and uncle bless my ridiculing these abominable practices.

Many building administrators receive extra payment when handing over apartment houses to the local authorities. To pocket the money as soon as possible, they attach a promissory note to the documents they give to the officials—a punch list of jobs to be completed "as the work progresses" (*v rabochem poriadke*). In reality, it means, "Once you sign it, catch us if you can."

People's cries for help flood the correspondence departments of all Moscow papers. Thus, *Soviet Russia* published my write-up about the Siberian city of Bratsk. Last fall, with great pomp, the city hall let people move into hundreds of newly built apartments. The dwellings were hardly ready to shelter stray dogs and cats, never mind humans. The new settlers had to light candles, not to make their housewarming more exciting but to avoid bumping into each other in the dark. Besides the electrical work, the plumbing was also on the punch list of unfinished work. When nature called, the new settlers roamed the adjacent streets frantically in search of public toilets.

When the summer began, they started overhauling the roof of an apartment building in the Moscow district of Kiev. However, as soon as they dismantled the roof, they abandoned the site and moved on to other jobs in the neighborhood. The first rain flooded all fifty-two apartments, from the top floor to the bottom. The rainwater dripped into basins, pitchers, washtubs, pans, and other improvised vessels. These staccato sounds made people join hands, not to break into square dancing out of joy but to catch absent-minded housing managers. The catching game and the flooding continued throughout the summer. Late into the fall, the dwellers would pin the scatterbrained workers to the damp walls.

"Fix the roof, for crying out loud," they shouted, "or else!"

I am relieved. Finally, I have found something. Neither Dad nor Uncle Misha can approve of such frivolous bonus throwing.

Upon thinking about it some more, however, I decide these stories would not work either. Most likely, when my dad and my uncle hear them, they will exchange glances in disbelief. It would be difficult for them to even imagine how these things could take place in their lives. Even at the height of summer, when they are in high demand, they would not even think of abandoning the apartment at hand. To start another job just for the sake of grabbing the upfront money? It is not only a matter of decency. If something like that occurred, they would have to kiss goodbye their future customers. . . .

Oh, I got it! I would give them my pieces published in the pages of the all-union newspaper *Labor*, the organ of the country's Central Council of Soviet Trade Unions. That is it! I have got it finally. Out of solidarity, my father and my uncle should empathize with the plight of hardworking, blue-collar people like themselves. When I composed those pieces, I was satisfied with the fact that I was standing up for the little man. It felt good to speak up against the tyranny of the local bosses, their rudeness and their disregard for their subordinates' human dignity.

Here are a few examples I ran in my practice. A wicked director of the sheep-breeding factory in the Orlov district of the Rostov region had mistreated one of his truck drivers. Now he was delaying reimbursement for the man's travel expenses. . . . Now he struck his name off the list of bonus recipients. . . . The reason was simple. When the Ministry of Agriculture's inspector general questioned the driver about his director's shenanigans, the man told him the truth and nothing but the truth. However, neither God himself nor the local authorities helped the man when the director abused him.

In the town of Gorlovka of the Donetsk region, a shop supervisor at the local machine-building plant pocketed his subordinates' bonuses. He did not even try to come up with some plausible excuse beyond the first thing he could think of—"That's the way it has to be done."

At the Kazan construction material plant, a tremendous attrition of workers took place year after year. When questioned about the reasons for it, the plant management shrugged, "It's a mystery!" However, the moment you step into the workers' shower room, the mystery dissipates. First, you are getting a shower way before you undress. On your way to the dressing room, you run into a spray of sprinkling water produced by the rusting pipes. . . . Things are not easier after you have taken your shower. To get to the benches with your clothes, you need to master solid ballet dancing skills. To cross over the huge puddle on the dressing room floor, you must use your ability to move *en pointe*. Then, you have to climb on the windowsill and, after cooling your heels in the puddle, run over the radiators to the benches on the other side of the room. If you are no good at making long ballet jumps known as *grand jetés*, you can brace yourself and wade through the puddles. However, it will make you need to take your shower all over again.

For a while, I rejoice. Finally, I have figured out how to make my loved ones see that my writing does good things. After all, I come to the defense of ordinary blue-collar workers, like them, who are persecuted, humiliated, robbed, and forced to work in dismal conditions.

Alas, this thought does not console me for too long. My heart sinks the moment I realize that all these stories reaffirm my dad's and my uncle's decision to stay clear of working for any Soviet enterprise. Yes, toiling privately, they do risk being fined or even jailed for running a private business. However, nobody will humiliate them or rob them of their hard-earned income. As to their working conditions, they wash up under the tap at the apartment they fix and go home where they take their shower without the need to have the ballet dancer's skills. . . .

The train is just an hour away from arriving in Odessa. I jog my memory desperately. There must be something I wrote that they will approve of, that at least some members of my extended family will accept. I am about to lose my spirit. One of my satirical targets has been the embezzlement of public funds. As in America, where some Congressmen use their election campaign funds to fly their families to the Swiss Alps for skiing, some Soviet officials also do not mind shoving their hand into a pocket not their own. For *Soviet Russia*, I have written about a certain Comrade Ivanova, chief of the Ishim District Board of Education in the

Omsk region. She used funds intended for needy students not only to buy a Volga sedan for herself but also to hire a private chauffeur. She put the man on the board's payroll, listing him as a school inspector. . . .

I feel this case is my sure bet. When this story reaches the ears of Big Abram, intolerant of any injustice, he would not be able to contain himself. I wager he would even shout something like, "They should throw that bitch in jail! It'd serve her right!"

With hope in my heart for my justice-loving uncle's outrage, I arrive in Odessa.

~

Comes June 4, my mother's birthday. All our relatives and family friends gather in our apartment. Everyone exchanges greetings with me. How are things over there, in Moscow? They ask me questions. Are the capital stores well stocked? Can you find buckwheat over there, for example?

Then they take their seats around the table. The usual toasting begins. To the birthday girl, to her husband, to her children. . . . Everyone enjoys my mother's cooking. They exchange the latest city rumors. Nobody asks me anything about my new journalistic endeavor.

It looks like my brother kept his word. He has not blurted out anything about it.

More time passes. Things move to dessert. I examine the faces of my uncles and aunts. Some of them avoid making eye contact with me— or am I imagining it? A thought enters my head that makes me blush from humiliation. What if they know everything about my involvement with the papers but they don't consider it worthy of much attention? They let it slide the way worldly-wise senior family members treat a young fellow's embarassing sexual indiscretions. They take a lenient view of it. The lad is wet behind the ears, a hothead. So, he has caught a cold in the pants. Well, things happen. He is still a lousy judge of women. It's okay. When the young fellow matures, he will learn to be more careful.

I am about to lose heart when my dad's friend Marshak, a former actor of Jewish theater, speaks up across the table. His dark eyes sparkle like bits of hard coal. He wrinkles his flattened nose, the kind a boxer often has.

"Oh, Emil dear," he says, looking over everyone cockily as if inviting the others to join him in his fun, "have you seen that movie clip about cows with wire in their stomachs? Oh, my God! I didn't know whether I should laugh or cry."

He refers to the most recent issue of the satirical newsreel *The Wick*, which has just hit movie theater screens around the country. The newsreel producers read my satirical article in *Soviet Russia* last spring and asked me to write a script for them.

The theme of the story, titled "The Iron Logic," is the poor quality of machines producing hay pellets for cattle feeding. The wire that ties up the pellets is of such dismal quality that it often breaks. Its pieces wind up in the cows' stomachs. It seems that, in their simplemindedness, the cattle mistake bits of wire in their hay for multivitamins aimed at cheering up their rather dull life. The result is quite dramatic for them: often, their lives are at stake. All pleadings with the machine manufacturer to do something about the wire have fallen on deaf ears. The problem has been dragging for such a long time that someone at the Moscow Veterinary Academy has already defended a dissertation titled "Extracting Metallic Waste from Cattle's Stomachs."

Here some other family members also shake their heads. They have seen it. They nod. They even grin. Is it because of Marshak's long-standing reputation as an entertainer at our family gatherings, or do they find the story funny?

(To this day, remembering that episode in my life, I am not sure what took place then. Did Marshak talk about the clip in *The Wick* just because I lived in Moscow, where they produce the satirical newsreel? Or my younger brother could not hold it in after all and blurted to Marshak's son Mark about my press activities? Maybe, with his artistic soul, Marshak sensed I needed the moral support of my loved ones?)

My vacation ends, and I go back to Moscow. There are still a lot of battles ahead of me. One of them is to break into the field of publishing not as a freelancer but as a staff member. I want to make a full-time job out of what I like doing. Is that too much to ask for in one's life?

10

A Mosquito in Amber

A mosquito in amber. . . . This image comes to my mind whenever I recall this episode of my Soviet life. . . .

I am back in Moscow. It is mid-June 1966. After the cooler weather of May, a heat wave has hit the city. Like tanks before a decisive battle, large cisterns of *kvass*—a fermented beverage made out of bread, much sought after in summer and as popular as Coca-Cola in America—roll out onto the street corners. The kvass sellers, hefty middle-aged women with double chins, settle themselves in front of the tap and take a deep breath while smoothing out the white aprons on their knees. They are getting ready for a day of trying work. On such a hot day, providing kvass for the cheeky Muscovites without damaging your psyche will not be easy. Even the fact that they have recently cracked down on hooliganism in the country is unlikely to help. The first Soviet automatic vending machines for seltzer water are now available in the streets, but everyone knows seltzer has no chance of competing with kvass, the cherished summer drink.

I emerge from the subway at Dzerzhinsky Square in downtown Moscow and head to the Chinese Gates. As far I as I know, somewhere under the gate arch should be the personnel department of the "Entrails of the Earth," Nedra Publishing House.

I am acting on the advice of my friend Victor's father, who works in the Ministry of the Press. Even though by now my satirical pieces have appeared in a wide range of papers and magazines, I cannot even dream of becoming a staff member over there. When I discover job openings in the feuilleton department of the places that have published my work, I tell the department heads I would not mind letting go of my boring engineering career and coming aboard. They laugh, thinking I am joking.

They slap me on the shoulder, saying, "Oh, man, don't play a fool! You know what's what."

And they are right—I do. It is not that complicated. No matter how you look at it, I am unemployable as a staff member in all those places for being both a Jew and a non-Party member. I should know that ideology is an essential part of any Soviet media outlet. And I have not one but two strikes against being qualified for a staff member at any of them.

So, one day, having learned about my situation, Victor's father has opined that I might want to use the back door to find my way in. For starters, capitalizing on my engineering training, I should try to get a job as an editor at some publishing house specializing in technology. Then, perhaps, I could move to a literary publishing house; all of them are under the same Ministry of the Press. A publishing house serving the same industry as my engineering job would be my best bet as a point of entry.

I do not know how realistic his advice is, but I decide to give it a try and approach the Nedra Publishing House. It specializes in the gas and oil industry, to which my research lab belongs. With my engineering degree and newspaper publishing record, I feel I have a fighting chance.

I am aware it would not be easy. It is not a great time to find a job for "persons of Jewish ethnicity," as they call Jews in the Soviet press. After World War II, there has hardly ever been a good time for that. A good many Jewish jokes address this sad state of affairs:

A man comes to the director of the Moscow Circus and puts a little suitcase on his desk. Little mice in black tuxedoes run out of the suitcase and make a semicircle. They take out their tiny musical instruments from tiny cases and play Tchaikovsky's "First Violin Concerto."
Director: "Unbelievable! Stupendous!"
"So, can I count on a job offer?"
"No, you can't. Your first violin looks Jewish."

Or another one:

A man walks into the HR department and says, "My name is Rabinovich. Do you need specialists of this kind?"

So here I am. I reach the Chinese Gates in the central Moscow district and enter the office of the Nedra Personnel Department. A little round mirror from her purse in hand, a hefty middle-aged woman fixes her makeup. The onslaught of the heat has ruined it. She powders her glistening nose, pretending not to notice me. It looks that she does not feel like even turning toward him—she acts like a heat-exhausted dog that disregards even the most threatening body approaching its fence.

Finally, the manager tears herself away to check out the visitor. She cannot believe her eyes. A man with pronounced Jewish physiognomy asks about job openings. She peeks into my documents. The ambiguity of the situation irritates her. How could someone who is not only Jewish-looking but also Jewish according to his passport have the audacity to apply for a job in the Soviet press? And he is doing it on such a hot day!

Her stern facial expression betrays her attempts to parse the situation at hand. Either it is just today's heat has melted the visitor's brain, or he is a certified mental case.

Idly, she cools herself with a handheld fan that smells of Indian sandalwood. Her hand exhausted, she brings her face closer to a portable electric fan on her desk.

Since the strange visitor shifts from foot to foot but does not spare her his presence, the manager tries to get rid of him with the time-tested technique known to all soccer goalies. In a dangerous situation, they do not risk throwing themselves under the feet of the forwards rushing toward the goal. Instead, they kick the ball hard, sending it as far away into the open field as they can. The bureaucrats call such a maneuver "booting it off," or "soccer-kicking" (*otfutbolit'*).

After fixing her hair and looking into her mirror, the manager powders her nose again and, without looking up, says: "Automatics and telecontrol, you say? Oh, you're in the wrong place. We have that department somewhere else."

"Where is it?" I say.

"Over there," she waves her hand toward the window. "On Kirov Street . . . Somewhere in the courtyard across from that tea and coffee shop."

Here, instead of picking up on her "*Hit the road, comrade!*" cue—I should have expected to be turned down—I drag myself from under the Chinese Gates toward Kirov Street with little enthusiasm. Luckily, it is not too far, a few blocks up toward the Nikitsky Gates.

I reach the tea and coffee shop. Then, I cross the street and enter the vast courtyard on the opposite side. I circle it, hardly believing I will ever find the editorial office they soccer-kicked me to. The yard turns out to have two exits, one of which leads to Bent-Knee (*Krivokolennyj*) Alley. I see the street sign and think to myself, *Well, they've kneed your ass with a bent knee, my friend. What else did you expect to happen, you fool?*

Outside of one hall, I spot a doorplate that reads "Nedra Publishing. Editorial Office of Literature in Automatics and Tele-Control."

I am surprised. Wow! They have not sent me to some Nowhereville, after all. . . .

I go up to the second floor. Like many stairways in the country, it is poorly lit and reeks of cat urine. I enter the dark corridor of a communal apartment. For lack of better facilities, they have quartered the editorial offices here. I knock on one door, then on another, until I find the department head, Lyudmila Bykova, an energetic, good-looking woman in her early forties, dressed in a smart, beige business suit.

I introduce myself, tell her that the house's personnel department has sent me to her, and put my résumé on her desk. She picks it up and gives it a quick look.

"Who do you say sent you here?" she asks, peering into my face, trying to understand what kind of creature, like a bat to the light, has flown into her office.

"Well, the personnel department," I say.

For a while, the muscles of her face freeze in a mask of uncertainty. The manager tries to figure out why in the world they have sent her someone with a Jewish surname to be considered for a book editor position.

She mulls it over for a while. Then, she makes a mistake many well-educated people do. She puts too much trust in the belief the world operates strictly according to the cause-and-effect principle. She does not allow for happenstance, which sometimes plays a crucial role in life. She interprets my presence in her office as the personnel department's recommendation to hire me. I have the qualifications. I hold a bachelor's degree in electrical engineering and have a long list of publications in the central press of the country.

The manager spends a few more minutes trying to figure out what is wrong with the personnel department. Then, in addition to her belief in the cause-and-effect principle, redundant information lets her down. As I am to learn much later, at this moment, not knowing what she should do, she remembers a trifle of a fact in her superior's life. Once, during a party in a private circle (only heads of departments had been invited), the director of the publishing house entertained his subordinates, recalling a recent episode of his family life.

They had sent him, a renowned chemical engineer, on a business trip to Egypt to build a local oil refinery. As usual, he applied for visas to the country for himself and his wife. To his surprise, he received a call from the City Party committee inviting him for a private talk. During the conversation, the authorities told him he had to get a new passport for his wife for this trip. A few things in her current one had to be changed. Two items—her patronymic and her ethnicity—specified in her passport were problematic. The thing was that, while her first name, Irina, and her Russian surname, which was her husband's, were proper for the forthcoming trip, her Jewish patronymic, Isaakovna, and the fifth item, her ethnicity, made it clear she was Jewish. And that was unacceptable.

About two years before that, Nikita Khrushchev had awarded the Egyptian president Gamal Abdel Nasser the title Hero of the Soviet Union. He had also decorated him with the Order of Lenin and the Golden Star. Thus, the Soviet leader had shown how much he respected the Egyptian president and how much the Soviet people loved their Arab allies. Now, however, as if not giving a damn about Nasser's dream to destroy the Jewish state in his backyard, a Soviet specialist would arrive in Egypt accompanied by his Jewish spouse. What a faux pas!

The authorities offered to fix the problem by issuing a new passport for the director's wife. In that document, her Jewish patronymic Isaakovna was to be replaced with Muslim one, Ismailovna, and, instead of identifying her ethnicity as being Jewish, they would make her an Azerbaijani.

I did not know what was guiding me when I was heading to the Nedra Publishing House—naiveté, despair, stupidity or perhaps a mixture of them. But it looks like Comrade Bykova, by all means an intelligent person, had a hard time imagining that a Jew could do something so outrageous as to ask for a job walking in from the street. That cannot be. The only explanation she could come up with was that the personnel department sent me to her because I must be some relative of the director's wife. It seems she recalled the director's story, the hiccup before his recent business trip to Egypt, and she thought of the proverbial Jewish nepotism stereotype. According to this tall tale, all Jews cover each other's back; they care about their own only.

To clarify the situation, Bykova picks up the phone and calls the personnel department.

"I have Samuil Abramovich Draitser here," she utters while looking at me. "He says he's come here on your recommendation."

I did not use the word "recommendation." The only explanation for why Bykova mentioned my full name, complete with my given name, my patronymic, and my surname, is that she wanted to signal (in an unlikely case they might have missed it) that I am a Jew.

So, what Bykova is saying is this: *I have an all-around Jew here in my office looking for a position in my department. Am I correct in understanding that you recommend him for a job here?*

If anything goes wrong, she does not want to be blamed for making the risky move of hiring a Jew.

A long, theatrical-length pause ensues. I guess that, made drowsy by the heat, the personnel manager tries to understand what the editorial manager's call is all about. Why does she ask such a strange question? How could anyone in their right mind hire a Jew nowadays?

Since the pause drags on, Bykova adds: "Generally speaking, we need a book editor. He has an engineering degree and quite a few publications."

She uses the adverb "generally" not by chance. It leaves room to add, "but the decision is up to the superiors."

To this day, I have no idea what took place. Maybe the personnel manager also recalled the director's story and was afraid to damage her relationship with him, or perhaps something else happened. Either way, they hired me.

∼

Two years later, when, as the Soviet cliché has it, I have already "bonded with the collective" (*vlilsia v kollektiv*), while clinking our wine glasses during our International Women's Day party, Bykova asked me: "Hey, Emil, how's Irina Isaakovna doing nowadays?"

Seeing I did not know what she was talking about, she froze for a moment. Then, she corrected herself: "Well, I mean 'Irina Ismailovna'?"

Since a big question mark remained on my face, she realized I had no fricking idea who "Isaakovna-Ismailovna" was.

For a minute, she looked at me with hostility, as if I had cheated her. Then she softened up. Anyway, they could not do anything at this point. It has been a year already since the Six-Day War waged by Arab countries against Israel had ended, and a movement to allow Jewish emigration from the Soviet Union had begun. In the political climate of the time, it was not clear how to deal with Jewish employees in Soviet workplaces. This question bounced from one official's desk to another, not unlike how one throws a hot potato from one hand to another, waiting until it cools down.

However, unlike a hot potato, neither the Jewish question nor the Jews themselves ever cooled down. So, the employers had developed a formula of "three not-to-dos" for Jewish employees—*do not to hire them, do not to fire them,* and *do not to promote them.*

That year, amber became trendy in the country. Everyone collected it, and the country's fashion mongers used it to make brooches and necklaces. People especially prized pieces of amber with some insect in it, a fly or a mosquito.

Now, by the time the head of my editorial department discovered she had blundered when hiring me, I had already slipped under the "three not-to-dos" radar: I had become the proverbial "mosquito in amber."

11

Apples of Discord

Now that, thanks to bureaucratic astigmatism, I am employed in the publishing industry, I attend to my satirical career with renewed enthusiasm. No matter the circumstances in which that fluke occurred, they took me, a Jew, in. They have accepted me as an equal. Times have changed.

I get more evidence of the shift in the country's political climate when I get a call from Sasha Shcherbakov, head of the feuilleton department of *Komsomol Pravda*. He invites me to stop by; he has something interesting for me. It means some promising material for a full-length feuilleton for his paper.

For a few years, the paper's editor-in-chief, Alexei Adzhubej, Khrushchev's son-in-law, infused it with the spirit of the Thaw, the cultural rejuvenation that came with the denunciation of Stalin's crimes against humanity. Designed to reach young people of Komsomol age, from age fourteen to twenty-eight, the paper became much livelier, eased up on the propaganda, and became more generous toward material that interests young people—sports, travel, and humor. The paper's circulation skyrocketed, reaching several million copies.

Among the topical satires I had published there recently was a piece that addressed both the shortage of hotels in the country and the utter lack of hospitality. To relieve these shortages, it was forbidden to check into a hotel in the city where you were a permanent resident. In the industry that should be hospitable by definition, they treat hotel guests terribly. I wrote a flash-fiction story and, on Sasha's advice (to avoid being accused of generalization), provided each paragraph with footnotes indicating the names of the hotels in which I suffered indignities during my journalistic travels:

ONE NIGHT ONLY

Every time I approach a hotel registration desk, a presentiment of
a hard, train station bench passes throughout my ribs. I have
already given up interpreting the NO VACANCY sign as two
ordinary Russian words. For me, it is some cabalistic mark, a bad
omen of forthcoming misery and humiliation.

But this time I was in luck.

"One night only!" came the voice to my side of the partition,
and they shoved me a piece of paper. "Sign this 'Promise to Vacate'
note!"

"Excuse me," I said, "why go through such a formality? If it's
only till the morning, so be it. I'm leaving your town early in the
day, anyway."

"O-ho-ho!" The front-desk clerk stretched out the exclamation.
"We know you well."

"Me?"

"All of you. You all say you'll leave, but then we end up having
to call the police to throw you out. Either sign the promissory
note or else!"

I gave in. The clerk copied everything she needed from my
passport into her thick ledger, then locked my passport in a small
desk safe, which would not have been too hard for some intruder
to walk off with, together with all its contents.

"Excuse me, why do you keep my passport?"

"W-well," faltered the manager, "just in case. Anything can
happen."

"But haven't you written everything down, anyway?" I argued.
"All my identifying marks and coordinates? If I abduct a towel or
an ashtray, then you can call for a police search."

"Oh, a search!" she cried, waving her hands. "They may spend a
year looking for you all over the whole country. And the country
of ours is vast, as you might be aware of. Meanwhile, I have to
show my books to my boss now. Got it?"

I did not get it. But, since, in some uncontrollable section of my
cerebral hemisphere, I harbored a sinful daydream about spending
a second night in this hotel, I grabbed my suitcase and set off to
find my room.

The first thing that caught my attention was a register in a gilded frame, which listed every object in the room. The register had a grand ring to it, and a tone of warning. I was seized with trembling. I feverishly counted every item in the room, and only on finding all in place was I able to calm down and go out to the hall to have a smoke.

I was about to strike the match when I was suddenly toppled onto the floor, nearly breaking my neck and raising a cloud of dust. When the cloud had settled somewhat, I could see the maid rolling the hall carpet into a tight cylinder.

"Why are you taking it away?"

"Just for the night," she said in a dramatic tone.

"Why? Who's going to take it?"

"Who! Who knows who all of you, the guests, really are?"

I walked up and down the hall for a while, here and there stumbling upon the sign

ANY UNPAID BED IS CONSIDERED VACANT

Ready to go to sleep, I pulled off the bedspread and cringed: on the pillow, there was something black and nasty. It was a stamp done in shoe polish, which read:

CITY COMMUNAL SERVICE
HOTEL "REST YOUR CASE"
INVENTORY #_____

There was no number. While drifting off to sleep, I realized with a shiver that it was a no-man's-pillow. Without fail, someone might swipe it from me in the night.

Just as the dawn broke, I found the maid standing over me. She was holding an elderly, unshaven man in a vertical position. It was clear he had spent a sleepless night. One of his eyes was closed, and the other gazed at me dreamily, though shrewdly.

"Just look at him!" said the maid in a scolding voice. "Still sleeping like a log, when it's another guest's turn already!"

At these words, the man smiled, dropped his suitcase, and, sighing, tumbled down onto my legs.

I caught up with my sleep on a park bench.

Now, when I enter Sasha's office, he smiles and hands me a letter to the editor. I read it and understand why he feels I am going to be pleased with it. The letter is a jewel for a feuilletonist; it would be a piece of cake to make people laugh. No need to steer your imagination to find some interesting plot. My job in composing a satirical article is only to inter-line the letter with short commentaries here and there.

However, reading the letter has a strange effect on me. While scan-ning it, I go through an admixture of contradictory emotions. Addressed to the head of a police precinct, the letter horrifies me, makes me rejoice, and saddens me at the very same time.

The horror comes from the realization that the letter in my hands is, in fact, a police denunciation, which hearkens back to Stalin's time. Back then, it was enough to send such a letter, even anonymously, to the local NKVD office, as the state secret police were named at that time, and the person against whom the accusations were laid would be snapped up in no time. He or she would be persecuted without the bother of following the protocols of investigation and court hearings. There was no time to waste on hearing out deliberations between prosecution and defense. After all, it did not matter whether the accused was guilty or innocent. The gulag camps were always in need of more slaves to toil on the gigan-tic construction sites around the country. That is how the material base of socialism was built in Russia, to begin with.

I rejoice that, even though now, in the year 1968, many Khrushchev-inspired relaxations of Stalinist political dogmas have been rolled back under Brezhnev, the savage treatment of citizens no longer occurs on the scale of the 1930s. The resumed winter of discontent is not as harsh in comparison. After all, the punitive organs dismissed the letter as un-worthy of their time and let the press react to it.

Still, I am saddened that such a letter could be written in our time. It opens my eyes to the fact that Stalin is still alive in some people's hearts. The author of the letter assumes that, as in the dictator's time, the puni-tive functions of the state machinery are at his personal disposal.

That the author of the letter discloses a private matter in public does not surprise me, however. The whole Soviet way of life emphasizes the prevalence of the collective consciousness over any private considera-tions, "A collective is always right!" The authorities have encouraged this way of thinking by introducing "comrades' courts" recently. Now, they can call you out to be publicly scorned at your residence for some family squabble or petty hooliganism. You may also be condemned by the general meeting at the place of work for your "antisocial actions."

All these things may explain why the border between the personal and the public in the so-called simple Soviet person's mind is washed out, like the coastal strip between the ocean and the estuary. No wonder people treat the institutions of power as ones that are supposed to serve their personal needs.

For example, it is not uncommon for an abandoned wife to turn in desperation to the Party committee at her fugitive husband's employment seeking help in bringing to order the irresponsible Party member "for immoral behavior." She expects the committee to force him, under the threat of being expelled from the Party (which would bring much more damage to his reputation than if he were not a Party member), to come to his senses.

The Party takes such complaints seriously. They do not take no for an answer. A true Communist must overcome any obstacles. As the Party claim has it, "There are no fortresses that the Bolsheviks aren't capable of taking over!" The following underground joke of the time illustrates this concept well:

> A woman complains to the Party committee at her husband's place of work that he neglects to fulfill his conjugal duties.
>
> They call the man in for a talk.
>
> "Comrade Ivanov!" says the Party committee's secretary. "We've received a complaint about you ignoring your marital duties. As you must know, we Communists stand guard over a strong Soviet family. What can you say in your defense?"
>
> "Hm," Ivanov says. "Well, you know . . . my age . . . I'm not a spring chicken anymore. . . . My health is no longer as good as it used to be. . . . Well, to call a spade a spade, I've got to admit I'm impotent."
>
> "Impotent? Ha!" the secretary says. "Don't you ever forget, Comrade Ivanov, first and foremost, you're a Communist!"

The appeal to the press to intervene in private life contained in the letter Shcherbakov hands me in is not the first one in my journalistic practice. One day, as I sat in the editorial office of *Soviet Russia*, proofreading the galleys of my satirical article, a tall, middle-aged woman entered the room. A crumpled paper in her hands, she approached me and slapped it on the desk.

"Write a feuilleton about the bastard!" she said. "All the details are here."

She seemed to make it clear there could not be a more important matter to which the paper should attend than the one she called for.

"I won't let it go like this," she said. "I'll fight! I'll make the rascal go back where he belongs—to his family."

And now, this letter to *Komsomol Pravda* has arrived. I feel compelled to publish it as is with my commentaries:

Apples of Discord

Thanks to the millennia-long efforts of humanity, a multitude of the trickiest problems has been solved. However, it remains a mystery what to do if your sweetheart does not reciprocate in kind.

Dear readers, just think of it! Nowadays, to split an atom is possible. . . . To make a round trip into space is also possible. . . . To summon a plumber from your building housing department is hard but, in principle, is also possible. But if some human being does not care much about your amorous feelings, in the vast universe, no organization can fix this disharmony. No one is there to turn to who could solve this issue in your favor.

Today, we hasten to cheer up our readers with the breaking news: thanks to the efforts of some strong-willed comrades, this most unjust, centuries-old glitch in human relationships is finally taken care of. From now on, as soon as you, a citizen in love, confirm your suspicions of nonreciprocity, follow the example of A. B. Sidorov, a resident of the city of Ashkhabad of the Turkmenian Soviet Socialist Republic.

Take a pack of writing paper, interleave it with carbon paper, and get down to business. In the upper right corner of the page, type out the position and the name—the last, the first, and the patronymic—of the main addressee, the head of the police precinct of the district where your hardhearted darling resides. A line below, show where the copies will go, as Comrade Sidorov has done in his letter:

(1) To the district prosecutor office of the [beloved's] place of residence;
(2) To the head of [her] housing department;
(3) To the house management;
(4) To the editor-in-chief of a newspaper (preferably an All-Union one).

After the heading "A Complaint," describe, as precisely as possible, the duration and character of your relationship with your paramour:

> When [we met and] she learned I was unmarried (single), she promised to come over to live with me in Turkmenistan, in the city of Ashkhabad. I left for my home alone. We corresponded with each other, and, over the year, I received 8 (eight) letters from her. In each letter, she kept promising to come to me, to the city of Ashkhabad. She mentioned in her letters that she worked and studied in the evenings. Finally, she wrote that she was employed as a senior engineer and received 120 (one hundred twenty) rubles, and soon she would receive 160 (one hundred sixty) rubles. I believed her, considered her an honest, good girl and thought she would make a good wife for me.

Once you have explained the source of your sublime feelings, show the specific signs confirming their depth and authenticity:

> I sent parcels and gifts to her and made money transfers. She received them, replied to my letters, and thanked me.

Now it is the time to get down to telling about sharp turns, ruptures, and dramatic collisions in your relationship with the human being dear to you but cruel at heart:

> I wrote to her I would arrive soon, but she wrote in her last letter I shouldn't come. I still could not help it. I traveled to Moscow and went to her address to look her up. She met me coldly, scolded me about why I came.

All the aforesaid is written for public organizations and the collective at her main place of work or residence. For the police and prosecutors, you need weightier evidence of deception. False promises alone would be not enough for them to open a criminal case against the ungrateful one:

> And what do you think! I learned there from the building super that she does not study at all, and she works not as an engineer but only as a yard-keeper. In short, there, on the spot, I found out she is a con artist. Perhaps she acts this way with others, and she deceives them as well.

That's it! The last phrase radically changes the nature of your letter. This is no longer a private complaint; it is an act of civic awareness. Your personal business has thus gained a social significance. Now, it becomes a report to the authorities, which each of the addressees must investigate. And, the citizen who dared not to respond to your feelings is bound to be visited by a police operative, at the very least:

> I hope that, upon receipt of this letter, you take the appropriate action and inform me about the results.

There is a nightmarish way to bring the conceited paramour to her senses at once. Only a real man, which Comrade Sidorov is, can bring himself to do it:

> I decided to tell you everything so that you take measures against her behavior, punish her for her chicanery, and make her return everything I sent to her.

And, right there, attach all your postal receipts, as Comrade Sidorov has done. This action should make a proper impression.

Don't you gasp, dear readers! It is a time-tested way of doing things. Before the resident of the city of Ashkhabad, Turkmenia, a resident of the city of Venice, Italy, a certain Othello, demanded from a certain Desdemona (of the same residence) that she returned to him his gift—a handkerchief. . . .

Well, you may object that all this took place between lawful spouses with common property rights. Therefore, Comrade Sidorov is all the more spot-on! Because he demands his own stuff, dear to him: eleven pounds of Turkmen apples, a vial of sample perfume, and a kerchief.

And, mind you, not some *hand* kerchief, which Othello had demanded from Desdemona, but a *head* kerchief, knitted, which, as the attached price tag proves, is worth one ruble sixty-five kopeks.

In my practice, however, cases like this one, where the source material requires only ironic commentary, are few and far between. Most often, you need to build a feuileton from the ground up, that is, to come up with a form that fits the content.

PART IV

In Hot Water,
1971

12

The Scatterbrain Debacle

"Hey, what's up, man?" says Sasha Moralevich in his usual warm and friendly manner when I stop by his office. Sitting in his swivel chair, he turns his whole body toward me. Sasha belongs to the *Crocodile* elite; he is one of the magazine's few special correspondents and a member of the editorial board.

I tell him I have just returned from one of my first out-of-town journalistic trips. Without asking for my travel impressions, he shakes his head. He knows it all too well. He has crisscrossed our homeland many times.

"A country of mice and frogs, isn't it?" he says shaking his head.

Sasha is young, only a year older than me; he is not even thirty yet. A tall, smiling fellow with the face of a teenager, which does not match his robust body. He more resembles a sportsman—an athlete, a boxer, or a wrestler—than an intellectual. He is vigorous and dapper, and his natural

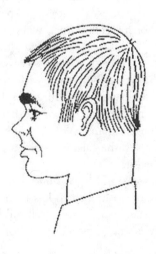

Alexander Moralevich,
Crocodile's special
correspondent (a friendly
cartoon by Vladmir Shkarban)

friendliness and self-confidence attract women. When I see him, sitting in his office, smiling, relaxed, and full of energy, it is hard to imagine he spends most of his time on the road. He visits the most remote parts of the country, be it a mountain range or the tundra. While traveling on his assignments, he finds time for hunting and fishing. It does not prevent him from filing a new double-spread feuilleton for every *Crocodile* issue, which comes out three times a month. And what a piece! A talented writer of satirical prose, Sasha is the undisputed king of the feuilleton genre. He has been awarded the prize for the best feuilleton of the year many times. All the *Crocodile* writers, both staff members and freelancers, envy him. His talent is self-evident and indisputable, and he radiates so much friendliness that it is hard to have ill feelings toward him.

Sasha places the highest demands on the genre of journalism he practices; he holds it in the highest regard. (As he jokes, being a genuine satirical columnist is the second most uncommon job in the world, the first being the Patriarch of All Russia. There have been only four for the past century.) In his view, even in America, a country of the free press, only two columnists are worthy of this high calling—Art Buchwald and Russell Baker.

Shortly after meeting me for the first time, Sasha confided in me his deep childhood wound. He spoke with that wide smile of his, even though his early life was hardly amusing. This big, strong, and talented man was once a two-year-old baby left to starve in his parents' sealed apartment. The year was 1938, the time of the Great Terror. One night, the NKVD operatives broke into his family's home, shouting, "Money? Jewelry? Weapons?" They arrested both of his parents and his grandparents. Later on, they shot his grandfather, who was accused of being an "enemy of the people," and they exiled his grandmother for fifteen years. They sentenced both of his parents to years in prison.

Sasha wrote about those early episodes of his life in one of his poems, "Amid the bandits and riffraff, I grew the way the weeds do." The tattoos on his arms appeared then (at that point in Russian history, only criminals sported them).

However, the calamities of his early age did not break his spirit; they hardened it.

Now, when I stepped into his office, I have just returned from a trip to Volokolamsk, a town less than a hundred kilometers from Moscow. Before that trip, I knew well only my native city, Odessa. I also lived three years in Kiev, the capital of the Ukrainian Socialist Republic, an

enchanting city, rustling with poplars along its boulevards. Now I reside in Moscow, its quarters spread around its center like a giant sun-
flower. When my train stopped in Volokolamsk, what I saw stunned me.
I stepped out of the train car as if a time machine had thrown me back
into the nineteenth—or even the eighteenth—century. On its beat-up
sidewalks covered with plucked grass, goats wandered, shaking their thin
graybeards. Rain blackened the rotting logs of the houses. A local church
had become so lopsided that it rivaled the Leaning Tower of Pisa.

Sasha listens and nods. It is clear he has seen lots of backwoods places
during his business trips around the country.

"Yes, buddy," he says. "Yes, we live in a country of mice and frogs."

~

A Soviet satirist is hardly the same as an investigative journalist in the
West. His job is not to dig out some unseemly truths about, say, corrup-
tion or abuse of power. Mostly, he ridicules things the state apparatus has
proved wrong and worthy of criticism. Like most Soviet satirists, I write
my pieces relying on documents of various kinds—local court decisions,
police reports, or protocols of the communal comrades' courts. The press
also receives plenty of documents from the Peoples' Control Committees.
These governmental organs are mostly concerned with violations in the
sphere of the state economy. There are also letters to the press about brib-
ery, red tape, drunkenness, and public rudeness.

However, they only scratch the surface. When I travel around the
country, I realize I know only a fraction of the true state of affairs in its
vast expanses. When on the road, no matter where I go, I find a stagger-
ing disparity between the quality of life in the provinces and that in the
country's capital.

You may arrive in a provincial town, whether by train or bus, and find
no taxis available. If you are lucky to find vacancies in a local hotel, they
throw you an unwashed towel. Water in the shower is rusty and luke-
warm, that is, if it runs that day at all. A half-asleep attendant sweeps
the corridor floor with a century-old broom. At the city diner, they steal
meat from the cutlets; they taste like papier mâché. A local department
store carries jackets, trousers, and overcoats nobody wants to wear. They
stock the bookstores with tomes nobody wants to read. You go to a movie
theater, and the film breaks a few times during the screening.

Add to this picture the ubiquitous shortage of essential goods. Year in
and year out, no matter how hard central and local planning committees

try, they all fail to predict the demand for the most necessary items in a given locality of the vast country. One time, traveling to the city of Perm, a city close to the Ural Mountains, I could not find insoles for my shoes. In Kuibyshev, a city located on the banks iof the Volga River, there was no underwear in my size. A small-town hairdresser may shave you with dull blades and cut your hair with clippers that yank it from time to time. If you attend a local theater, you will wait for a tram (or any other means of transportation) for a long while after the show is over. Not to mention the quality of provincial cultural life. . . .

When it comes to the cultural domain, highly placed critics and Party censors vet major productions in the country before they see the light of day. The only targets open to satirical arrows are garden-variety, run-of-the-mill creative works with no political agenda. I have made forays into satirical reviews of the latter. A year ago, the Moscow regional paper *Lenin's Banner* published my review of a children's book. You will have as much fun reading the book as you do when checking out a train schedule. The railroad association comes to mind because of the time-stamped instructions for what any boy's daily routine should look like. They appear on the book's pages with the regularity of telegraph poles flickering beyond the express train's windows:

7:30 a.m. Wake up! Breathe deeper! Don't forget to tell everyone "Good morning!"
8:30 a.m. Tell everyone, "Bon appétit!" Don't forget to chew your food well! . . .
9:50 a.m. Learn a poem by heart!

And so on. . . .

Soon after that, *Crocodile* published my review of a Soviet-made movie, a spy thriller. It was so packed with clichés it was easy to confuse it with a parody of the genre. However, nothing in my past had prepared me for what I experienced in the city of Belgorod.

Located in the Russian Federation's south, near the border with Ukraine, the city boasts three hundred thousand dwellers. When I try to recall sometime later how the whole thing had started, I conclude that my short nap on the hotel bed was to blame for what happened next.

~

It is Monday, February 1, 1971. The purpose of my business trip is to meet with the author of a book I am editing for the Nedra Publishing House. The man, chief engineer of one of Belgorod's plants, could not come to Moscow to work with me on his manuscript, so they have sent me over.

I arrive by train early, at five in the morning. I shiver from the cold, pull my head into my shoulders, and come out onto the railroad station square. There is no taxi in sight at this godless hour, but the city trams have begun their routes. In the company of blue-collar workers, sullen from their Sunday overdose of alcohol, I reach my hotel where a room has been reserved for me.

I check in and, after breakfast, go to town to meet my author. We work on his manuscript in his office until the afternoon, taking only a short break for lunch.

My train back to Moscow is in the morning. I return to my hotel room. There is nothing else for me to do for the rest of the day. I have to find something to kill time. I decide to take a short nap first.

I wake up at the most inappropriate time—around 5 p.m. It is getting dark outside already. An empty evening in a foreign city is in front of me. The boredom sets in. Maybe I should shake it off by going to the theater?

The thought of a theater comes by default. I can hardly count on any possibility of seeing a new movie here; they premiere in the country's capital.

However, unlike most regional backwaters, the city is the center of the Belgorod Province. Thus, it may have a drama theater or maybe even two. I recall seeing black-on-yellow posters in the streets, announcing the opening night at the local drama theater. The name of the playwright, Victor Lavrentiev, rings a bell. After some effort, I recall he has authored a play titled *Honor Thy Father*. It has nothing to do with the Ten Commandments, however; the play is about the generation-gap problem in a working-class Soviet family. . . .

Well, I decide, perhaps the new play is worth a try. Otherwise, I might die of boredom in this place.

It is hardly good weather for a night out. It is slushy outside. A blue-gray haze envelops the city. Luckily, the theater building is not far from my hotel. The classical columns of its facade promise a solid theatrical experience.

What I see on the stage that evening bewilders me. My travel all over the country has made me get used to the low grade of provincial cultural life. Yet, now I am totally flabbergasted. The nonsense of the stage goings-on makes me think my daytime nap is not over. I feel like I am stuck in the most bizarre dream of my life. The play I see that night in Belgorod gives both the children's book and the thriller a run for their money. It is unparalleled in its utter stupidity and vulgarity; it is a pitiful example of aesthetic penury. No wonder only a handful of spectators fill up the first two rows of the otherwise empty theatrical hall.

~

I return to Moscow, unpack, and rush to my typewriter. I do the first draft of a piece lampooning both the text of the play and its staging. For its title, I use a quote from the play, "Shut up, You Scatterbrain!" (*Sklero-tik, zakroj rotik!*)

After a few rewrites, I take it to the head of *Crocodile*'s Department of Culture, Alexei Khodanov. He reads it, laughs out loud in some places, and gives it the green light.

Then my piece moves to the desk of the main reader, the magazine's editor-in-chief, one Manuil Grigorievich Semyonov. A writer of humorous novels himself, an ethnic Kalmyk, he is of small height, an unassuming and quiet man of good disposition. I do not remember him ever raising his voice at any of his subordinates—writers and artists, people unruly by their temperament.

The next day, Manuil summons me to his office. As is his style, he does not play the big boss with me. He seats me next to him at the long table covered with papers and, looking over my work, says: "Emil, here's the thing. When a satirist shoots, he shoots to kill. No middle ground. Give it all you have. Take no prisoners."

I take my work home. I labor over it for a few more days and bring it back to the magazine.

This time, Manuil signs off on it and sends my typescript to the printing shop.

~

A coupe of months pass and on May 18, 1971, the issue with my feuilleton hits the newspaper stands around the country. They have given my piece a prestigious place; it occupies the whole bottom half of the magazine spread.

SHUT UP, YOU SCATTERBRAIN!

A Tragicomic Sonata in Three Acts

CAST

Artistic Director of Belgorod Regional Drama Theater, Leonid
   Moiseyev
Producer and Director Vladimir Ilyin
Actors and actresses of the theater

ACT ONE

(The theater hall. On the proscenium, Artistic Director presses a
manuscript to his chest. The Actors and Actresses take the
orchestra seats.)

ARTISTIC DIRECTOR. Well, let me tell you, comrades! Stanislavsky
   may have a point, stating that theater should start the moment a
   spectator steps into the foyer. But theater begins with having a
   good play in hand. Here it is! The one we've been waiting for so
   long. The one we all have been craving—a play on a
   contemporary topic!
      Here it is, our daily bread! No, it's a delicious, high-calorie
   bun with raisins in it! As the author tells us in his staging
   directions, it's a "tragicomic rhapsody"! He calls it "rhapsody"
   because, as in music, it makes us think deep philosophical
   thoughts. Of good and evil. Of patria- and matriarchy. . . .
   You've all read it by now. But let me recap. The heroine of the
   play is Alevtina Mironovna Vyatkina. She's a businesswoman—
   as the playwright defines her, she's a "hybrid of a mother and an
   official." She makes sure that matriarchy reigns in her household.
   Alevtina is the head of the family. . . . That's the title of this
   rhapsody. She is the head of the family because she earns three
   times more than her husband, a nice guy, modest, but down on
   his luck. . . . She plans to celebrate their silver anniversary. It is
   here that things get complicated and emotions boil over.
      The fact is that, twenty-five years ago, Alevtina, who wasn't
   yet a "hybrid," had three candidates for her hand and heart.
   But she chose the man with a sensitive and searching soul—
   a pharmacist. As his character description has it, he was "keen

on exploring unique medicinal substances." She preferred him to others for reasons that remind us of high Greek tragedy, such as the works of Sophocles.

"Little Makar," she recalls, "tested on himself a new sleeping pill he invented. He slept and slept, and that made it impossible for him to propose." While this midsummer night's dream lasted, the nervous bride also swallowed the sleeping pill invented by her groom.

Awake a day later, Alevtina announced her choice. The couple's hypnopaedic declaration of love had the most terrible consequences for the two rejected suitors. One, Obukhov, had a nervous breakdown. A psychiatrist had to treat him for five years. It didn't help much: for the rest of his life, the man's psyche remained damaged beyond repair. Another rejected man, Strekalov, developed severe stuttering. To cool down his heart, which Alevtina had set on fire, Strekalov set off for the Far North, to the icebergs. There, he studied the "behavior of people under permafrost conditions." He authored several scientific articles, and the Canadian government invited him to a conference in Montreal.

On his way to Canada—at this point, the events in the rhapsody reach their climax—the tundra specialist drops by his hometown. Now, in all the splendor of his international fame, he wants to appear before the woman who rejected him a quarter-century ago. He mysteriously makes his way through the closed doors of the Vyatkins' apartment and tries to persuade the virtuous woman to leave her loser of a husband and their two children and elope with him.

He prevails. "I abdicate!" Alevtina exclaims. "I renounce my throne. I make my revolution." She rushes to the home of the "permafrostnik." However, here—I remind you it's a "philosophical rhapsody"—the forces of the good fight for her soul. Her husband, Makar, who only looks demure and henpecked, embodies these forces. Having predicted the course of events, he has moved the hands of the wall clock two hours ahead. Thanks to that, gripped by fatal passion, his life companion misses her tundra seducer. The combined forces of good destroy the former suitors, one after the other. Here is where the curtain goes down. Questions?

ACTOR. Pardon me, but it's not clear from this rhapsody whether the pharmacist-husband's invention is of any worth.

ARTISTIC DIRECTOR. Well, you don't understand the spirit of the play yet. It's devoted to the future. The husband—Makar, that is—invents a remedy of no use now but, possibly, valuable to humanity in the future. His mother-in-law nudges him to continue his research. "So many people shake at night because of this damn threat of the nuclear war!" she says. "And, with these pills of yours, everyone would be asleep." His father-in-law explains the delay in Makar's research, "They vetoed it. They didn't allow it to be used. Too powerful a remedy. Imagine the country on high alert, and everyone is sound asleep. The military and the firefighters objected to it."

Unlike Jesus Christ, who allegedly turned water into wine, Makar did the opposite: he converted alcohol into water. He had to. Otherwise, everyone around him would turn into drunkards. His father-in-law drinks. Their housekeeper, Nyusya, swills it as if to say, "It shouldn't only be the men having fun." Even the daughter asks the heroine, her mother, to stock up on alcohol, telling her, "We'll be the most hammered people in the world!" Her mother responds that she has had enough, "You'll drive me to it. I'll turn into one big hammer." How could Makar afford not to think of a way to prevent alcoholism!

YOUNG ACTOR. I'll have the part of Vyatkina's son, Alaric. I don't get it. Why do all the characters have regular names, but only the devil knows what kind of name the son has!

ARTISTIC DIRECTOR (*affectionately*). The devil has nothing to do with it. The name is the author's subtle hint. An allegory, if you wish. In ancient history, Alaric was the chieftain of the Visigoths, who destroyed ancient Rome. By naming the Vyatkins' son Alaric and their daughter Rogneda, the author makes the point that today's children are barbaric.

YOUNG ACTOR. But this is such a vulgarity! The play is rife with platitudes. "Excommunicated from the conjugal bosom," the husband, Makar, calls the ottoman on which he sleeps "a barometer of marital bliss." Calming down his father, Alaric says that, though, in the grip of passion, his mother won't do something silly, that she's not a young girl. The father answers, "When they're aging, they're worse than young girls."

ARTISTIC DIRECTOR. Easy, easy, young man! Victor Lavrentiev has written this rhapsody. It's published in the September 1970 issue of the *Theater* journal. Its editorial board knows better than you and I where vulgarity is and where it is not! The debates are over! Let's start the rehearsals!

ACT TWO

(Same and the Artistic Director.)

ARTISTIC DIRECTOR (*rubbing his hands*). Here we go, comrades. The play is a winner. There's plenty of room for a director's imagination. Do we have some young character in this play? Yup. Rogneda, the daughter. The stage directions say, "She comes in her dressing gown." Way too puritanical! (*To the actress playing the part of the daughter*) Come out wearing your lingerie! . . . Do we have other women? Grandmother? Well, let's keep her clothes on. . . . The only other female part is that of the heroine, the head of the family. (*To the actress playing the part of Alevtina*) The playwright's remarks say, "It's morning time; Alevtina Mironovna emerges from the bedroom." Here, it begs you to come out in your nightie! (*A light noise in the hall.*) It isn't too much. Don't say no to it! Put on your pink lace negligee. The spectators from the last row of the orchestra could spot it right away.

　　What else can we come up with? Aha, I have it! What a spectacular scene! "Strekalov comes up to Alevtina, hugs and kisses her." What kindergarten playfulness! What is the sofa on the stage for! (*To the actor playing the part of Strekalov*) Keep her down while kissing her until the audience applauds. . . . Well, it looks like we've hiked up the erotica. (*He flips through the pages of the play script.*) We need to make the text funnier. . . . True, the author has a few cheerful gags. Miron, Alevtina's father-in-law, cries out now and then, "Where is my coffin?!" Or here, the plumber says to the housekeeper Nyusya, "You, the bipedal vacuum cleaner!" It would be good to toss in something short and memorable. . . . Something that the audience would pass on to their friends and family. . . .

A VOICE FROM THE AUDIENCE. "Shut up, you scatterbrain!"

ARTISTIC DIRECTOR. Ha-ha-ha! Hilarious! It is for you, Nyusya, a great riposte! Well, shall we begin!?

ACT THREE

The Belgorod Theatre on the third day of the premiere. In the
hall, a few high school pupils and students from the local
vocational school are scattered here and there. There are two more
rows of casual theatergoers. . . .

For a few days, I enjoy compliments from my fellow satirists. Besides
Grisha Kremer, I hear good things about my piece from Sergei Brudny,
one of the *Crocodile* staff writers. He is a young man with the mellow
manners of a person who grew up in the stable and well-to-do family of
a movie star. Tall, balding early, with the remaining bits of his hair slicked
back with pomade and his nails manicured, he is known for his good
manners. When he lights his cigarette, he makes sure he does not blow
smoke into his companion's face.

Though our backgrounds are different—he is the son of a movie star
and I am the son of a housepainter—during my visits to *Crocodile*'s offices,
we have gotten to know each other and become friends.

"Good work, Emil," says Sergei. "Keep it up, my friend. I'm proud of
you."

~

A whole month has passed since my "Scatterbrain" piece appeared on the
pages of *Crocodile* when an early morning knock on the door brings me
back to that momentous point of my journalistic life.

13

Who Has Done It?

"Telephone! It's for you." My neighbor knocks on the door of my room in the communal apartment.

I receive this phone call early in the morning on June 18, 1971.

My neighbor is a wheezy old man. We have become friends through our interactions in our communal kitchen while I brew my morning coffee and he warms up his rice porridge.

I wonder who would call me so early. From my small, pencil-box-like room, I step into the windowless hallway with paint peeling on the walls and pick up the phone. It is mounted on the corridor wall and serves all eighteen occupants of the six rooms of our communal apartment.

I recognize the voice of Arkady Polishchuk, the managing editor of the journal *Asia and Africa Today*. I met him at the House of Journalists, and soon we became friends.

Journalist Arkady Polishchuk, c. 1970 (courtesy of Arkady Polishchuk)

"Congratulations, man!" he says with a chuckle and a hint of benign envy. "They've denounced you in the *Literary Gazette!*"

"What?" I say. "Denounced? Why? What are you congratulating me for?

My voice sounds hollow, not my own. I am half-asleep, and I am trying to make sense of how such a friendly voice could relay such alarming news.

"Well, don't you know, man? Nowadays, if they attack you in the press, you're famous anyway. . . . They tore you to pieces in the *Literary Gazette*."

At this moment, without yet knowing why the *Literary Gazette* has trashed me, I am seized with fear. It is not even with my fear but the fear my parents would most likely experience if they heard these words. They still remember the Stalinist era when a critical article in the press often contained a rhetorical question about whether the particular offender was fit to be part of the great socialist society. As soon as such person saw his name in the paper, he packed his bag with some warm underwear and a jar of currant jam. It was only a matter of time before, in the middle of the night, a KGB black sedan, nicknamed "Black Maria," would roll up to his home and take him to a place where vitamins were in short supply.

Stalin's time of limitless ferocity has gone, but, for my parents, the Soviet power remains a loose cannon. Who knows what kind of trick it will play on you!

Luckily, my parents do not read the *Literary Gazette* or any other Soviet paper. They trust none of the words in them anyway. Besides, they also do not know my pen name.

"But cheer up," Arkady goes on. "Do you remember my friend Vadik? Yeah, the guy from my journal. . . . We had coffee the other evening at the House of Journalists. He hangs out with none other than Vasily Aksyonov. Yes, that Vasily Aksyonov. One of our most popular young writers. . . . Well, Vadik told me the other day that Aksyonov had read your 'Scatterbrain' piece and asked him to say hello to you. He said, 'Good job! That's what all those damn bastards deserve!'"

Since my feuilleton in *Crocodile* ridicules a play written by one of the most propagandistic Soviet dramatists, I know whom Aksyonov has in mind. He is thinking of the old literary guards. They keep a big padlock on the doors of Soviet publishing houses. They curb the influx of new literary blood and suppress young, talented writers' careers.

Under different circumstances, the praise of a famous writer would please me. But the news unsettles me. An assault in a paper widely read by the intelligentsia is not something to be taken lightly. It may well end my journalistic career or, at the very least, deal a severe blow to it. I throw a light jacket on my shoulders, pop out into a drizzling rain, and run to the nearest newsstand. I grab a fresh, still-smelling-of-typographical-paint copy of the *Literary Gazette*.

I take a step away from the kiosk and, on the go, unfold the paper. My eyes jumping over the headlines, I scan all its sixteen pages.

Finally, I find the note.

At first glance, its title, "With Ease Extraordinary," seems not threatening. Peaceful. Even playful. But this is only at first glance. The title is sarcastic. The inversion—placing an adjective after the noun—gives the innocent phrase a sinister glow. "With Extraordinary Ease" sounds like a compliment, but "With Ease Extraordinary" is a disapproving rebuke. It is as if to warn me, *Hey, man, you better watch what you're saying!*

I hold my breath and run through the text once. Then a second time. I cannot quite grasp what they are accusing me of. The author of the note is one Isidore Shtok.

To begin with, it is not clear what he has to do with it. He is known for his plays staged by the Moscow Puppet Theater. It means he is a member of the Playwrights' Guild, as is the author of the play I have lampooned. Does that mean he wrote it to stand up for his fellow playwright? Well, let us see what it is all about:

> The favorite magazine, entertaining and usually just, has published E. Abramov's feuilleton "Shut Up, You Scatterbrain! A Tragicomic Sonata in Three Acts." It is about the play *The Head of the Family*.
>
> Of course, a thorough analysis of a literary work is not part of a satirist's task. It is the business of literary critics and literary scholars. It is essential to capture the spirit of the work, and, if the work is a failure, if it is vulgar, this needs to be shown to the readers. And the more convincing the feuilleton's tone, the more compelling the quotations, the more effective it will be.
>
> However, the feuilleton falls short. E. Abramov does not even try to pretend to be objective. He wisecracks, and he snipes; he shows his outrage with remarkable ease.

As I read, I cannot grasp it right away: does he scold me or praise me? What should a satirist do if not to snipe at what deserves to be sniped at and show his outrage where it is due?

The writer quotes my feuilleton and, again, he either reprimands or praises me: "In assessing the behavior of the actors and their characters, the feuilletonist does not mince words."

Good grief! If a *satirist* should avoid mincing words, then who should not do it?

Then comes the recapitulation of my sins:

> E. Abramov randomly pulls individual cues, phrases, and words from the text. Another second, and he proclaims the playwright the chief culprit of vulgarity and schlock in our theaters.

Why "randomly pulls"? I have given the reader the whole storyline. And why the "chief culprit"? They stage a lot of plays across the country. Why should anyone take a cue from the works of Comrade Lavrentiev in particular?

I reread this sentence. I sense that, while defending the honor of the playwright's uniform, the author of the note expresses his own thoughts about the writer. He adds in things I do not have in my text, which, it seems, he would have liked to see. To cover up this intention, the First of May parade of the playwright's accomplishments follows. In Soviet literary criticism, it is customary to turn to such pomp when covering up someone's slipshod work:

> They published the well-known playwright's Victor Lavrentiev's *The Head of the Family* in the journal *Theater*, No. 9, 1970, and staged it in several theaters. V. Lavrentiev is the author of many well-known plays, such as *Honor Thy Father* and *A Man and a Globe*, staged at the Moscow Art Theater, the Moscow Maly Theatre, and dozens of other theaters.

Now, when they introduce an author sheltered from criticism in the full radiance of his orders and medals, a short democratic nod to the press is in order. The writer of these lines assures us he is not some airhead. He understands that the media should give objective information about events, in this case, on the country's cultural front. However, this reverence for

the press makes it clear that liberties have their limits. His aim is to remind the reader who the bosses in the country are. In a public rebuff, to
prevent any pushback, it is customary to cite the resolutions of the most
recent Party Congress. Here, he cites the one that has been adopted just
a few months earlier, in April 1971:

> One can argue about the merits and demerits of this or that play;
> one can and should be critical. Still, one must firmly keep in mind
> that setting high standards for people has to be combined with
> trusting and respecting those people. All of this creates a
> constructive and friendly atmosphere that allows the fullest use of
> one's faculties. The XXIV Congress of the Communist Party has
> raised this issue precisely that way.

Now it's time for the concluding knockout:

> In the feuilleton "Shut Up, You Scatterbrain!," there is not a trace
> of trust, respect, or genuine and principled exactitude regarding
> the maintenance of high standards. E. Abramov wrote about
> V. Lavrentiev's play unconvincingly and rudely. Such "criticism"
> cannot benefit either literature or theater.

I am at a loss. Isn't criticism of a play that is hardly more than smutty
schlock a true instance of "principled exactitude"? Neither Khodanov,
the head of the culture department, nor Semyonov, the editor-in-chief,
found my writing rude. Moreover, the latter advised me to splash gasoline on the fire, to give it more spice.

What could this *Literary Gazette* publication mean? No matter how
hard I try, I cannot recall a case where anyone has dared to take a swing
at the almighty *Crocodile*.

I call Sergei Brudny. He works on the staff of the magazine and may
shed light on the matter. Sergei hems. He also cannot remember any media
attacks on *Crocodile*. He promises to find out what is going on.

I call Arkady back. He is much more experienced in journalism than I
am. You could say he cut his teeth on it. He has worked in the field for
almost fifteen years longer than I have. Although he does not specialize
in satire, he is a seasoned journalist. Maybe he has a better idea of what
happened.

When he picks up the phone, I ask him about something that struck me as being odd when I saw the name of the note's author for the first time.

"Listen, Arkady," I say. "Can you explain why Isidore Shtok of all people has scribbled that note in the paper? He writes for the puppet theater. Why specifically did he, not some other playwright, write the piece? What's in it for him?"

"Um," Arkady says. "Gee, I hadn't thought about it. I'll ask around."

I invite him for coffee with éclairs at the pastry shop in my Stoleshnikov Alley. All Muscovites with a sweet tooth patronize the shop; its éclairs are the best in town. We agree to get together after his work hours.

To calm my nerves, I do not take the subway as I usually do but walk to my workplace. It is a long walk. My mouth dries up from anxiety. Here and there, I stop to cool off at the vending machines selling seltzer. My journalistic career is in trouble. The *Literary Gazette* is not the all-powerful *Pravda*, but it is widely read and influential. I do not know how *Crocodile* will react to the note.

It also registers with me that there is quite a bit of irony in the situation. Up to this point, I have published more than a hundred satirical notes and feuilletons in Moscow periodicals, *Crocodile* among them. Now, my satirical targets and I have traded places. I have become the object of public scorn. And it does not sit well with me. . . .

At work, I keep a low profile. Now I find it a blessing I sign my publications with a pen name. My colleagues at the editorial office here, at Nedra, have no inkling that the person denounced in today's *Literary Gazette* sits in the same room with them. . . .

Finally, the workday is over. The pastry shop is packed at this time. I appear early to secure a table for my friend and me.

Although the shop is crowded, being tall, Arkady glances over the heads and waves his hand. He is thin, tall, sporty-taut (in the winter time, he is keen on skating), with a lively face and laughing eyes. He wears beige summer pants and a blue, British-made polo shirt. A booklet sticks out from under his armpit.

"I've dug up something for you, man," he says, sitting down. "I have some thoughts about what happened."

"Thank you for coming," I say, shaking his hand. "I can't wrap my head around it. Nothing like this thing has ever happened to me."

We both know that, if someone tries to give a rebuttal to the publication in a paper or magazine, usually they send an angry letter, a "wagon" (*telega*), in our journalistic parlance, to the editor of the paper. They attach to it some documents for justification. But what could they attach here? After all, in my feuilleton, I quote the published text of this stupid play.

"Calm down, man," Polishchuk says. "Take it easy. I understand you're hurting. But let's sort things out. Let's see who is the true object of this press attack here."

"What do you mean, who?" I say. "Isn't it me, the author of the feuilleton, and *Crocodile* magazine, which published it?"

"Well," Polishchuk chuckles, "I'm afraid you're wrong about the second party. The author of the note makes it clear from the beginning he's not attacking the magazine itself. Look, to avoid any ambiguity, he precedes his remarks about your piece with a whole bouquet of compliments to the magazine. He calls it 'favorite, entertaining, and usually just.' You don't sweeten up like that even a lady whose heart you want to win. No, the author of the note has no intention to accuse *Crocodile* of any wrongdoings. Who in the world could even harbor such a stupid idea! Which organization uses *Crocodile* as its mouthpiece?"

Arkady says it in a mocking tone, turning his ear and cupping his hand around it to hear me better.

"Every young pioneer in this country knows that the satirical magazine is the instrument of the Central Committee of the Communist Party," he continues. "Who then, being in his right mind, would dare to criticize *Crocodile* in the open press? And who would let it happen? Let me clarify, doing it in a Soviet publication, not in some *Wall Street Journal* or *Der Spiegel*."

Arkady smiles sardonically and continues: "So, they waged an attack only on you as the author of the feuilleton. Now, we have a detective's task in front of us. We have to answer three conjoined questions. The first one is, 'Who's attacked you?' The second one is, 'What was their motive?' And, perhaps, the most important one, 'Who's ordered the attack?' . . . So, let's start with the first one—'Who's done it?'"

"What do you mean, who?" I say. The publication has upset me, but not so much as to cloud my thoughts totally. "Isidore Shtok, as you know."

"No, no, dear man." Polishchuk wrinkles up. "It's signed by his name. Most likely, with his permission. But I believe he didn't lay a hand on this nonsensical, poorly concocted write-up."

"Who's done it then?" I blurt out. "Some mystery game they play!"

Polishchuk grins. His spectacles flash with the hidden pleasure of an experienced investigator holding a thread he hopes will help him solve the case.

"How long have you been freelancing?" he asks.

"About seven years, I guess." I am trying to concentrate.

"Well, here it is. And you still don't understand that what you see on the pages of the Soviet press is only the shadows cast upon the cave wall in front of the readers."

I recall that, before taking up journalism, Arkady graduated from the philosophy department of Moscow State University. He wrote his thesis about Aristotle's aesthetics. Now, it appears he paraphrases one of Plato's ideas. People believe they see the real world, yet they are just chained prisoners sitting in a cave and facing the bare wall. What they see are their own shadows and the shadows of what happens behind them, cast by the fire.

"Yes," Arkady goes on, "the note isn't anonymous, it's not an editorial. Isidor Shtok signs it, but I doubt he wrote it. Think about it. Shtok is a professional writer. He's an artist, a wordsmith. I doubt he's composed the letter. Some Party bureaucrat did it—someone in charge of overseeing the cultural field. . . . Pay attention to the language of the note, to its icy tone, nonliterary, the one reserved for Party functionaries of all ranks. It's packed with the Party bureaucratic clauses. It's dull like hell. Look!"

Arkady reaches his hand across the table and takes my copy of the *Literary Gazette*, opens to the page where they printed the note.

"I don't doubt some Party rat in charge of watching over the country's cultural scene has scribbled it. Think about it. Could a true wordsmith write this paragraph, for instance?

One can argue about the merits and demerits of this or that play; one can and should be critical. Still, one must firmly keep in mind that setting high standards for people has to be combined with trusting and respecting those people. All of this creates a constructive and friendly atmosphere that allows the fullest use of one's faculties. The XXIV Congress of the Communist Party has raised this issue precisely that way.

"This is, as you understand yourself, nothing but the Party barking, saying, 'You better watch your step, comrade journalists!'"

He's right, pops into my head. The style of writing betrays its real author.

"You're within your rights to ask," Polishchuk continues in the same measured tone, "why Shtok? Well, I assume they pressed him to sign this rubbish. They obligated him to do it. They forced him. Why did he agree? I suppose the only reason is that they made him clean up his stained political reputation. To show his loyalty and dedication to the Party. Whether he is a Party member is irrelevant. Any artist better follow their instructions. Right, Comrade Abramov?"

For the first time, Arkady smiles compassionately.

"Most likely, they pressured the man to sign this garbage," he adds. "And I guess he had no choice but to do it. . . . Well, did you see his play, *The Divine Comedy?*"

"Is this the one that Obraztsov Puppet Theater staged?" I say. "No, I only read about it. Well, it had run in Moscow before I moved here. I know, though only puppets are on the stage, it's a play for adult theatergoers. It's based on the comics of Jean Effel, the French artist. It's the story of the world's creation, the biblical version. An antireligious satire."

"Well," says Arkady, "the anticlerical theme serves as an eyewash there. Here, for you, I sought it out in the Actors' House library. I advise you to peruse it."

With these words, he puts the booklet he has been holding under his armpit onto the table.

It is a printout of Shtok's play. There are a few bookmarks in the brochure. Smiling a bit patronizingly, like an older brother, he opens it up and says: "If you read it carefully, my dear friend and comrade in pen, you'll see that, from the time the play appeared, Shtok has been in hot water. He sinned against the Party line."

I shrug. What kind of stigma could one attach to a play for a puppet theater with the most Soviet theme of them all, the antireligious one?

As if to answer my unuttered question, Polishchuk clarifies: "It's true, the theme is foolproof. I'd even say it's the staple of our country's Propaganda Department. What could be more ideologically safe for a play than antireligious satire?"

He opens the brochure to the first bookmark: "But let's take a look. . . . The carefree little couplets in the play's prologue are there to create a happy atmosphere, one of carnival where everything is just for fun:

Theater, this earthly heaven,
Will be our paradise twice over:
We'll show you the comedy
Of how Adam and his wife lived in Paradise.

"This opening, I assume, is to relax the censors' vigilance. And for a good reason. Later in the play, there are a lot of perilous allusions. Here, in the first scene, the Creator . . . well, since, as I'm sure you know, the word 'God' is undesirable in our Soviet vocabulary, he evades it. So, in the play, the archangels roam around the Creator, who is bored stiff. Their small talk has all kinds of hints."

Polishchuk reaches for the other bookmark and reads:

ANGEL A. What can be interesting over here? Sheer emptiness.
    (*He whimpers.*)
ANGEL B. I've heard, in other galaxies, there's a lot of action.
    The planets fly around. Life's bustling. And what we have
    here?
CREATOR. Why don't you fly over there and find things out?
ANGEL B. Why! Is it even possible for us to fly there!
ANGEL A. Alas, it's impossible.

"Isn't it a hint," Arkady looks round and, his voice lowered, continues, "that we, Soviet citizens, would enjoy being over there," he nods toward the café window, "where things are buzzing, not like over here, where they're hardly audible? . . .

"Let's move on," he takes to the brochure again:

ANGEL B. All day, it's the same thing over here, "What's new?"
    Nothing! Ours is the most backward galaxy. We fear everything,
    and we snitch on each other. That's all we're up to. You're the
    "Creator," my foot. What have you created? The only thing you
    can do is insult and threaten us.
ANGEL A. He's laughing at you, Creator. He's saying, "With
    leadership like Creator's, we can hardly fly too high."
CREATOR (*to Angel B*). Repeat what you've just said.
ANGEL B. He's lying through his teeth.

CREATOR. I dare you to repeat it! If you know what's good for
    you . . .

"Well, what are you saying now?" Arkady asks.

"Hm," I say, quite surprised. "Here even a fool would figure out which
galaxy the archangels have in mind."

For the Muscovite public prone to reading between the lines, there are
plenty of allusions here. If "galaxy" means "country," then it is clear what
kind of a country the author has in mind. Where else, if not in the USSR,
is everyone afraid of everyone and people rat each other out? What other
country could the Moscow creative intelligentsia have in mind when it
sighs in secret that life is boring? That visiting another (Western!) country, the one where life is in full swing, is next to impossible? It is clear
what game Shtok is playing here.

It is quite possible the censors realized what dangerous game the author
of the *Divine Comedy* was playing here and informed the Writers' Union
about it. He must repent and do something useful for the authorities. He
has to prove his loyalty to the "galaxy" in which he lives, because, just like
his fellow citizens, he has nowhere else to go. And he never will . . .

"Well, well." Arkady stretches his legs, takes up his éclair, and, gulping
down his coffee, says, "Well, all this is just a warm-up. . . . Are you done?"

He glances around at the crowd in the pastry shop and lowers his
voice: "There are some more things we should talk about. Let's get out
of here."

14

Who's Ordered It

We leave the café, turn right, and stroll toward Dmitrovka Street. It is getting dark already. Here and there, the lights in the driveway entrances to the courtyards switch on.

"Here it is," Arkady says, looking around to ensure nobody hears him. "My girlfriend, Galina, works at the Actors' House. She tipped me off regarding your guy. I mean, the one who signed the anti-Abramov note in the paper. What I'm about to tell you, dear satirist, even Salvador Dali, with his wild imagination, couldn't conjure up. Do you know that, in the very first reading, the censors had slaughtered another play by your Comrade Shtok? It was a sequel to the *Divine Comedy*, titled *Noah's Ark*."

I shrug. Who the hell can tell! The ways of the censors' brains are even less predictable than earthquakes and tsunamis. They could ban an artistic work on a whim, on any idiotic pretext.

"That's the case here too." Polishchuk reads my mind. "So, here's what happened. When they got acquainted with that play, the Ministry of Culture banned it from being produced by any theater in the Soviet Union. The reason?"

Polishchuk looks above my head at the thinning crowd of passersby and says, lowering his voice: "The Censorship Committee determined the play is riddled with dangerous ideas of . . . Zionism."

I stop in my tracks.

"Did I hear you right?"

Arkady laughs: "As they saw it, Shtok's play promoted the Zionist agenda. And it did so 'at the time when our ideological enemies have launched a smear campaign around the so-called Jewish question in the Soviet Union.' They said that 'now when we are threatened with an embargo on trade relations with our country,' Shtok tried to play the Zionist card."

In 1967, after the Six-Day War, in which Israel defeated the Arab armies, an anti-Zionist campaign was launched in the country. They had branded it "anti-Zionist," but everybody was aware it was a fig leaf. Everyone knew the term "Zionist" stood for the term "Jewish."

I snicker nervously. "So, what sort of Zionism did they find in the play about Noah? The deluge is the deluge. Isn't it the story of Noah saving a pair of each species? Right?"

"Yes, yes," Polishchuk nods, "a pair of each species. But that's about the animals. In Shtok's play, Noah and his family survive."

I stop in the middle of the sidewalk, almost colliding with a solid-looking man with a briefcase in his hand. I excuse myself. The man mumbles something to himself and leaves.

"But isn't the same thing in the Bible? So, where's Zionism here?" I say. "I bet that, during the deluge, even Mount Zion itself also wound up under water."

"Aha!" Polishchuk snaps his fingers and laughs, foretasting the pleasure of seeing my reaction to the clue he has kept up his sleeve. "Here it is. The commission decided that the fact that, in Shtok's play, only *Noah's* family survives, is not by chance."

"I don't get it." I shake my head. "Isn't that the way it is in the Bible?"

"It is!" Polishchuk says again, raising his index finger. "But! Who *is* Noah?"

"What do you mean, who? A biblical character, isn't he?" I say, not sure where he is going with this. "Who else is he?"

"Bah, it looks like you're out of your depth in biblical matters, satirist Abramov," Polishchuk says. "Noah is also the representative of the Judaic tribe."

I stop again and look at Arkady in puzzlement: "What, that's the way it's stated in the play? Judaic?"

"Good God, no!" Polishchuk laughs. "You think Comrade Shtok's lost his marbles? I get you're angry at him for allowing the use of his name to sign the damn note. But try to be objective, my friend. Who, being of sound mind, even utters the word 'Judaic' nowadays? Never mind putting it in a play. . . . No, man. The Commission's arrived at such a logical conclusion on its own. Here's their line of thinking. Where does the story of Noah come from? From the Old Testament. Well, what religion claims it as the most sacred of books? Foremost, Judaism! Therefore, this means that, by using the Noah story, the playwright thrusts the theatergoers into an 'ideologically harmful direction.' By following the Bible, the playwright insinuates that all humanity owes its survival to none other than the Judaic tribe!"

"Listen, Arkady," I say. "Are you sure it isn't some flapdoodle? Couldn't someone give the Bible to that dumb Commission to read, if they haven't ever read it or have forgotten what they've read?"

"Dear satirist!" Polishchuk says. "They tried. Sergei Obraztsov, our celebrated director of the puppet theater, wanted to produce the play. He tried hard to get permission to stage it."

"And what happened?"

"Well, the Commission members responded to him with something like, 'Excuse us, Sergei Vladimirovich, but, for us, the Bible isn't a holy book, as you may have imagined. We cannot allow anyone with the help of such dubious sources as some biblical legends to provide grist for the mills of our capitalist ideological opponents.'"

"I can't believe my ears," I say. "Is it possible for people to be that dumb?"

"Trust me, Emil, it's possible," says Polishchuk. "Nowadays, even this case is not the most stupid one, believe me."

He puts his hand to his chest in a comedic gesture of piety.

"Wait a minute." I stop again, recalling an old street poster. "Wasn't the *Noah's Ark* play staged eventually?"

"It was," Polishchuk nods. "But, as my Actors' House source informs me, it took place only after Sergei Obraztsov wrote a letter to the minister of culture of the Russian Federation, Comrade Kuznetsov. He assured the minister the new, revised text of the play was a far cry from the old one. He wrote that his theater collective had introduced sixty-four substantial corrections to the original text. Did you hear? Sixty-four! . . . Well, they permitted them to stage the play. But the ideological stain on Shtok's reputation remained. And, how can you get rid of such a stain in our time? Mind you, it's not some drop of ice cream that landed on the lapel of your jacket. You can't take it to the dry cleaner. To clean up your smudged ideological reputation, you must commit some redeeming act. I bet that's why the ideological watchdogs pressured Shtok to sign the anti-Abramov scribble they had prepared for him."

We reach Strastnoy Boulevard and stop. Arkady looks at his watch and, since the mystery of the *Literary Gazette* demarche is far from being solved, he suggests we go to the House of Journalists, which is nearby. Its café closes late.

The opportunity to attend this club, which is closed to the general public, is one of the few perks a member of the Union of Soviet Journalists enjoys. They accepted me to the union two years ago, five years down the road after my first piece had appeared in the Moscow press. In the life of an average Soviet citizen, even a modest benefit, such as having access to a professional club, is at a premium.

The House of Journalists, *Dom zhurnalista* (*Domzhur*, as we call it for short), is in the center of Moscow, near the Nikitsky Gates, in an old aristocratic mansion. It is a famous place. The mansion has preserved its beautiful ballroom, which has become a concert hall. There is also a fireplace room, the pink and blue guest rooms, and the grand staircase. In 1831, the greatest Russian poet, Alexander Pushkin, brought his charming wife, Natalie, here for the first time after their wedding. After the revolution, the biggest twentieth-century Russian poets, Alexander Blok, Sergei Yesenin, and Vladimir Mayakovsky, held public readings of their work here.

The House of Journalists, Moscow

Now, from time to time, actors give their concerts here. There is an excellent restaurant whose beef chops Souvaroff are considered the best in Moscow. Here, they also screen foreign films barred from general release. (This circumstance has yet to play a big part in one of the most fateful decisions in my life.)

We turn left and, strolling along Tverskoy Boulevard, head toward the Nikitsky Gates. There, crossing over Bolshaya Nikitskaya Street, we soon find ourselves at the mansion entrance.

"So," says Polishchuk as soon as we take a table at the café and order our coffee, "let's move to the second question of our investigation. Why did they launch the attack on your *Crocodile* article? It's hardly plausible they have a personal grudge against you. Well, doesn't this phrase strike you as strange?"

He points to the opened page of the copy of the *Literary Gazette* that I still hold in my hands. Taking on the comic air of a prosecutor who does not doubt for a minute that the offender would not be able to hide from the all-seeing eye of the law, he puts on his glasses and reads: "'Another second, and he,' meaning you," Arkady says grinning, "'he proclaims the playwright the *chief* culprit of vulgarity and schlock in our theaters.' Doesn't the adjective '*chief*' seem strange to you in this context? Why '*chief*'?"

"Ahem," I mutter. "It *is* weird. I thought this too. Why is this play-wright the 'chief culprit'? Why should any author emulate Comrade Lavrentiev when we have dozens of other playwrights like him?"

"Well, what does it mean then?"

I shrug, "The devil only knows!"

"Forget about the devil," Arkady says. "It'd be useful for *you* to know it for your own sake first. I guess, when you wrote your piece, you didn't quote the lines from the play by memory, right?"

"Of course not," I say. "I've gotten a hold of the journal *Theater* where the play is published. I checked every line I quote in my piece."

"Good for you, man," Arkady says. "But, while doing that, by any chance, did you bother to look up who the journal's editor-in-chief is?"

"Why should it matter? The play is a piece of crap. Regardless of who the editor-in-chief is."

"Well, it does *matter*, my dear friend," Arkady says. "It matters a lot. Because the editor-in-chief of the journal *Theater* is none other than . . ."

For effect, he makes a pause before declaring it: " . . . the same Victor Lavrentiev, the author of the play."

I lean back in my chair. I'll be damned!

"Well, what of it!" I say. "That makes things even uglier. The man wrote a potboiler, a stupid and vulgar play, and he published it in the journal he edited. What he says goes. He should be ashamed of himself two times over!"

"Heh-heh-heh, dear comrade satirist," Arkady says. "How many years have you used your satirist's hot pen? Seven? Well, I must tell you— you're still wet behind the ears, my friend. A Soviet satirist, like no other journalist, should know by heart whom he can and cannot touch. Do you get it now why, in this *Literary Gazette* write-up, they have that phrase 'the chief culprit of vulgarity and schlock in our theaters'? The sole purpose of the note is to dry-clean the reputation of the editor-in-chief of the country's leading theatrical magazine."

Polishchuk pauses before proceeding in his detective's tone: "So, once we have established this circumstance, we can answer the third question, 'Who ordered the attack on you and your lampoon?'"

He takes another pause. Looking at my face, the face of a neophyte brought to the bosom of a new faith for the first time, he says: "All right, I'll ask you a leading question. What organization does the journal *Theater* represent?"

I shrug again. Why should it matter whose instrument the journal is! The play is trash regardless where it is published. . . .

Arkady leans over the table and brings his face close to mine: "Here it is, my friend. The journal is the organ of two organizations—Writers' Union and . . ."

Here, for effect, he takes a dramatic pause: " . . . and the Ministry of Culture! Thus, the journal's editor-in-chief is part of the ministry's *nomenklatura*. To criticize him for whatever sin is to blame the minister for picking wrong personnel. Clear enough? Now, who serves as this country's minister of culture today, young man?"

Arkady is back to mocking me a bit again. Then, realizing I am not in a mood for jokes, he adds in a peaceful tone: "Well, as everyone knows without looking it up in a reference book, it's Yekaterina Alekseevna Furtseva. And, as you might hear it by now, this former weaver is not to be messed with. Instead, she'll make a mess out of anyone in her way."

I say nothing to Arkady. That Furtseva is a simple weaver in her past and comes from the deep provinces does not lower her in my eyes. I am also not of a princely family and grew up a thousand miles from the country's capital. My father is a housepainter. However, he keeps himself from the Soviet authorities as far as possible, and she, thanks to them, has made a dizzying career. People joke about her. As one jest has it, on an art exhibit's opening day, the usher asks a man at the door for his ticket.

"I'm Picasso!" he says.

"Prove it!"

Picasso draws his famous dove of peace, and they let him in.

Next comes Furtseva, also without a ticket. When the usher asks for it, she says: "Hey, comrade, I'm the minister of culture of the USSR!"

The usher: "Well, we let Picasso in and will do the same for you as well if you prove it."

"Who the hell is Picasso?" she says.

"Come on in, Comrade Furtseva!"

Arkady shakes his head: "I'm sorry to say it to you, young man, but you got yourself an all-too-mighty nemesis. She's not only this country's minister of culture. She is also a member of the Central Committee of the Communist Party. Under Khrushchev, she was even a member of the Politburo for four years. They decorated her four times with the highest award in the country—the Order of Lenin. She also received the Order of the Red Banner of Labor, the Order of a Sign of Honor, and countless medals. Nothing to sneeze at. . . . Alas, my friend, you've stirred up a hornet's nest. Do you know what a temper this lady has? She'd have a half-dozen people like you and me for breakfast. And she wouldn't even notice it. She would slip us down her throat smoothly like oysters."

For a moment, I see myself as an oyster disappearing down a monster's throat. The very thought of it makes me shudder.

"By the way, do you know by any chance what she's done to Baboch-kin?" Arkady continues.

"Which Babochkin? . . . The famous Babochkin? The star of that pre–World War II blockbuster, *Chapayev*?"

"The very same. The country's darling. A celebrity of the highest order. The People's Artist of the USSR, mind you. . . . Well, to his misfortune, in one play, the man dared to portray some Soviet official in a satirical vein. Boy, how she got up in arms against him! She hunted him down all over the place. As if he were a rabbit and she were a hungry hound! . . . First, she attacked him in a *Pravda* article. Then, she followed his career, making sure she killed it. She cut off the oxygen from him everywhere. Ordered all film studios and drama theaters of the country to turn him down whenever he asked for a part. . . .

"And what about Rostropovich? A world-famous musician, mind you. . . . Just because he housed that 'renegade Solzhenitsyn' at his dacha, and she made the world famous musician unemployable in his own country. Can you imagine that! . . . Have you heard how she handled the Theater of Satire after they produced *A Profitable Place*, a play written in the last century? When staging it, the director had the gall to make some satirical references regarding today's moral climate in the country. So, right away, she ordered to shut down the play. . . . Well, if that's not enough for you, guess who didn't let either the Beatles or the Rolling Stones tour our country? The very same iron lady. . . . Do I have to go on?"

I shake my head. I have had enough. Besides, it is getting late already. The waitress has already removed her apron and looks at us as if to say, *Have some conscience, comrades. Your time's up, and I need to close.*

We leave *Domzhur*. I see Arkady off to the subway station. When parting, he shakes my hand in sympathy and advises not to lose heart. Who knows, maybe it will pass, somehow?

After saying goodbye to him, crestfallen, I plod along to my home. I try again to sort out what happened. I recall the blue-gray haze of that fateful evening in Belgorod. . . . The slush on the streets . . . the show at the almost-empty hall . . . my return to Moscow and my feverish writing . . . Khodanov laughing when reading my piece . . . Manuil's advice to add more heat. . . . Is it possible he did not know who the playwright was? That you could not touch that man with a ten-foot pole without enraging the omnipotent minister of culture?

Here, one more thing pops up in my head. It makes me feel even more anxious. I suddenly realize that I have upset Catherine the Terrible not for the first time. About a year ago, *Crocodile* published my feuilleton "A Candlestick as a Memento." In it, I described the deplorable state of security at museums in the country. Taking care of them is the direct responsibility of the Ministry of Culture. For example, two of my hometown museums—the Museum of Western and Oriental Art and the Archaeological Museum—had no alarm system or other protection. The museum windows and displays were dilapidated. Recently, 2,500 ancient Greek coins were stolen from it. From the Museum of Peter the Great near Moscow, they pilfered a bunch of early eighteenth-century artifacts—

smoking pipes, antique candlesticks, jewelry boxes, and design ink sets. At the Museum of the Krasnoyarsk Territory, thieves got away with antique medals, ancient coins, and rare books.

It is obligatory for the government to respond to the press criticism. *Crocodile* reported the response under its rubric "Following Up Our Publications." The ministry acknowledged the criticism as valid and added in the blah-blah-blah language of bureaucratese that it "has obligated the museums to improve safeguarding, to take better care of their exhibits."

And, now, a year later, here is another *Crocodile* attack on the same ministry, another feuilleton with the same byline—"E.—*May he be damned!*—Abramov!"

This time, to respond with the usual formulaic reply would hardly work. To write again, "*Obligate* [whom?] *to improve* [the play?]"? Even when the order comes from the almighty minister, how can one improve a piece of theatrical crap? How can you enhance it?

So, they inspired a counterattack. They published a denunciatory note in a prestigious place, the *Literary Gazette*. Not only writers and journalists but the whole Soviet intelligentsia read it from cover to cover.

It is clear that my satirical career is at stake. Will it survive? Will the *Crocodile* fight back? Will it intercede on my behalf?

15

Crocodile Responds

A few more nervous days pass after Shtok's note appears in the *Literary Gazette*. What is next? Will the *Crocodile* fend off publicly the cavalry swoop of the *Literary Gazette* or abstain from it and try to handle it behind the closed doors?

I call Sergei Brudny a few times. In the corridor of the communal apartment, leaning against the wall on which the phone is mounted, covering the speaker with my palm, I ask him whether there is any news. He cannot tell me anything substantial. Manuil, the boss, has made a few trips to the Central Committee recently, but he has not bothered to inform his subordinates of the purpose of his visits. It is quite reasonable to expect he has tried to clean up the magazine's reputation from an unwarranted smear.

To be called on the carpet is part and parcel of Manuil's job. After all, he edits a magazine with a license to criticize people at the outer end of the usually permitted in Soviet press. *Crocodile* happens to cross this boundary from time to time. Thus, Manuil has defended his most brilliant staff member, Sasha Moralevich, more than once. He is the rarest Soviet feuilletonist who abhors self-censorship. He could not care less about what other people think he should or should not ridicule. He leaves it to his editor to make the last call.

~

It takes a few more days before a new issue of *Crocodile* appears on the newsstand near my place. Though my journalistic career is under threat, I try not to give in to my anxiety. I force myself to walk there in measured steps, not to do what I feel like doing—to rush there headlong. I approach the stand, buy a copy, and, my heart pounding, leaf through the magazine pages until I come upon an editorial note titled "On the Same Topic" (*Po tomu zhe povodu*).

I give it a quick read. It is clear right away that, in his administrative wisdom, Manuil has skewed any confrontation with the all-powerful minister of culture. He has played down the acuity of *Crocodile*'s attack on the vulgar potboiler that Furtseva's subordinate had composed and, abusing his position, published in his journal:

> In the magazine *Crocodile*, #16, a feuilleton was published that criticized some flaws in the director's work and shortcomings of the stage version of the play by V. Lavrentiev, *The Head of the Family*, staged at the Belgorod Regional Drama Theater.

I am too agitated when I read it to appreciate the verbal tightrope-walking or to marvel at how skillfully the magazine maneuvered, presenting the feuilleton as a critique of the staging, not of the play itself. The linguistic zigzags that follow pursue the only goal—to dry-clean the uniform of the theater's editor-in-chief, to make believe the fiasco of the play was the fault of the provincial theatrical director.

However, the tightrope walker who wrote the note—was it Manuil himself or someone from the office who cooked it up on his orders?—slipped off the rope when he mentioned "the stage version of the play." What gibberish! Isn't any play written to be staged? It is another desperate attempt to shield the playwright, to make the Belgorod theater alone be the guilty party.

I read on:

> As the deputy chief of the Belgorod Regional Council on the Arts, Comrade P. Uvarov, informs our editorship, the feuilleton was discussed by the Party organization and creative collective of the theater. The criticism of the play and its staging is recognized as basically on target, although the Council on the Arts also agrees with the publication in the *Literary Gazette* addressing the said feuilleton.
>
> Furthermore, it is reported that, at present, the theater continues to work on the staging of the play, looking for a more correct interpretation of individual scenes.

I read this paragraph and perk up for a moment. The local Council on the Arts and its Party organization admit that the "criticism of the play and its staging is basically on target." And the theater continues to look for a "more correct" interpretation of the scenes. So, after all, my piece did hit the nail on the head!

I feel sorry for the Belgorod Regional Council on the Arts. Poor folks! Go figure which of the Moscow bosses to please first! They try to maneuver between the Scylla of *Crocodile*, the almighty instrument of the Party Central Committee, and the Charybdis of the Ministry of Culture, who is behind Shtok's commentary in the *Literary Gazette*. How the hell are they to know which of the two powerhouses will prevail?! That is why, in their letter to the editor, they have "on one hand but on the other hand" rhetoric and such stylistic pearls as "*more* correct interpretation" (it is either correct or not, isn't it?). They also report working on improving some "individual scenes." They try hard to reassure readers that it is not the whole play that is a piece of junk; it is only some tiny parts of it that need to be tuned up a bit.

It is also clear that, by citing the Belgorod letter, Manuil lets his curator at the Central Committee know that he, Manuil, is blameless. Over there, in Belgorod, they agreed with the magazine whose professional honor remains squeaky clean. But, at the same time, he nods to his curator: yes, I understand you are also under pressure. The letter from Belgorod alone might not be enough to fend off the enraged and all-too-powerful minister who is breathing down your neck. She does not give a flying fuck about what over there, in the Belgorod province, they think. It is clear Furtseva demands blood be spilled. To calm her down, it is necessary to throw her a conciliatory bone. Something along the lines of "Well, we might have stepped over the boundaries a bit but please rest assured we'll punish the culprits whoever they might be." To leave no doubt that he is responding to the minister's barking, Manuil repeats the *Literary Gazette's* accusations word for word:

> Having discussed the response of the Belgorod Regional Council on the Arts and I. Shtok's note in the *Literary Gazette*, the editorial board of *Crocodile* deems the feuilleton not written convincingly enough and its tone disrespectful to the author of the play. Sanctions have been imposed on the members of the editorial staff who, without due rigor, prepared the feuilleton for publication.

I assume the *Crocodile* curator and the minister herself hardly care that, besides the head of the culture department, Alexei Khodanov, the other "employee" who "without due rigor prepared the feuilleton for publication" was no one else but . . . Manuil himself. In fact, he read it twice, suggested peppering it up, and then he signed off on it for publication. So, does this write-up mean he has imposed sanctions . . . on himself?

(I cannot help but recall here a character from Gogol's *Inspector General*, the noncommissioned officer's widow, who, according to the town's mayor, has flogged herself in self-punishment.)

The note in the magazine could have stopped here. Perhaps that would have been enough to pacify the enraged minister. But, to be on the safe side, to ensure that her fury calms down, Manuil has decided to shed some sacrificial blood. Luckily, the author of the satire that disturbed the minister's peace of mind is a freelancer. That makes it much easier to make believe that tarnishing the name of the honorable editor-in-chief of the *Theater* was a sheer blunder. Why tiptoe around the freelancers, after all? They are a dime a dozen. Thousands of journalists around the country dream about being published in *Crocodile*. . . . The minister should rest assured we will punish that troublemaker, that *no-goodnik*. How does he dare imply that the minister entrusted editing the journal *Theater* to the author of a stupid and vulgar play! We will teach him a lesson.

So, Manuil lay the sacrificial lamb, the author of the feuilleton, on the altar of the wrathful celestial being by adding one more line:

> The author of the feuilleton, E. Abramov, is no longer welcome to contribute to our magazine.

Manuil's sentencing depresses me. First, I pace the sidewalk in front of the building where I live. Then I head for the adjacent Petrovka Street. There, mingling with the crowd, I try to sort it out one more time. What the hell has happened? I rerun the whole sequence of events in my head. I saw the staging of an awful play, perhaps the most stupid and vulgar I have ever seen. I lampooned it in my piece. The editor-in-chief of the most potent satirical outlet in the country read it and suggested making it even more devastating. I followed his advice. The magazine published my article. Both the theater and the local cultural authorities accepted my criticism. And yet, the magazine has cut me loose and smeared my journalistic name for being "unprofessional." Why? What on earth?

The only conclusion I can draw is that the most essential qualification for a Soviet satirist is to know beforehand whom he can or cannot touch. "The stronger always blames the weaker." That moral of the fable titled "The Wolf and the Lamb" by Ivan Krylov, which we all learned by heart in secondary school, runs in my dejected head.

Another excruciating day passes. Then yet another. I go to work at the Nedra Publishing House; I sit at my desk editing a book typescript filled with electronics circuits, but, like a mosquito swarm in the warm evening, my thoughts rush around in my head. It is a blessing again that I publish my work under a pseudonym. My colleagues at the Nedra editorial offices are blissfully ignorant of the fact that, within the last month, I have been defamed not once but twice: first, in the *Literary Gazette*, with a circulation of a million copies, and, second, in *Crocodile*, which has a run of six million copies.

At home, I shudder every time I hear someone's footsteps behind the door of my room. I am waiting for a knock on my door summoning me to the corridor phone to take a call from the *Crocodile* editorial offices. However, I still hope for a miracle. Maybe, just maybe Manuil has changed his mind and will call to say he is sorry for having yielded to the pressure of the all-powerful minister, that they forced him to cut me loose . . . that he did it for show only, to pacify the furious Furtseva. And he will suggest I change my pen name and continue to write for the magazine. . . .

One time, popping out into the corridor to be closer to the phone to be sure I hear this redeeming call, I see a familiar figure. A tall man, broad-shouldered, with a powerful torso and a small head, is walking toward me, returning from our communal restroom. Though our corridor is poorly lit, I recognize him right away. Sasha Moralevich!

For the first minute, I am just startled. What is he doing here, in my communal apartment? We have a warm and friendly relationship, but we are not close enough to visit each other at home.

Then, I guess it at once. At the end of the corridor where Sasha is heading lives Nina, a beautiful young model whom I admire from afar. But Sasha is a different matter. His flamboyant personality captivates women.

Without thinking, I ask him what I know already: "Sasha, what brings you here?"

In a gentleman's way, Sasha takes no notice of my question and asks me: "Well, how are you doing, man?"

I am at a loss for what to say. Sasha looks at me with sympathy.

"My advice to you, Emil," he says, "spit on them! The dog barks, but the caravan goes on."

I am silent. No matter how I try, I fail to assume a relaxed look.

Sympathy in Sasha's face soon yields to an expression of disgust. As if some leech had appeared in his mind's eye . . .

"B-bitches!" he utters, forcing the swearing through his lips, putting all his contempt into it. "B-bitches!" he repeats, drawing out the first consonant. And, thinking that is not enough, he adds, "Wh-h-ores!"

He shakes his head and says: "Spit on them, old chap!"

I hear the music of the current smash hit. The door at the end of the hallway, the one to Nina's room, opens; her head sticks out the door, "Sasha, where are you?"

Sasha again gives me his sympathetic smile, takes my hand into his big hands, shakes it, and walks away.

This brief meeting with Moralevich calms me down for a while. No matter what you say, the moral support of the king of the feuilleton genre is worth something. . . .

A few more dithery days pass. At the end of the week comes another knock on my door. It is the same old neighbor who woke me up early in the morning on that day when Isidore Shtok's note appeared in the *Literary Gazette*. He says again, "Telephone for you!"

This time, when I pick up the phone, the voice of Masha, Manuil's secretary, comes on. I danced with her more than any other woman at *Crocodile*'s New Year party last year. She is about forty, a raven-haired, beautiful woman with a small waist and big blue eyes, in which I, a bachelor, drown. . . .

As soon as I hear her voice, I sense she has nothing good to tell me. In the tone of a person who somehow feels guilty (though what does she have to do with it?), she says Manuil Grigorievich asks me to stop by his office.

By the end of the next day, I enter the office of *Crocodile*'s editor-in-chief. I walk past Masha. Upon seeing me, she lowers her head. Manuil sits at his desk, surrounded by the galley proofs of the forthcoming issue. He raises his head for a moment, then buries his eyes in the galleys again

and mutters that I should surrender my *Crocodile* correspondent ID to
Masha. He produces this phrase in a muffled tone that signals how much
he is discomfited by the situation.

"The play's a piece of crap, of course," he mumbles without looking at
me. "But who could have known!"

It is clear he does not finish the sentence with what he wants to say but
cannot, "that the playwright has such a powerful protector."

He spreads his hands in the air, his pen still in one of them, and shakes
his head in distress. That is the way a priest in an ancient Greek temple must have shaken his head when letting his congregation know that,
though he is the high priest, he is powerless to predict the will of the
whimsical gods. . . .

At this moment, stepping over the office threshold but remaining near
the door, appears Alexei Khodanov, the culture department head, the first
person who read my work, signed off on it, and passed it to the editor-
in-chief. A broad-shouldered, handsome man of above-average height,
his widespread thick eyebrows remind me of an eagle's wings at takeoff.
Unburdened with heavy reflections, his face with its square jaw seems
to belong to the posters depicting young builders of communism. Miles
of fences around all Moscow construction sites are pasted up with such
posters. Their captions read "Communism Is the Youth of the World,
and They're the Ones to Build It!" (*Kommunizm—ehto molodost' mira, i
ego sozdavat' molodym*).

Khodanov stands in the doorframe for a while and kneads his fingers in agitation, like a schoolboy on the threshold of the teacher's office.
Then, with a Komsomol member's naiveté, he argues that, besides composing a garbage of a play, Lavrentiev had the gall to publish it in the
journal he edits. "What I say goes; I'm the boss, ha?" Khodanov says with
fierceness. "He should be ashamed of himself twice over!"

Manuil interrupts proofing the galleys, hears Khodanov out without
looking at him, and, without saying a word, returns to his work. His is
the way a well-brought-up person reacts when plain stupidity is uttered
in his or her presence.

To compose myself, I linger at Manuil's desk for a minute. I feel he
is not looking in my direction because he is ashamed of his powerless-
ness. What can one do? That is how things stand at the current moment.
It seems he is taking the setback in stride. In his line of work, you are

bound to run into a wall now and then. It is a fact of an editor's life. Take it or leave it.

I exit the editor-in-chief's office and head toward the elevator. I step carefully as if there were not a wooden floor underneath me but a trampoline, and I have to watch my balance.

At that moment, I do not know yet that I am destined to interact with both Manuil and Khodanov one more time. However, under quite different circumstances. . . .

16

In a "Domestic" Way

For a few days following my visit to *Crocodile*, my mind has been in a tumult. I am distraught. I try to recall at least some precedent for when a newspaper or magazine refused to defend its author and gave him away, a lamb to the slaughter. In the Soviet press, retractions—of any kind!—are rare. A retraction compounded by a public dissociation from a contributor is just unheard of! The system of control over what gets into the pages of a Soviet press organ is airtight. To deal with any press mistake, the guardians of bureaucratic reputations in the higher echelons of power fight each other tooth and nail. If it comes to it, they handle the conflict in a "domestic way." It does not come to a public scandal.

Once, in my practice, I had seen how it was done so that no dirty linen was aired in public. They settled the conflict in a way so that the wolves were sated and the sheep intact. . . .

The fate of my short documentary, part of issue #90 (April 1970) of the satirical newsreel *The Wick*, is a case in point. I based my script on my feuilleton published in *Lenin's Banner*. The article ridicules the appalling quality of tourist goods made in the country—the backpacks, the tents, the works. The backpacks weighed a ton. Since their straps were too narrow, they dug into your shoulders. It felt as if you were dragging a tank on your back. Instead of portable pots for cooking soup, porridge, and tea, you had to schlep full-size buckets. Putting up a tent was sheer torture; unable to bear its weight, the racks bent. The pegs for tying the tent to the ground were made so poorly the rope wore out in a few days. Even a drizzle made the tents leak; you had to carry pieces of some plastic material for that eventuality. Thus, hiking with such awful tourist equipment meant not so much enjoying nature as fighting your gear.

As always, the question arose of who was to blame for such shoddy quality of the tourist wares produced in the country. As with any other goods, the manufacturers did not give a rat's ass about the quality of these products. With no market-based competition, customers faced a Hobson's choice: to buy whatever is available and consider yourself lucky or do without. Soon there may well be not enough even of this junky stuff to go around.

In the Soviet system of the centrally planned command economy, incentives were in place to increase the volume of production. If a factory did not meet its quotas, the workers should forget about their bonuses— all of them, be they monthly, quarterly, or annual. However, few stimuli existed for improving the quality of the products. In the case of tourist gear, the planners established some bureaucratic control over quality. They entrusted such authority to the Board of Tourist Affairs at the All-Union Central Council of Soviet Trade Unions (VTsSPS). By definition, it should care about the recreation of the toiling masses.

That is why, when making the video, we interspersed footage showing the horrific quality of tourist goods with footage from the interview with the chairman of the Board of Tourist Affairs.

For example, at one of the tourist sites, our cameraman approached a tent and splashed a cup of water on it. At once, an enraged tourist popped out from the tent, swearing. The episode cut to the official in charge of tourism. Looking at a piece of paper on his desk, he pronounced in a solemn tone, "I'm convinced our Soviet tourists will be satisfied with our care for them. Our industry will significantly increase the production of such tents. Three hundred and fifty thousand of them will be issued in the coming season alone."

As a punch line to the clip, we used the soundtrack of a favorite tourist song of the time. We made its refrain, "Mom, I want to go back home!," the clip title:

Once again, uphill the trails,
We schlep our backpacks.
Only Cyclops can do it.
Mom, I want to go back home!

After we finished shooting the video, they printed a few copies of the new issue of *The Wick* and screened the video in some Moscow movie theaters.

Overnight, a thunderstorm broke out. Either the chairman of the Board of Tourist Affairs himself or some of his subordinates saw the documentary and were furious. The chairman grabbed the hotline phone designed for the country's elite (they called it *vertushka*), rang up Sergei Mikhalkov, editor-in-chief of *The Wick*, and raised hell. He threatened to get him into hot water, to call up the Central Party Committee to back him up.

Sergei Mikhalkov was not your regular Ivan, mind you. The man carried a lot of clout. A famous children's poet, he also authored the lyrics of the national anthem approved by Stalin himself. They decorated Mikhalkov with several of the highest orders of the country. He was a Hero of Socialist Labor, awarded three Stalin Prizes and a Lenin Prize. However, the man was still vulnerable when facing the all-mighty Central Party Committee. He needed support. So, he ordered his staff to find some highly placed officials to defend him.

The next day, they summoned me to the Mosfilm Studios, where *The Wick* was produced. They made me part of the makeshift fight-back squad. They drove us to the offices of another bureaucratic organization, the Central Committee of People's Control. This governmental watchdog body checked on how state industrial plans were fulfilled. They also looked for violations of financial discipline and performed other similar tasks.

It was unclear how these officials could help us, but we showed them the clip in question. They enjoyed it. They chuckled during the screening and promised to protect us from the angry gods.

The next week, they called Mikhalkov on the carpet before the Central Party Committee. Upon his return, he ordered us to tone down the criticism in the clip. Mosfilm stopped printing copies of the reel. Reportedly, they made mild alterations and gave *The Wick* its usual countrywide distribution.

~

I will revisit the theme of the quality of Soviet tourist goods three years later. In the summer of 1973, as part of a cultural exchange, a traveling expo called "Tourism and Vacation in the USA" took place in several Soviet cities. I attended it during my summer vacation in Odessa. To call the American exhibit a hit would be a huge understatement. Its success was smashing in the literal sense of the word. While Odessans stood in a mile-long line to get a glimpse of the way the Americans vacation, quite a few exhibited items—tents, skis, and boots—disappeared into thin air. To give the show at least some protection, the local law enforcement units dispatched police "volunteers" (*druzhinniki*). Among others, they drafted my brother, Vladimir, a young engineer. To save it from being stolen, he helped to bolt down every piece of American equipment.

~

A half-year before the *Crocodile* betrayal, I received a call from Yuri Zolo-tarev, head of the feuilleton department of the central trade-union paper, *Labor* (Trud).

"Hi, Emil," he said. "Do you have a few days off? How about spending some time not under our gloomy Moscow skies but under the sunny southern ones?"

When I stopped by his office, Zolotarev handed me a letter to the paper. It had arrived from Ochamchiri, a small town in the Abkhazian Autonomous Oblast, a part of the Georgian Soviet Socialist Republic. I read the letter—and I could not believe my eyes. The author of the letter was alerting the Moscow paper about one of the local collective farm chairmen. When he had had one too many drinks, he sometimes ran out into the streets brandishing his handgun at the farmers. One time, it even came to him shooting and wounding one of them.

At first glance, every single circumstance in the letter was bizarre. Unlike the American Constitution, the Soviet one did not grant citizens the right to bear arms. Also, where the hell did the collective farm's chair-man get hold of his weapon? Unlike in the States, in the Soviet Union, the only gun you could buy in a store was a toy pistol. No weaponry, besides rifles for holders of the hunting licenses, had ever been for sale. Also, why hadn't the local police taken care of the fellow a long time ago? Why hadn't they disarmed him and locked him up?

Then, I recalled that the action had taken place in the Caucasus, the Soviet Wild West of sorts. They could buy and sell everything under the table over there, including the gun and the local police chief. . . .

So, the letter looked promising. When verified, it could offer exciting material for a feuilleton. It was worth the effort to visit the place and check things out.

In a few days, I flew to Ochamchiri, a typical Soviet provincial town— dilapidated buildings, narrow streets, poorly paved sidewalks. It had local color, however. In its ancient past, the town had attracted a score of con-querors. On its outskirts, there were ruins of Roman baths and the rem-nants of a medieval fortress. The town's name betrayed its Turkish origin; it came from the Turkish word *shamshir*, "boxwood," which overgrew its locale. In Soviet times, they had built some industry here—an oil extraction plant, canning and tea factories, and a tobacco fermentation plant.

Once I checked into the hotel, I contacted the author of the letter and offered to meet in the hotel lobby.

In a short while, a young, soft-mannered brunette appeared. As I learned, she was a student at Tbilisi University. She explained that she was compelled to write the letter. One victim of the unruly collective farm chairman was her relative who had gotten himself into trouble by being in the wrong place at the wrong time.

The next day, I traveled to the collective farm and talked to the villagers and to the chairman himself. I do not think that, being loaded with *chacha*, the local moonshine distilled from grapes, he understood my questions.

I also visited the nearest police precinct. The officers confirmed they had tried to confiscate the perpetrator's pistol, but to no avail. The man refused to give it up, claiming his gun was a toy, shooting with blanks.

When I returned to my hotel, a phone call came to the front desk. A polite male voice invited me to visit the regional Party Committee.

I hesitated for a moment. Why a Party Committee? I was not a member of the Party myself. And I had arrived in Ochamchiri representing not a Party paper but that of the Central Council of Soviet Trade Unions. However, I knew I'd better not mess with the Party reps. Like any other Soviet person, I knew well what organization was the true master of the country.

I asked about the committee address, but the man on the phone told me not to worry about it. A car would wait for me in front of the hotel in the morning.

The next day, they brought me to a white building with columns in the town's center, just a few blocks from my hotel. I could have reached it on foot, but I understood that I had to follow protocol.

Once in the foyer, the chauffeur handed me over to a young secretary. A frozen smile on her face, her lips pursed, she showed me into a large office equipped the way all important offices in the country were—leather upholstered doors, dark knotty-pine paneling, framed pictures of Leonid Brezhnev and other Politburo members on the walls.

Behind a dark, polished wood desk in the room's center sat a well-dressed, middle-aged man—a three-piece suit, a white shirt with shiny cufflinks, a tie of subdued colors. There were hardly any pieces of paper on the desktop. I had long observed that the less paperwork there was on an official's desk, the more critical the position he occupied.

The man sprang to his feet to greet me. His face radiated joy at having me as his guest. He remained on his feet until he saw that I was comfortable in the armchair in front of him. To his left, keeping a respectful distance, sat two other men. One of them was about the same age, apparently his deputy. Another, younger man, judging by the sheepish look on his face, was most likely an intern.

The officeholder's face was lit up with the joy of extending his Caucasian hospitality to me, a guest from Moscow. With a wide grin on his face, the man asked me whether I would be kind enough to share with him what had brought me all the way from our country's fabulous capital to their provincial backwoods. As part of the hospitality ritual, the secretary brought us tea in small tulip-shaped glasses.

I told him what I had found so far. As I was talking, his tea glass cupped in his palms, the officeholder nodded at some places and shook his head at others. His face showed no emotion as he listened with great interest to what I had to say. The intern looking over his shoulder, the deputy scribbled something in a large notebook on his lap.

When I finished, to show how precious for him my visit was, the Party secretary asked me sorrowfully when I was leaving them and whether I planned to revisit their godforsaken town any time soon. It would be an honor for him to have another happy opportunity to have me as his guest.

That was all. The next day, I flew back to Moscow and, in a few days, composed my feuilleton, typed it out, and brought it to the *Labor* editorial offices. Zolotarev read it in my presence, nodded in satisfaction, and signed off on it for the printers.

The waiting time for a feuilleton to appear in the paper's pages after its approval usually was not long. However, I checked the paper at the newsstand every single day for a week with no results. Then another week passed. Nothing! I waited a few more days and called Zolotarev.

"Well, Emil," he said, "the thing is that we won't be able to run your piece this time. But don't worry. By the end of the month, go to our cashier's office. No, no, it won't be just a kill fee. We'll pay you in full. The piece won't go for reasons that have nothing to do with your work."

He said nothing more.

Since it was happening for the first time, kill fee or not, I did not know whom to turn to for an explanation. Zolotarev was not willing to disclose whatever he knew about it.

When I came to the *Labor* editorial offices to receive my honorarium, I ran again into Grigory Kremer, now Kroshin, who was also there to collect his pay. When I told him all the details of my Ochamchiri story, he laughed and slapped me on the shoulder.

"Wow, my friend!" he said. "Looks like we're milk brothers now, doppelgangers in our satirical business. A similar thing happened to me some time ago. Not here, at the *Labor*, but at *Izvestiya*, the central instrument of our government. From the city of Ufa, the capital of our Bashkir Autonomic Republic, a letter arrived. A paper reader described, in minute detail, horrendous violations of law. Among many others, there was even a beating up of detainees at one of the district police precincts.

"So, I traveled to Ufa on the paper's behalf," Grigory continued, "checked things out, and, upon return, filed my feuilleton. I had already proofread the galleys when, back in Ufa, the Bashkir regional leadership got worried the revelations would damage their reputation. They called the man overseeing their republic at the Central Party Committee. Then, a phone call came to *Izvestiya*'s editor-in-chief. The man got cold feet and threw out my feuilleton from the issue before it hit the presses. Case closed.

"Well, my friend," Grigory said after a pause, "it looks like your Ochamchiri travail is a carbon copy of my Ufa story. I can tell you what happened the moment the door of your Ochamchiri Party boss's office closed after you. The dude picked up the phone and called his Party boss in Sukhumi, the capital of Abkhazia Autonomic Region. He duly reported about your visiting the area of his patronage. As the chain of command has it, the Abkhazia Party boss called Tbilisi, the capital of the Georgian republic. He briefed his boss, the First Secretary of the Republic's Party Committee, about the goings-on.

"No local Party honcho wants to have his region dragged through the mud in the papers. The Georgian chief contacted his republic representative at the Central Party Committee in Moscow. As you know, the paper that sent you to investigate the scandal in Ochamchiri is weak-powered. It's not the organ of the Party; it's just that of the Central Council of Soviet Trade Unions. As I'm sure you agree, the Loch Ness Monster myth has more credibility than the claims of the Central Council of Soviet

Trade Unions to independence from the Party. So, the fate of your publication was sealed. That's how it goes, my friend."

~

I recall that conversation with Grigory now when I am struck by the
Crocodile editorial demarche that let me down. I come home after visiting *Crocodile*, where I had surrendered my journal's correspondent ID,
and try to calm down. I call Grigory first. I am at a loss as to what to do
next. What would happen to my journalistic career? I also call Sergei
Brudny. Both fellows had joined the satirical battalion a few years before
me. They might have some insight into what could be in store for me.

Since the conversation is not one you can have over the phone, we
agree to meet at the café of the House of Journalists. I still have my ID as
a member of the Union of Journalists. So far, no one has asked me to
return it, although that could happen now. As Lensky sings on the eve of
the duel in the opera *Eugene Onegin*, I also do not know "what will the
coming dawn reveal."

17

The Pecking Order

I make my way to the House of Journalists from the Nikitsky Gate sub-way station. It is drizzling. I think of that light springtime shower under which, seven years ago, I had headed to the editorial offices of the *Mos-cow Komsomol Member* for the first time. Now, I do not have that youth-ful enthusiasm in my heart anymore. I am torn up inside. As a Russian saying goes, "Cats are scratching at my heart." And their claws are enor-mous. . . . No matter what you say, when you are thrown to the dogs by the mightiest journalistic outlet in the country for no good reason, there is not much to be jolly about. . . .

Having already drunk too many cups of coffee, I sit in the café waiting for my friends. Grisha appears first. He lowers himself into the seat next to me. His body language tells me he is sorry for me and wishes he knew how to help. I may look like a terminally ill patient.

"Well, how's it going, man?" he says. "Don't let it get to you. Don't worry about it too much, will you?"

"I cannot understand what happened," I mumble in dismay. "Before they published the piece, both Khodanov and Manuil himself read it twice."

I am annoyed with myself. I have asked this question myself too many times already and found no answer.

"Trust me, buddy," Grisha sighs. "I figured it out a long time ago. The Soviet satirists' business is not that much different from that of the sappers. Today you have hit a landmine; tomorrow it could happen to me too. None of us has indestructible protective gear. I wish they would publish a special reference book of the *Who's Who* type. The kind they have in the 'rotten West,'" he giggles. "Without it, who knows who the untouchables are? You can survive if you spot the mine on time. Before you step on it, that is. The whole secret is to know in advance whom you can nip in your writing and whom you better stay away from. . . . Well, yes, the head of the feuilleton department knows in advance when he gives you an assignment most of the time. But if you find material for a feuilleton yourself, then you are on your own. Well, certain things you must know by heart. For example, could you tell me the highest official rank you're able to make fun of in the pages of our press?"

The question catches me off guard. I have never given it a thought.

"Don't strain yourself, Emil!" Grisha waves his hand. "I'll tell you, anyway: little people. A chief of some housing department . . . a manager of a local culture club . . . or some careless maintenance engineer. . . . As the expression goes, we criticize no one 'of a rank higher than a building super' [*ne vyshe upravdoma*]. Besides, all these people should live in distant provinces."

As Grisha is talking, I mentally scan my published pieces.

"Well," I say, "once I did a feuilleton for *Evening Moscow* that put the heat on the chief technologist of a Moscow plant."

"Okay," Grisha nods. "Let's talk Moscow. Could you tell me what kind of plant it was?"

I try to recall, but Grisha waves his hand in my direction again: "Relax, I'll tell you myself. I bet the man was an engineer at some plant of not even secondary but tertiary importance. Of some brick-producing factory or the kind that makes electrical bulbs. I bet on multiple occasions you've skewered some director of a grocery store or a vegetable warehouse. For mismanagement, for violation of financial discipline—right? And that's your whole game license. But, tell me, have you ever lampooned even one Moscow Party functionary, whether he was on a city or even a district committee? I bet you haven't. . . . Okay, forget about the Party! What about some head of the city hall executive committee, not just some of his clerks? I bet, none! . . . Now let's put aside the city government. Let's go down to Moscow city districts. Did any paper ever give you the green light to write about any wrongdoing, even on a small scale, that took place in two Moscow districts, Perovsky and Bauman?"

I try to say something, but Grisha waves his hand at me again: "Don't scratch your head, Emil. There's nothing for you to recall here. I couldn't understand myself why these districts had always been protected from criticism. However, it shouldn't have been hard to figure out. Our esteemed Comrade Grishin, first secretary of the Moscow City Party

Committee and a member of the Politburo, runs for a seat at the Supreme
Soviet always as a delegate of Moscow's Perovsky district. Ask yourself a
question. Could even a minor violation of the socialist order on that territory be exposed in the press? Not a chance!"

"Well," I say, taken aback somewhat. Seven years writing satire and I
am still learning all the intricacies of our government's workings. "What
about the other district, the Bauman one? Some other big shot is a
Supreme Soviet deputy of that district as well?"

"You got it, buddy. And the man is none other than our revered Leonid
Ilyich Brezhnev, a humble servant of this district's citizens at the Supreme
Soviet."

Finally, Sergei Brudny shows up at our table. As usual, he is dressed
up. He wears a dark-blue blazer with shiny sea-captain's buttons.

"What's up, gentlemen?" Sergei sits down and undoes his blazer button. "Why all this noise with no fight?"

"What fight?" Grisha says and shakes his head. "It's only a fight when
you can hit back. You don't call it a boxing match when your spar-
ring partner's hands are tied up. . . . I'm explaining to our colleague why
two particular areas of our capital are shielded from any press attacks by
people like us, the 'lovers of unhealthy sensations,' as they call us behind
our backs."

"Little Emil," Sergei turns toward me and, in a measured, somewhat
languid, tone, says, his nostrils flaring in light mockery, "it looks like it's
our burden of native Muscovites, mine and yours, Grisha, to widen the
horizons of our dear Rastignac. He got it in his head to conquer the
press of our capital. You say, they block two urban districts in Moscow
from satirical nips in the press? Big deal! What about closing a whole
region? Even *Crocodile* can hardly touch any organization of some oblast
or even a national republic. Manuil has a list of posts and regions that his
magazine must not touch. For example, he can't let a bad word about the
Krasnodar Territory appear in his magazine. You may ask, why is that?
What's so special about Krasnodar? Why can't even a yip about it appear
in the press for that one of many regions in our immense country? Let
me remind you, gentlemen, that *Crocodile* is not some city or region
paper, like *Evening Moscow* or *Lenin's Banner*. It's the organ of the Central Party Committee. However, the sinless sun always shines over the
Krasnodar Territory. Why? Because, for many years, the first secretary of
the Territorial Party Committee has been Comrade Medunov, one of

our dear Leonid Ilyich Brezhnev's close friends. The same applies to the Dnepropetrovsk region. Why? Should I explain it to you or would you like to guess it yourself?"

He is right. There is no need to strain my brain about it for too long. Everyone knows Comrade Brezhnev began his Party career in Dnepropetrovsk region. So, the whole area now is a solid preserve where not only are you forbidden to scare some bird sitting on a tree branch but you should also be careful not to trample the grass under that tree. . . .

"You have to understand, man," Sergei continues, releasing a stream of smoke toward the ceiling. "Only *Pravda* can criticize whomever they feel like with no one's approval. On its pages, a feuilleton appears on a Central Party Committee's cue only. A critical piece in *Pravda* isn't a court hearing. No deliberations take place. No floor is ever given to a defense lawyer. There it is the final verdict, not subject to appeal. . . . That's not quite the case with *Crocodile*. Though it's the publication of the same Central Party Committee and it must follow general Party guidelines, it can propose certain topics and choose certain objects of criticism. But that's about it."

Sergei exhales smoke again and, seeing we are all ears, continues: "Well, Manuil has plenty of experience. He is a pro. He has a dog's nose for the stuff. He knows whom you can just yap at, at whom only growl, and whose leg or even whose butt you can nip with no precautions. The man toiled as managing editor in the national press biggies, like *Komsomol Pravda* and *Izvestiya*, for many years. He is a member of the powerful Writers' Union. Two Red Banner of Labor orders and a full hand of medals . . . nothing to sneeze at, my friends. Like a mole in the ground, he senses which of his burrows he can pop out of safely and which ones he's better off staying away from. They could trample you down to death. He knows whom *Crocodile* can bother and whom it's better not even to touch. To be on the safe side, he ventilates all the forthcoming issues with his curator at the Central Party Committee."

"What do you mean, he 'ventilates'?" I shrug. "What kind of ventilation can there be with your boss? Unless like that popular joke, 'What is an exchange of opinions?' 'You enter your boss's office with your opinion and leave it with his.'"

"That's what it is," Grisha perks up. "Here's another bit on the same topic. If I'm your boss, then you're a fool. If you're my boss, then I'm a fool."

"You're all smart alecks over here, I see," says Sergei, flicking ashes into an empty coffee cup. "Put yourself in Manuil's place. He has to walk a tightrope of his own. His magazine is satirical. It's *Crocodile*. So, he has to at least show some teeth. But if you bare them at the wrong guy, you can get a good smack in the teeth. So, when the new issue of the magazine is typeset, before sending it to the print shop, Manuil locks himself up in his office and sits down at his *vertushka*, the hotline, that is. He calls his curator up there." Sergei rolls his eyes toward the ceiling. "'Greetings, Ivan Ivanovich,' he says. 'Here's the thing. We're about to run a piece that may be of some discomfort to the XYZ Province Party Committee. Do you have any objections?'

"A busy man, the curator may ask him to give the gist of the piece in question. If he feels it's only a slap on the wrist, he may give it the green light. If the matter is complicated, he may ask that they rush the galley proofs to him for his perusal. His butt is also on the line, you know."

"All right, all right," I say. "I get it that the higher echelon of the Party cadre is off limits. What about some government employees in the ministries? I don't recall ever writing about any of them. Can it be that all of them are sacred cows? Even in some of our national republics? Say, Uzbekistan?"

"You're right, Comrade Abramov," Sergei says humming. "Not all. You can't touch any heads of the country's ministries. Neither the All-Union ones nor those of the national republics. *Crocodile* can poke some deputy of a republican ministry, say, that of Turkmenia or Kazakhstan or Uzbekistan, if you wish. But, not any All-Union ministers. . . . Officials of the Heavy Industry Ministry and the Ministry of Defense are untouchable. All our special correspondents, the most trusted ones, our elite, know this all too well. When they're on the road and workers for these ministries approach them seeking justice, they can't help them."

Arkady Polishchuk shows up at the café. He joins us at our table and pats me on the shoulder, trying to cheer me up.

"It's not yet the end of the world, my friend," he giggles. "Chin up!"

He learns what we are talking about and says: "May I add my two kopecks, comrades? . . . Speaking of hazards," he turns toward me. "Do they know at your workplace . . . what's the name of your publishing house, again?"

"Nedra," I say.

"Oh, yes. Nedra. Do they know about your freelancing?"

"Heavens, no."

"Brilliant of you, man," Arkady says. "In our times, your job security means keeping your mouth shut. I've learned that the hard way, my friend."

And he tells us how, some fifteen years earlier, when he had just started his journalistic career, *The Young Leninist*, the regional newspaper of the city of Kostroma, hired him to run its correspondence department. One day, a letter arrived at his desk signed by three young writers. They all complained that the Kostroma regional publishing house had given them a hard time. They could not publish their works there, try as they might.

Arkady investigated the case. The chiefs of the local literary association turned out to be miserable hacks. They saddled the publishing house and turned it into their private gravy train. Up to 70 percent of the honorarium budget allotted to the publisher wound up in their pockets.

"I'd tried to read the work of those chiefs' of the association," Arkady continues, "but, oh boy, no matter how hard I tried, I couldn't get to the end of any of them. I even called on a few of my friends, all of them literary scholars, mind you, graduates of Moscow State University. I proposed a competition of sorts. The prize for reading a novel by one Andrei X, reading all the way to the last page, was a dinner on me at the best Kostroma restaurant.

"Well, two of them took up the challenge. They tried to trick me. One read it from the beginning and the other from the ending. But I exposed them. I asked them about the action in one chapter in the middle. Neither of them could make it that far in the book. They both got stuck in the swamp of horrendously boring socialist realism rubbish. . . .

"Well, I composed a feuilleton on the subject and sent it to the *Literary Gazette*. They published it. After that, strange things started happening to me. In the magazine *The Female Worker* (Rabotnitsa), they threw my essay, typeset already, out of the issue. I asked the department head over there what was going on. She narrowed her eyes and said, 'I didn't know you were *that kind* of person!'

"Then, at my place of work, at my paper, suddenly they cut my salary. When I tried to find out why, the editor said, 'My advice to you, Arkady, is this: do yourself a favor and quit. It's for your own good.'

"I quit. Then, wherever I'd apply for a job, they'd tell me the same mysterious phrase, 'We know what kind of person you are.'

"With great difficulty, the magazine *Life of the Blind* took me aboard. I guess they sympathized with me. I'd walked into so many walls, they sensed I was one of their own," Arkady grins. "I worked there for a year until my university friends helped me to get on the staff of my current journal, *Asia and Africa Today*. It's a scholarly publication, no journalism. It looks like they took me on to temper my journalistic zeal.

"So, my friend," Arkady pats me on my shoulder again. "We're all tightrope walkers. And we do it without the safety net."

⁓

Time drags on. A few hours later, one by one, my friends leave, asking me again not to take *Crocodile*'s betrayal personally.

Well, it is easier said than done. Who else can I turn to in such a low moment in my life? I am a stranger in the capital, a migrant from Odessa. So, I call Boris, my compatriot and friend.

He invites me over right away. As usual, right as I step over the threshold of his apartment, he gives me a big hug and says: "We'll feed you, Emil."

We sit and talk late into the night. He hears out the whole story about my last *Crocodile* publication, Minister Furtseva's fury, the *Literary Gazette* demarche against me, and the way *Crocodile* let me down. He sighs with compassion for me, and then he says prophetic words: "You're upset now, my friend. You're pissed. And you have all the right in the world to feel that way. If something like that were to happen to me, I'd feel that way too. But, trust me, the time will come, and you'll be proud of what you have done, what you have written."

I shake my head in disbelief.

⁓

A few months pass. I lie low, licking the wounds on my injured ego. Through Sergei, I hear about a new scandal involving *Crocodile*, this time one on a much larger scale. When I learn the details, I am a bit comforted. Another slip in the well-oiled mechanism of controlling the Soviet press has taken place. This time, it is not some freelancer like me who has gotten into hot water but one of the most important bona fide members of the staff—the magazine's managing editor. It turns out that even he is not immune to bringing upon himself the wrath of the all-powerful Central Party Committee.

At the epicenter of the scandal is Vladimir Nadein, one of the country's best feuilletonists. I like the man. My first publications in *Crocodile* passed through him when he was the head of the magazine's economics department.

There was nothing hawkish in Nadein's appearance. Despite the acidic style of his writing, this tall, a bit plumpish, dark-haired and dark-eyed man was kindhearted with his fellow journalists. I was not surprised they promoted this brilliant journalist to the second-highest position at the magazine.

One day, Nadein learned that the Ukrainian Republic's Regional Party Committee in Poltava was robbing blind a local collective farm. To improve the nourishment of the Committee members, they had created the following routine. A few days after the Poltava Regional Party Committee placed a call to the chairman of the collective farm, a truck would drive up to his office. The chairman would sigh and shake his head at the fact they had designated his farm as a wet nurse of the mighty Regional Party Committee. He would scribble a note to his storekeeper, something like, "Supply the bearer of this paper with these many pounds of butter and these many jars of honey."

After some time, under unclear circumstances—either the chairman of the collective farm fell ill or he did not face the auditors for some other reason—they discovered that a lot of the farm's products were missing from the warehouse. They arrested the storekeeper and took him to the local police precinct. The man maintained his innocence. As proof, he produced his boss's notes.

When the police precinct's chief tried to get to the bottom of the mysterious disappearance of honey, butter, and other nutritious foods, they demoted him. The reason for his career setback was his narrow-minded understanding of the "Thou shalt not steal" commandment.

The man did not realize it should not be called "stealing" when something as important as enhancing the diet of Party functionaries was in question. After all, "The Party Is Our Helmsman," as the posters around the country reminded the Soviet population. Undernourished, the helmsmen might lose their grip on the wheel and make the ship of state crash.

Instead, feeling unjustly punished, the precinct chief made photocopies of the notes the farm's storekeeper had given him, all those notes that had ordered him to cough up the butter and honey for the Party brass. He then sent the evidence to Moscow, to the editorial offices of the omnipotent satirical magazine *Crocodile*.

This story was so outrageous that Vladimir Nadein, the managing editor, did not send some freelancer or even one of the special correspondents to Poltava—he hit the road himself.

He reached the collective farm and dug. However, there was no need to dig too deep. It was easy to see that the storekeeper was innocent. He had stolen nothing. Instead, what had taken place was a clear case of extortion, a highway robbery of the collective farm goods.

Nadein returned to Moscow and published a feuilleton titled "So, Who Are We Talking About?" (*Tak ob kom ehto my?*)

Soon, a letter arrived from the Poltava Regional Party Committee. The jaws of both the author of the feuilleton and the magazine's editor-in-chief dropped. "Having heard it out and discussed it," the letter informed them, "we have disciplined the chairman of the collective farm as a Party member."

God dammit! Why did they punish the man? How was it his fault? How could he have ignored the demands of the Party bigwigs? Such injustice! After all, hadn't he been the Party committee's nourisher?

Nadein and Manuil scratched the back of their heads. Was it possible they had overlooked something the first time around? And Nadein flew to the collective farm again. He dug and dug again. Upon his return to Moscow, he published another piece defending all three victims of the Poltava Party bosses—the collective farm's chairman and his storekeeper, who had carried out the orders of their superiors, and the police officer who had been removed from his office unjustly, just because he did not punish the innocent.

Apparently, the first secretary of the Central Party Committee of the Ukrainian Republic decided he had had enough. That make-believe freedom of the press, my ass! Without bothering to provide any proof, he complained to the All-Union Central Party Committee in Moscow. The *Crocodile* journalist, he claimed, "has cast a shadow over the entire Party organization of the Ukrainian Republic." The members of the Poltava Regional Party Committee, the lovers of free-of-charge butter and honey, were not to be blamed. It was all the fault of the journalist who had publicized their love of nutritious food, free for the taking.

They summoned Manuil to the Central Party Committee and ordered him to throw Nadein under the bus. To fire him. End of story.

Now, after all the details have sunk in, I realize why the Central Party Committee sided with its Ukrainian Party comrades. Nadein had spilled the beans about the way many Party functionaries around the country were using their power to rob the local collective farms blind.

This story also proves that—beyond any reasonable doubt now!—no matter how worthy of criticism your target may be, and no matter how well protected you may feel by the press organ you write for, you are hardly safe from the wrath of the gods who reside high in the Soviet heavens—the Central Party Committee of the USSR.

PART V

Not for Want of Trying, 1971–73

18

Writing between the Lines

No matter how unjust *Crocodile*'s derailing of my journalistic career is, in hindsight the "Scatterbrain" debacle is a blessing in disguise. It wakes me up to reality. I should have never taken in earnest the Party call to criticize anyone "regardless of rank" (*nevziraia na litsa*). The "Scatterbrain" incident pushes me over the edge. Many doubts have been creeping up on me for a long time. Year after year, I have written satires aimed at the same targets. It makes me ask myself, *What the hell?* How many times can I work myself up over the same thing? As soon as winter comes, all major papers are flooded with readers' letters complaining about the same things, over and over. If you wonder where the tomatoes grown on the collective or state farms are, especially in the northern part of the country, look for them not on the store shelves but in the fields under the first snow of the season. They are left there to rot on the ground because of mismanagement.

Bad management is not the only weak link in the socialist economy. Plodding along the satirical path, I have encountered problems such as poor workmanship and the inefficiency of socialist enterprises. When I collected material for my feuilleton "A Candlestick as a Memento," published in *Crocodile*, I found that many museums were unprotected. They were also grossly underfunded. Some of them, like one in my hometown, the Odessa Archaeological Museum, had tried to beef up their budgets by setting up a souvenir shop. They wanted to make copies of their artifacts for sale—a statue of a Scythian wooden god or an African statuette or a miniature of an Egyptian sarcophagus. However, they got a rap on the knuckles. The local financial organs balked. The reason was simple: every Soviet enterprise must fulfill (even better, overfulfill) its production quota. Nobody knew what kind of business plan to impose (*spustit' plan*, in the

Soviet lingo) on the souvenir shop. So, to protect the sacred cow of the socialist system, they did not allow the souvenir shop to open. Thus, short of funds, the museum could not afford to protect their exhibits properly.

In this case and many others like it, the buck never stops at any Soviet official's desk. It is customary to blame some little man for any of the system's faults. When I compare notes with my comrades-in-satirical-arms, we call a spade a spade. We come to the same conclusion: in the pages of the Soviet press, the only person you are allowed to blame for any fault of the system is the proverbial "switchman." This folk expression, "It's all the switchman's fault" (*Vo vsem vinovat strelochnik*), stretches back to tsarist times, when the first railroads appeared. The officials in charge of railroad maintenance attributed any derailments to some poor switchman's oversight.

What should I do now? I cannot go on like this any longer. I do not even feel like trying to get my foot in the door of some other paper's feuilleton department, even if they take me in. Now that I have realized the truth about the limits imposed from above on public criticism, I feel it is immoral to keep blaming little people for the faults of the system.

~

One day, I run again into Sasha Moralevich, the *Crocodile* special correspondent. I find him in the same place as the last time—leaning against the wall of the poorly lit corridor of my communal apartment and smoking. It looks like he has grown fond of my beautiful neighbor Nina.

We chat for a while, and I mention my predicament to him. Sasha nods in assent.

"Well, Emil," he says, "do you know what Manuil Semyonov, our editor-in-chief, told me after he'd hired me and I brought him my first piece? He read it, got nervous, and then uttered, 'Sasha, stay clear from any generalizations! Stick to a particular locality and the facts at hand.'"

Sasha pauses and adds: "'The only place where generalizations of any kind are done,' Manuil said, 'is up there'"—Sasha points his big finger to the ceiling—"'at the Central Party Committee of the USSR. Period. Understood?' That's the bitter truth, my friend," Sasha says and pats me on the shoulder. "And we have to live with it for the rest of our lives, pal."

Here, I recall the sardonic pronouncement of Vitaly Reznikov, my satirical godfather: "All is fine; it's just in some stores you can't find some sausage" (*A v otdel'nykh magazinakh net 'Otdel'noj" kolbasy*).

Now, Sasha and I stand silently for a while as if mourning the current state of satire in the country, the genre we had both fallen in love with.

Then Sasha puts his cigarette out, pats me on my shoulder again, and heads for Nina's door.

~

Many years later, when the Soviet archives were opened to researchers, I learned about another sinister use of state-sponsored satire. The émigré Russian scholar Irina Pavlova makes it clear:

> In their research, Western historians focus on the disorder, crime, mass thievery, and lawlessness. For anyone brought up in Western civilization, such factors indicate that the regime is not able to establish order in society and solve urgent social problems. But for the Stalinist regime, all these manifestations of disorder were just "the chips that fly when you're chopping wood." First, this disorder was provoked by state power itself; and second, it took a lenient view of it as an unavoidable by-product of its policies. Stalin even tried to use the situation for his own ends. There is evidence that he told Kaganovich [one of his main associates]:
>
> > "See to it that *Gudok*, *Industriia*, and the other newspapers print as much as possible about our sloppiness, deficiencies, glitches, shoddy work, and so on. . . . We don't want those dopes abroad to see the forest for the trees. Our real figures and achievements are to be kept secret, while our petty problems—of which we have plenty, of course—should be glaringly apparent. 'Soviet chaos,' 'transportation in ruins,' 'abominable industrial output,' the works."
> >
> > "With photographs?"
> >
> > "Well, why not? In our position, a subtle policy is needed. You can't win if you don't cheat." (I. V. Pavlova, "Contemporary Western Historians on Stalin's Russia in the 1930s [A Critique of the 'Revisionist' Approach]," *Russian Studies in History* 40, no. 2 [Fall 2001]: 80)

It seems that the Stalin-blessed use of state-sponsored satire is another reason for its proliferation in the decades of Soviet history that followed.

~

Back to 1971. Awakened to the reality of what Soviet satirical journalism is all about, I find that my first impulse is to stop writing altogether. However, soon I find it is too late for that. The writer's bug bit me a long time ago, and it does not look like it will let me go anytime soon. Seven years down the road after my first publication in the *Moscow Komsomol Member*, I have become used to seeing my writing in papers. I cannot stop cold turkey now. So, I say to myself, maybe I should pick a safer genre? Why not popularize new developments in science and technology? My engineering background should help me enter the field. Journals such as *Technology for the Youth* (Tekhnika molodezhi), *Science and Technology* (Nauka i tekhnika), and similar publications are highly popular.

One day, on my way to work, I stop at the editorial offices of another technical magazine, *Inventor and Innovator* (Izobretatel' i ratsionalizator).

Well, it turns out they need a satirist much more than another popularizer of science. As soon as they have learned that *Crocodile* has published me, they want me to write about an inventor who was cheated out of his fee. I feel compelled to help the man. His bricklaying machine has made home construction skyrocket around the country, but he has not seen a kopeck of pay yet.

They send me to Uman, a picturesque town 150 miles southeast of Kiev, the capital of Ukraine. I have always wanted to visit the town where my mother was born and raised. She used to shake her head in nostalgia recalling the beauty of its centerpiece, Sofievka Park. Back in the eighteenth century, the Polish Count Potocki built it for his lover.

I travel to the city and talk to the abused inventor and all the bureaucrats involved in his case. The magazine publishes my report. To my dismay, I have found describing how the brick unloader works much less enjoyable than ridiculing the bureaucrats who cheated the inventor out of the compensation he was entitled to receive. Perhaps my Odessan genes have kicked in, and grudgingly I come to terms with the fact that I have been lying to myself about having any desire to write about science and technology. It is like offering a wolf the opportunity to graze instead of giving him a slab of juicy lamb.

What should I do now, that is the question! Is it at all possible to write without mentioning the names of people responsible for wrongdoing, yet not be accused of generalization?

~

To my luck, such an opportunity comes up soon. The Thaw, which had begun in the mid-1950s with Khrushchev's denunciation of Stalin's crimes, had ended. In late 1964, they accused the man of "voluntarism," that is, of doing whatever suited his fancy, and ousted him from office. Leonid Brezhnev, a thick-browed Party bureaucrat from Dnepropetrovsk, replaced him. In contrast to Khrushchev's lively, albeit often incoherent orations, the speeches of the new country leader were lengthy and mind-numbing. The man had a formidable talent of sorts: he could bore his listeners to death. As we joked among ourselves, at one time, the US Department of Justice considered eliminating lethal shots administered to death row inmates and forcing them instead to listen to Brezhnev's speeches. But the project was promptly dismissed from the agenda. Everyone agreed that the American public would not approve of such a cruel and unusual punishment.

There was nothing funny, however, about what Brezhnev had done. Under him, the Stalinists reinvigorated their ideological grip on the country's cultural life. In September 1965, they tried the writers Andrei Sinyavsky and Yuli Daniel for publishing their work abroad. Their only fault was ignoring the principle of socialist realism. That is, they depicted life not as it should be according to the Party's wishes but as they saw it.

Then, in August 1968, the events in Czechoslovakia had the effect of a wake-up call. The Soviet invasion pricked the balloon of idealistic dreams. The illusions of the generation that came into public life in the 1960s (these people were called the "sixtiers," *shestidesiatniki*), full of hope for the democratization of the country's life and dreaming that, having condemned Stalinism, the Soviet authorities would become humane, were dispelled. As soon as the BBC (which we all listened to despite the jamming) reported that Soviet tanks had rolled onto the Prague squares, it became clear that Stalinism was still alive and well.

Soviet papers portrayed the suppression of the Czechoslovakian attempt to "give socialism a human face" as an act of "brotherly help." The refusal to trust any official pronouncements led to an explosion of underground jokelore unprecedented in Soviet times. Since it was unsafe to gather in public, the like-minded met around the tables of our cramped kitchenettes and peppered their debates about current affairs with antigovernment jokes. The mostly good-natured underground quips of Khrushchev's time were gone. It had been replaced by an outburst of biting comments like,

"What are our troops doing in Czechoslovakia?"
"They're looking for people who invited them."

Or,

> Did you hear? The state travel agency Intourist has come up with a new ad, "HURRY TO VISIT THE SOVIET UNION BEFORE IT VISITS YOU!"

The pessimism of the public mood had set in forever, it seems. The old underground oneliner about the low productivity of the Soviet working class, "They pretend they pay us, and we pretend we work," has now morphed into, "They pretend they're building communism, and we pretend we believe them."

Russian literature, traditionally held in high regard by society, has always been in tune with the cultural zeitgeist. To circumvent the stringent censorship, the Russian artistic community has now turned to the fallback technique characteristic of Russian culture during tsarist times— Aesopian language. This mode of writing has been used to create works that seem innocent on their surface but that, in fact, conceal the treatment of topics a writer could not touch openly. Russian writers often used parable or allegory, inviting the sophisticated reader to read between the lines. The greatest Russian author, Alexander Pushkin, wrote the "History of the Village of Goriukhino" and later Saltykov-Shchedrin penned his *History of One Town*, both scathing satires on tsarist Russia. In fact, many passages of the *History* read like a satire on the regime we live under in the current time.

Quite in line with this literary tradition, in 1969 a short story titled "On a Summer Day" by Fazil Iskander appears in the journal *The New World* (Novyi mir). The author describes the ways the Gestapo blackmailed Germans, turning them into informants on their close friends and family members. Any Soviet reader familiar with the practices of the KGB recognizes the similarities between the secret police tactics of both regimes.

It seems that the author of the story has been able to circumvent the censors taking advantage of the strictly observed political correctness. An underground joke that circulated during the Great Terror in 1937 under Stalin illustrates this quite well:

Rabinovich appears in Red Square and shouts: "Down with the dictator! Down with the executioner! Down with the bloodsucker!"

In no time, the police grab him and take him downtown to the precinct.

"Are you out of your mind, Comrade Rabinovich? Do you even hear what you're saying?"

"What's with you, comrades?" Rabinovich says. "I'm protesting against that damned Adolf Hitler! Gee, who else do you think I had in mind?"

Humorous format became another means to conceal a satirical sting. Since the early 1960s, to project confidence about the so-called mature socialism, the Party had allowed Soviet media some levity. In 1961, they began televising a show titled *The Club of the Jolly and Resourceful* (KVN, Klub veselykh i nakhodchivych). This improvisational comedy program gained great popularity. The program was a contest that showcased the wit and erudition of teams of college students. A wave of cheerful humor won over the TV viewers. In 1964, the radio station named The Lighthouse (Mayak) inaugurated its Sunday program *Good Morning!* It combined favorite tunes with humorous pieces. In January 1966, it aired the first Soviet TV sitcom, *The Pub of 13 Chairs* (Kabachok 13 stul'ev).

Soviet press also followed suit. To give readers some respite from the gravity of the rest of the material, "Humor Nooks" (*ugolki iumora*) appeared in many Soviet publications. They used the humor of everyday life (*bytovoj iumor*), poking fun at family spats, relationships between the sexes, the misadventures of drunks, and such.

All these developments had set the stage for appearance of Aesopian satire in the cultural life of the country. The *Literary Gazette*, the organ of the Union of Soviet Writers, also inaugurated a humor page. In honor of the famous satirical novel by Ilya Ilf and Evgeni Petrov, they named it "The 12 Chairs Club." They introduced it as an outlet of humor geared toward the Soviet intelligentsia. It occupied the last page of the paper—the sixteenth, but, as its popularity grew, many readers turned to that page first.

The game the editors played with their censors was that of hide-and-seek. They published cartoons and flash fiction, entertaining on the surface but hiding a satirical sting. For example, because it was impossible to publicize the fact that desirable goods such as oranges were hard to find in Soviet stores, short verses by one Vladimir Lisichkin, ostensibly written for children, appeared on the club page:

> If you want an orange, kid,
> If you have this need indeed,
> Get playdough in a store,
> Make one orange or make more.

Emma Moshkovskaya wrote another children's verse on the scarcity of food in the Soviet Union:

> If your bowl seems scarce of soup,
> Get yourself a bigger loupe.
> Now, looking through such a loupe,
> You'll see a lot of soup.

Perhaps the most daring was the publication of a flash fiction titled "A Monument" by Andrei Kuchaev. Seemingly, it is another story about a drunkard's misadventure, a favorite topic of the "humor nooks" in many papers. On a cold winter night, while raising his hand to catch a taxi, a boozer spots another poor soul nearby in the same pose—with his hand outstretched. No car in sight, the boozer grabs his fellow in misfortune and, through the snowstorm, drags him to his home. In the morning, he discovers that, in his drunken haze, he has pulled a monument from its pedestal.

This short piece had its readers in stitches—not only because the story is hilarious but because of its political overtone. Anyone familiar with the typical Lenin monument could see that the story pokes fun at the "holy leader" of the October Revolution. His pose, with the outstretched hand, is interpreted sardonically. He is not calling the Soviet people to march "toward the shining heights of communism." He is just trying to catch a taxi. . . .

This publication caused a public scandal. A group of retired honorary Party members, the Old Bolsheviks, accused the paper of treating Lenin's image sacrilegiously.

However, after much turmoil, the editors of the page, and of the *Literary Gazette* as a whole, survived. The editors faked innocence. Their defense ploy was the same one used in the underground Rabinovich joke cited earlier. How could such an unholy thing as mocking the great Soviet leader even enter anyone's mind! Nothing is farther from the truth! The statue in the story is just some pedestrian plaster sculpture of an athlete; many city parks around the country feature one.

On one of my visits to Boris, my old Odessan friend, I mention the story in the *Literary Gazette*.

"Gee," I say, "Isn't it something? Good for them. How the hell could they pull it off? Lucky sons of bitches!"

We both laugh in satisfaction, and Boris says: "Well, I can think of at least one time the topical humor helped safeguard the satire. Have you ever wondered why they let the *Welcome, or No Admittance* flick run in the city theaters?"

I remember wondering about it myself. Back in October 1964, after its release, I saw the movie. I could not believe my eyes. How had the filmmakers pulled it off? Were the censors drunk or what?

The film takes place in a young pioneers' camp run by an overly demanding director. He orders children to obey camp rules to the letter. He expels one boy from the camp because he arbitrarily left the camp grounds and swam across the river, although the children are forbidden to do this because of the fear that it is unsanitary. The man believes that the boy's unruly behavior can serve as a bad example for other children.

It does not take much effort to see that the movie plot is a paraphrase of Soviet society at large. The young pioneers' camp is the whole country driven by the ideological preceptors. The constrained life of the youngsters in the camp is not much different from their parents' lives outside of it. They too have to watch every step. They too are subjected to fearmongering. They too are reminded all the time of the threat the outside capitalist world presents.

Through his social circle, Boris, a screenwriter himself, had learned about how this film had made it to the theaters.

"After they produced the movie," Boris says, "they screened it at the studios for the censors who promptly shelved it. What was Elem Klimov, the movie's director, to do?"

I jog my brain, but I cannot think of how anyone could possibly ever reverse any censors' decision. Their verdict is usually final.

"Well," Boris continues, "as the Russian proverb goes, 'You may get by without a hundred rubles, but not without a hundred friends.' Some of Elem's acquaintances knew someone who knew someone. In a word, he found a way to approach the supreme leader, Nikita Khrushchev, himself. It was around the end of September 1964; the man was still in power. So, they talked him into watching the movie at his summerhouse, his dacha in the countryside. They said nothing about the studios nixing it. They promised Nikita good laughs for himself and his dacha guests—close family members and other relatives."

"Good laughs, ah!" I say in disbelief. "That's all?"

"Well," Boris says. "They didn't lie. The movie is funny as hell. Isn't it? It's hysterical. Kids' comedic adventures, dimwitted adults. . . . Well, they screened the movie there, and everyone had a good time. They laughed aloud. And Nikita laughed together with everyone else. When it was over, he asked the man who brought the copy, 'Is it in theaters already?' 'No, Nikita Sergeevich,' the man played dumb. 'Well, at the studios, they put it on the shelf for some reason.' 'Ugh, how come?' says Nikita. 'Why keep it on the shelf? It's hilarious. Get it rolling!' And the next day, on October 9, 1964, the movie hit the screens of Moscow theaters."

I strain my memory and recall that I saw the film under somewhat unusual circumstances. It was at a regular movie theater, all right, but they screened it during matinee hours only. The theater was full of schoolboys.

When I tell Boris, he laughs at my gullibility.

"But of course, Emil, my dear friend! As you know, they screened the film just a week before they kicked Nikita in the ass and demoted him. That could mean pulling the politically ambivalent movie he allowed to run on the country's screens. They spent a bunch of money on this film production. So, they came up with an ingenious way to recover at least part of the expense while editing out the satirical bits."

"What do you mean?" I say. "I don't think they tampered with the movie."

"No, they didn't do any cuts, Emil. But please recall, when did you see it," Boris laughs. "What time of day? In the evening, after work hours, like every other adult in the country?"

"No," I say, still flummoxed about where he is going with this. "I believe the movie ran in the morning only. It was one of my days off."

"That's the trick!" Boris laughs. "They came up with an ingenious scheme. They ran the movie in the morning hours when primarily children attend the screenings. And kids could hardly comprehend that a comedy set in a pioneer camp was a send-up on their parents' everyday life."

～

These individual cases of success in tricking the censors make me want to try my hand at something similar. Soon after I see Boris passing by a long line to the barrel of kvass, I overhear the vendor shouting, "I'm running out of it! Stop lining up!"

It was a hot day, and a thought crossed my mind: What would happen if they still kept coming?

I came home and jotted down what I thought would most likely take place. I gave it a humorous twist.

After a few rewrites, I call Boris and read my piece to him. He giggles and says: "I bet they'll kill it. But it's bordering on the acceptable. But why not try it? What are you going to lose?"

The next day, I travel to Trubnaya Square, where the editorial offices of the *Literary Gazette* are located. I meet Ilya Suslov, the deputy editor of the "The 12 Chairs Club." A good-looking man of above-average height, with a head of curly brown hair, he gives me a penetrating look over his horn-rimmed spectacles. His subdued smile means only one thing—he wants to be sure I am aware of the game he plays on "The 12 Chairs Club" page, and I am not to waste his time by bringing him some toothless humoresque.

Since the piece is hardly longer than three typed pages, he has me sit in the chair at his desk and reads my whimsy right there and then.

"Not too shabby," he says. "Not too shabby at all."

He reclines in his chair and gives me another testing look.

"The 12 Chairs Club" logo

Ilya Suslov, "The 12 Chairs
Club" editor (courtesy of
Nancy I. Suslov)

"Wonderful, Comrade Abramov," he says. "Now, when we have all
reached the stage of 'ripe socialism,' our Soviet people can afford to have
a good laugh here and there."

He utters this in a pronouncedly orchestrated, ironic tone. I am barely
able to hold myself from bursting into laughter. It would spoil the game
he is playing. Nobody addresses anyone nowadays casually as "Comrade
Such-and-Such." By using the formal greeting, the man signals I should
not take anything he says at face value.

That is how we all talk nowadays—using the Soviet newspaper clichés.
In everyday situations, the stilted language of Party pronouncements
sounds comic.

"We'll try to see that your piece goes through," he continues. "But I
can't guarantee it. Is that okay with you, Comrade Abramov?"

Again, he smirks and smiles. I nod and leave.

To my delight, a week later, my piece appears on the page of "The 12
Chairs Club."

A Mug of Kvass

It was summer; a hot day, and everyone was thirsty. A vendor stood next to the barrel of kvass. A long line stretched to the vendor and his barrel.

"We're running out of kvass!" cried out the vendor. "There won't be enough for everyone."

From the long curving line, a citizen wearing a hat made of newspaper yells out: "Don't get excited, comrades, we'll ration it so that there will be enough for all. And we'll manage it justly. I'll count you off into three groups—group one, group two, and group three. Everyone given the number one will drink first. All number twos will drink after them, and the number threes can slurp up whatever's left."

"So why do the people who are picked first get to drink first?" came another voice from the line. "Just because they get the first number? . . . It should be this way—the thirds drink first; the firsts drink third, and the seconds drink second."

"Don't listen to them," cried an old lady to the kvass vendor. "Give only half a cup to each person. This way, everyone will get something."

"If we divide the amount of the remaining quantity by the approximate number of citizens," said a student while holding a multiplication table in his hands, "we come up with three hundred twenty-seven thousandths of one large mug per person, or six hundred fifty-four thousandths of a small mug."

"I'll hit you with a mug in a minute!" said the vendor to the student. "Don't make me nervous with your numbers, or I won't give you anything to drink at all. My shift ended a long time ago. I keep working because I feel sorry for you."

"No, comrades, numbers and measurements have nothing to do with it," reasoned a citizen with a skinny face. "If everyone is to get kvass, we must add water."

"Why on earth would I fill up on water?" said an agitated old man in a cap with a long brim. "Kvass has strength; it's got oomph!"

"What's going on over there?" The line was becoming restless. "Keep pouring! If people want a drink with a kick, let them run to the liquor store before it closes," came the quick reply from the other end of the line.

The vendor stood stock-still.

"And what if there's an inspection? They're sure to get on my case."

"Who cares about an inspection?" they all shouted. "Let the inspectors wait as long as all of us do. Then they'll know!"

With surprising agility, the vendor threw the hose into the open hatch and turned on the water.

And the crowd of people grew larger and larger.

"It's pure water now!" the vendor announced half an hour later, raising a mug. "I'm closing up shop."

"You have no right to leave people thirsty," said the old man in the cap. "Get back to business."

"You'll get me indicted," the vendor moaned. "Have you ever heard of water being sold for the price of kvass?"

"Sure, I have," the old man calmed him down. "And lots worse, too!"

"Brothers," the vendor croaked out, "spare me. I've got a wife expecting a baby in her eighth month. And two small children. You'll destroy me!"

"Pour, Uncle!" the line persisted. "We don't have the time; we're thirsty!"

The vendor's nerves could not stand it. He grabbed a handful of change and stuffed it into the pockets of the people standing nearby: "Here, take it, citizens! Let's pretend I'm giving you change. The barrel was half full of pure water from the beginning. It's the work of the devil. Me and my damned greed."

And the line of people grew longer and longer.

The vendor cried while continuing to rinse out mugs. The flow of water turned to a trickle, then into droplets, and then it stopped. The vendor looked up in fear. The familiar figure of the quality control inspector stood by the hose. He pressed it with his foot. It was now his turn to drink.

"That does it!" the vendor gulped. "It's dry. There's nothing left to do business with."

And the line grew longer and longer.

The inspector thought for a moment and freed the hose.

"The main thing, Petrovich," he said to the vendor after drinking down his mug of water, "is not to shortchange people; give everyone the same amount. Nowadays, there are severe penalties for that thing. Pour equally to all people."

I am pleased to have pulled it off. At first sight, "A Mug of Kvass" is only a humorous sketch meant to evoke a knowing smile from the reader. *Yes, I know, I stood in a line like that on a hot day.* . . . But, being well aware that the *Literary Gazette* is hardly the place for a humoresque on such a pedestrian subject, the sophisticated reader will recognize that, beyond the comic setup, the story makes fun of the socialist mentality. It hints at the falsehood of the equality principle traded in for the quality of life. People accept being poor as long as everyone is poor. They cheat themselves because of it—they are willing to pay for kvass while they are drinking tap water.

After a while, I get lucky again. Another piece of my writing makes its way onto "The 12 Chairs Club" page.

The Sun Shone

The sun shone, and all was okay with the world. A gardener watered his flowerbed. A limousine drove past. A scientist sat next to the chauffeur. He read a book by his favorite author.

"Daisies and violets," the gardener thought as he sprinkled the flowers. "Shrubs and bushes . . . leaves and stalks . . . what a blooming bore! He has it good," he thought, glancing after the chauffeur in the limousine as it passed. "Something new every day. He gets to see the world. Perhaps I should learn to be a chauffeur. While there's still time . . ."

The car had already rolled down the next street. "Got to change the left rear tire. It's pulling left," the chauffeur mused. "On second thought, to hell with it. This crate can fall apart for all I care. I'm just a highfalutin' flunky. A coachman is a coachman, no matter what he uses—whip or gas pedal. But him!" He looked at his passenger. "He's got a purpose in life— conducts experiments, searches for something. It's sure better than hugging a steering wheel all day long. Maybe I could be a technician, work in a laboratory. Then take more courses, find myself a field."

"So what if I discovered the formula for that wax," the scientist thought as he sat with the book in his lap. "Big deal I've published twenty-three research articles. What if I'm about to finish a post-doctorate? If only I could write a single story like this, then I'd feel it's all been worth something."

At that moment, the writer looked down the street from his study window.

"Still and all, what he does is the most sublime kind of work in the world. Creates beauty, which needs no reviews, artists' committees, or critique sessions."

He gazed at the gardener watering the flowers.

The sun shone, and all was okay with the world.

Like "A Mug of Kvass," though seemingly quite innocent, the story has a subversive subtext. It flies in the face of the socialist realism doctrine. Here, all the characters, regardless of their place in society, are dissatisfied with their lives. The circular plot is more in line with the Old Testament pronouncement "What goes around comes around" than with the call for "progressive movement toward the shining heights of communism" (*postupatel'noe dvizhenie vpered k siiaiushchim vershinam kommunizma*). The only thing shining in the story is the sun. The piece poses provocative questions, "Is it possible to make every person happy? Isn't it human nature to see that the grass is always greener on the other side of the fence?"

Inspired by these successes, I compose a few more pieces in which I express how I feel about our Soviet way of life. To my surprise, the editors do not give me a hard time. They publish them even though I dare to touch on certain ideological taboos.

Here is one example. Back in October 1917, as soon as the insurgent cruiser *Aurora* fired off a volley of blanks signaling the beginning of the Winter Palace storm, thus announcing the start of the new era, Soviet propaganda declared a new social order. From that moment in history on, not landlords and capitalists but blue-collar workers and peasants were proclaimed to become the true masters in the country. Labor, especially physical labor, was always promoted as "a matter of honor, a matter of glory, valor, and heroism." However, in my time, to be a blue-collar worker is hardly glamorous. I addressed this issue in a short story titled "Aesop."

One Stepanov, a machine shop manager, visits his superior, the factory's director, Koryagin, and asks to give him back his lathe operator job. The director is baffled. Why on earth would anyone want to give up his cushy white-collar post and go back to being a simple blue-collar worker? No matter what Stepanov tells him—that he enjoys working with his hands, that he comes from a family of lathe operators, that, on top of that, as a highly skilled lathe operator, he would make more money than he does in his current position—his boss refuses to believe him. He is convinced there is something else behind the crazy request. It is just the man expresses it in an oblique, roundabout way, like the ancient Greek fabulist Aesop, through some parable. The director is sure the man is hiding the true reason for his odd desire. He orders an audit of Stepanov's office, telling the inspectors to study his books, to pore over his inventory. The inspectors find no wrongdoing. Then,

> Koryagin undid the middle button on his jacket and, sighing, seated Stepanov on the sofa in his office.
> "Excuse me, my friend, I hadn't noticed. I looked at your face, but I didn't see it. Now I see," he said, studying Stepanov's visage. "You're tired, my friend, I can see it now. Take some time off, go on paid leave; you deserve it. Where would you like to go? Maybe to the Black Sea resort or to the Caucasus Mountains, eh? Or splashing around at the mineral springs in Kuialnik near Odessa? Just tell me where you want to go."
> "Back to the lathe," Stepanov said.

Eventually, the director gives up. He signs off on the manager's petition, convinced it is only a matter of time before he will figure out what kind of skeleton the man has in his closet. He still hopes to find the true reason for his subordinate's bizarre desire.

They publish this piece in "The Eccentric" (Chudak), the humor section of *Literary Russia*, the literary supplement of *Soviet Russia*.

Soon, I compose another piece. It addresses many frustrating aspects of everyday Soviet life: the long lines for the most essential goods, overcrowded public transportation, the practice of cheating customers in stores, the dismal government-run mail service, and widespread alcoholism, including on-the-job drunkenness.

TRIPLE SEVEN

I met him at the cleaners. I guessed right away who he was, though his cap was pulled down over his eyes and an overcoat hid his figure. I examined him with curiosity. He didn't notice me staring, it seemed. He tossed a raincoat over his shoulder and left. He walked briskly: I followed him at a light trot.

Soon he entered a pawnshop, took off the raincoat, and got money.

"What are you gaping at?" someone asked behind me in line.

I removed my jacket and shoved it through the pawnbroker's window.

I overtook the same guy at the check-cashing office, where he was paying his utility bill. I remembered it was time to pay mine, too. In the store, he bought half a pound of choice sausage (I bought premium), a dozen ready-to-cook cutlets, and two packages of frozen dumplings.

"Not bad," I thought, looking at him. "Not bad at all!"

Then I was confused. He bought a bottle of Triple Seven Port, uncorked it, and gulped its contents in one movement. Then he threw away the bottle.

Second-rate work! He could at least recycle the empty bottle. But why does he need port to begin with?

I puzzled over this mystery and, following him into a big apartment house, put this question to the man who had opened the door for us.

"Oh, that's his fuel," the man said. He took off the guy's cap, pushed him out of his overcoat, grabbed him around the ribs, and stuck him in the closet.

"You can't surprise anybody with robots nowadays," said his master, pouring himself a shot of Triple Seven Port. "There are well-known models that wax and polish the floor or write prose and poetry. Once I had this great idea: to use automatons to help protect myself from all negative emotions in my life."

He asked the plastic-coated robot to get back out of the closet. It obeyed with little enthusiasm.

"I have already forgotten about the stress of waiting in line, about being shoved around in stores or squeezed in buses. For a month already, my blood pressure has been normal, and I sleep like a baby. In my dreams, I don't curse the salesclerk anymore. To make me pay more, when weighing a piece of meat, the clerk would try furtively to pull the scales down. A robot doesn't leave the counter until it gets the exact weight of the purchased goods. . . . My heart tremors have vanished, the ones I used to have after any contact with the mail carrier. In the morning, the man would bring me the evening paper, and, in the evening, the morning paper. A telegram would take three days to arrive, and a money order thirteen days. Now this guy," the master tapped the robot on the shoulder, "picks up the mail right away at the post office."

I inquired about the reliability coefficient.

"I wouldn't say he has no feelings," the master of the house replied. "Sometimes the body overheats from the frequent turning on of the lighted tableau on his chest, the one that reads, 'PLEASE DON'T BUG ME; IT'S USELESS, I'M A ROBOT.' Overall, he is a real lifesaver. Three-quarters of my work time goes into scanning through the catalogs when choosing a design type. The robot handles that easily. Not to mention that he computes several times faster than me. In fact, my boss is happy when he shows up at work instead of me. No telephone nonsense, no cigarette breaks. . . . You can understand how convenient it is for me: I spend my free time searching for new ideas. The robot even picks my kid up from kindergarten while on the way home. They get along together. And, as you witnessed, it's not too hard for him to grab something for dinner along the way."

"But why does he gulp down port?" I said. "There are solid batteries."

"True, he used to run on batteries," said the inventor, pouring what was left in his bottle into three glasses and offering one to the robot. "I was forced to fall back on port. The thing is, I used to send him down to call the plumber on duty. You can tell what plumbers run on from a whiff of their breath. So, the evaporated alcohol oxidized some of my robot's contacts and screwed up the solenoid that spits out the three-ruble tip for the plumber. I was forced to run down to maintenance myself. Now, when port is inside its body, the contacts are kept moistened with a uniform solution, and they work fine."

The man checked a slot in the robot's shoulder and picked up an oilcan.

"I don't understand why the motors that run his legs are not quite in sync," he said. "As I'm sure you've noticed, he swerves a little when turning. Several drops of good old pickle juice, our national hair of the dog," he shook the oilcan, "is enough to eliminate the defect."

"Still, he threw out the bottle," I said, filled with envy.

"Oh, don't worry," the inventor smiled. "The salesgirl at the store likes him. She doesn't charge him the deposit, anyway."

I was so annoyed that my shock-resistant plastic body almost burst.

Translated from the computer language by E. Abramov

The story appears not in some obscure, jerkwater publication but in *The Week* (Nedelia), the literary supplement of the All-Union paper, *Izvestiya*, the central government paper. They have no problem with my satire. Go figure!

Upon thinking about it for a while, I conclude that the humorous setup did it. That it was a story about a robot written by another robot eclipsed the satirical intent. It looks like, for a satirist, writing in a comic mode can be self-defeating. Making things laughable has its pitfalls. It can soften the satiric bite. Satire should express intolerance of the social ills it attacks; humor signals the grudging acceptance of the imperfect world.

My euphoria at finding a new literary device that makes it possible for me to continue writing satire begins to subside.

19

Slippery Slope

Soon, I find the writing-between-the-lines mode altogether unsatisfying. I feel it is hardly more than a literary game. It looks like the Party overseers of literature do not mind opaque criticism of the system. It seems they brush it off as harmless and let it die its natural death. I imagine them chuckling to themselves, "Whatever makes them, the little fools, happy . . ." When I meet Grigory, Arkady, and Sergei at the café of the House of Journalists, we compare notes. We discuss the goings-on in this satirical world of ours. We conclude that the camouflaged satires we write amount to "flipping the bird in one's pocket" (*pokazat' kukish v karmane*). Whether or not we want to admit it, we *are* servants of the vile Soviet power, of Sofia Vlasievna (from *Sovetskaya vlast'*), as we euphemistically call it among ourselves. The dame does not give a damn about the jokes we crack behind her back. The Russian variant of the old Arabic proverb, "The dogs may bark, but the caravan moves on," is "Whatever a dog barks about, the wind carries away."

The only consolation is that we are not the guard dogs of the regime, like the authors of *Pravda* editorials. But they treat us, the country's satirists, like harmless, domesticated doggies, some poodles whose owners do not mind their cute yapping. We try to slip a mickey into our writings, that is, to come up with some means to relax our editors' vigilance. However, they have learned how to deal with potentially inciting literary work. They have become skilled in plucking the subversive sting out of our writing, turning a cobra of satire into grass-snake humor.

When one of the most prestigious publications of the time, the magazine *Youth*, which rivals "The 12 Chairs Club" in popularity, accepts my new story, I am elated. Wow, they are taking the chance to publish my piece that aims at a non-kosher target. My story makes fun of the perennial curse of Soviet life—chronic shortages of many consumer goods. For as long as I can recall, these shortages have compelled my compatriots to place their names on waiting lists for scarce stuff. Just the rumor that rare merchandise is about to become available is enough to start one of these lists. Weeks or even months before the item in question goes on sale, people compile these rosters of aspiring consumers. In the interim, those lucky enough to have their names included must return to verify their position on the list. If they fail to show up, their names are just dropped. These lists are no laughing matter to the Soviet people. They have been a part of everyone's life for a long while.

The plot of my piece takes the form of a practical joke the narrator plays by pretending to start one of these lists. The frenzy his act creates makes him forget that his trick is the only reason the whole thing began.

One day a friend and I were sitting in a café and, during a lull in the conversation, I pulled out a notebook and made a list of errands my wife had asked me to do for her.

"What are you writing?" asked my friend, trying to look over my shoulder. "What list is this?"

"It's nothing," I replied.

"I think you're trying to put something over on me." My friend moved closer. "What's the list for?" he said, winking.

"For nothing."

"Put my name down."

"Don't be a jerk."

"Emil," he pleaded, "come on. Put my name down."

"Leave me alone."

"So that's the way it is," he said. "When you want something, you come to me, but when I ask you to put me on your list, it's another story."

"Will you cut it out?" I snapped. "Stop bugging me about the damn list."

"What's happening, comrades?" inquired an elderly citizen who had stopped at our table. "What list is this?"

"It's not a list," I retorted.

"Understood," said the citizen. "My name is Glossky. Put it down."

To get rid of him, I scribbled something on the page.

"Thank you," said Glossky. "When do we come in to check on our names?"

"Tomorrow morning . . . at 6:30 a.m. Sharp!" I said the first thing that came to my mind.

"Thank you," said Glossky, taking his leave.

Before he was out of sight, two more people came up and demanded that I add their names to the list. I wrote them down, then leaned my elbow on the open notebook.

"Emil," screamed my friend, who was turning green, "what are you doing? Why are you torturing me? Please, as a friend, put my name down."

"No, I won't."

At that moment, a heavyset man came up to our table and pulled the notebook from underneath my elbow.

"Give it to me," he said. "My handwriting is neater."

This portly fellow sat down in a corner of the café and added his name and those of two young women he knew.

Glossky appeared again.

"Excuse me," he said. "Can I put my wife on the list?"

"No," I answered.

"Why not? We have different surnames."

"In that case, it's okay."

Glossky grinned and skipped over to the heavyset man, around whom a crowd was sprouting. When the pages of my small notebook were filled, someone got a piece of wrapping paper at the counter and used it to continue the list.

"I will never forgive you for this!" screamed my friend, looking back toward me as he pushed through the crowd. His perspiring face bore an angry expression.

Just then the heavyset man announced: "We have two hundred names. No more. That's all we can take."

"Write me down," my friend begged as he reached the list maker. "Somebody may drop out."

"I suppose we could keep going," the heavyset man agreed, "but then we must check in at five in the morning. There will be quite a crowd, you know."

Glossky reappeared.

"Can I enter my wife's sister? She has the surname of her husband."

"Where is she registered as a resident?"

"In Moscow."

"Go ahead," I nodded.

Soon someone started another list; then a third one appeared. People argued over which list was valid.

"Could I see your palms, comrades?" asked an old man, pulling the stub of an indelible pencil from a toothbrush container in his pocket. "We will mark your number on the palm of your hand. Experience has shown that this is the best way to keep track of the line."

"Why there?" said Glossky, extending his palm for marking. "Sometimes palms perspire from nerves, you know."

"Because it's a good spot," said the old man, clenching his fist. "No one will see your number."

It was drizzling when I left the café. A long line of people stretched from the entrance and continued around the corner. Among those waiting were an old woman knitting a sweater in the feeble light of the street lamp, two young men playing a game of chess on a portable board, and a substantial-looking citizen who sat on a folding chair while reading a magazine.

I passed them by. Then a terrible thought rushed through my mind. I knew my list was a fraud, but what of the others? What if one was for real? I exclaimed to myself, *Oh my God! My name's not on any of those lists!*

I turned and ran down the street toward the café.

"Citizens," I screamed, "who is last in line?"

Expecting that a piece on such a hot topic would have a hard time passing into print, I have titled it as casually as possible, "The List." When the magazine with my story reaches me, I see that, without asking me, they have altered the title; now it is "A Psychosis." With such a simple switch, they have redirected the satirical arrow. Instead of aiming it upward at a government incapable of eliminating shortages, the title points downward. It is not the poor management of the country's economy, inept at putting an end to chronic shortages of essential goods, that is at fault here. It is just that people are obsessed with forming lines of any kind. People are funny!

First, I think about calling Victor Slavkin, the editor of the humor department of the magazine, and making a stink. Then I decide against it. Most likely, the title switch was not his fault. His superiors, the managing editor and the editor-in-chief, know what they are doing.

I calm down and reread the piece. Well, if I am to blame someone for slanting my story, I should start with myself. Here I make fun of the victims, not the perpetrators of the systematic mismanagement of the country's economy. That is why it was so easy for the editors to turn a satirical piece into a humorous one. Yes, when writing it, I had hoped that, by poking fun at people's behavior, I would make the readers think of the real reason for the obsession with list-making. How cowardly of me!

After beating myself up for a while, I feel that maybe I am too harsh on myself. After all, it is a tall order—to publish a satirical piece aimed at those who have full control of every printed line in the country. (At one point, I had learned the Censor Bureau had to approve any text headed for the Soviet press—even the sticker warning about accidental forest fires placed on matchboxes.)

Maybe I should find a better, smarter, and more sophisticated way to point the arrow of my satire?

One day, I read in the *Inventor and Innovator* about "brainstorming," an unorthodox method of solving technological problems. Engineers often have a hard time thinking outside the box. They are packed with knowledge of their field of expertise. All those physical laws of nature, mathematical axioms, and theoretical postulates bind their thinking. Sometimes they invite to their conferences someone unburdened with excessive knowledge. Such a person might throw out some crazy thought that might solve the problem at hand. That is how they came up with cold-welding wires. An idea for the vice-grip pliers was born when someone jokingly suggested clamping wires with one's teeth.

As I read about it, the proverbial light bulb flashes in my head. It makes me think of the only class of people in the country making a living by doing not much—all those ubiquitous Party overseers. The whole army of them populates the numerous district, regional, and republican committees. All they do is watch over other people's work to ensure the toiling masses do not deviate from the Party line in the slightest.

I draft a story about a modern-day Ivan the Fool. It is about some lazy and incapable fellow. Even his father had given up on him early on, telling him he had as much chance to become someone as a chicken had to turn into a fighter jet. The boy grows up incapable of doing anything that requires any smarts. The only job he can hold down is that of a drawing copyist. After placing tracing paper over a new engineering drawing, he goes over every line with ink so that, later on, blueprints could be produced. The lines on the tracing paper must match the original; that is, they must be no longer, no shorter, no thinner, no thicker . . .

Such a setup is a nod to the Soviet metaphor of "sticking to the line," which is a paraphrase of the propaganda cliché repeated ad nauseam in the papers—"sticking to the Party line."

One day, the copyist's superiors summon him. After double-checking that he is truly ignorant, they invite him to attend a meeting of technical experts. They explain to him what brainstorming is all about. During the meeting, the engineers discuss ways to cool down a piece of equipment that often overheats. The clueless young man blurts out the first thing that comes to his mind, "We have to blow on it, that's what!" By free association, the phrase makes the engineers think of a way to solve the technological problem. They thank the fellow and, grateful for his help, give him a big bonus. After all, he assisted them, even if only by chance.

The rumor about the successful brainstorming session spreads like wildfire. As a result, the tracer's career thrives. They promote him. They make him head of a newly created Department of Funky Ideas. He enlarges his staff and hires two leading ignoramuses and four senior boneheads. Each of them brings in half a dozen regular dimwits.

The department receives requests for help from all over. Soon, an acute shortage of people qualified for such work leads to opening a school for clueless kids with a single goal in mind—to make them learn nothing over the course of their studies. The story protagonist signs up his older son for the school, hoping that, if he takes after his father, he will also grow up to be a successful nincompoop.

In the meantime, the man's career skyrockets. Now he grows into a statesman, the head of the Ministry of Offbeat Ideas. The story ends with the protagonist confiding in the reader:

Perhaps you're curious about my appearance and my whereabouts. Well, what can I say, dear comrades! Alas, I can't help you with that. The day has not yet arrived to reveal myself to the public. I generate ideas on such a high level that sometimes I dizzy myself. I guess you could say vertigo is the side effect of my profession. I'm solving many problems. I'm on call to help with issues of the highest matter, of great importance not only to our country but to the whole planet!

"So, dear comrade," the powers-that-be ask me, "what, in global terms, do you think of such-and-such problem?"

As always, I close my eyes, go limp and blurt out something, the first thing that pops into my head—and they giggle with joy. More often than not, they use my idea. That's if it doesn't go too much against the general line, of course. As a former copyist, I understand that. You must stick to the line. It should be no bigger and no smaller, no thicker and no thinner. . . .

I rewrite the first draft a few times, then type it up on my Olympia. Where should I take it? There are two places for sophisticated, between-the-lines satire, "The 12 Chairs Club" of the *Literary Gazette* and "The Green Briefcase," the humor department of *Youth* magazine. The club editors have limited space to play with; they do not want to see anything over a thousand words. My piece is at least twice as long. So, I take it to *Youth*. After all, they already know me over there; they published my piece on the list-making mania.

Slavkin reads the story, giggles, and asks me to leave it with him. Exhilarated, I go home.

A few days later, he calls and says he has already placed my story in the next issue of the magazine and sent it to the printers.

I rejoice. I have been able to disguise the satirical sting of the story so well that the editor has found it safe enough to appear in the pages of such a prestigious magazine.

A week later, Slavkin calls me to come over to proofread the galleys of my story. As I walk into his office, he places them in front of me. Here it is, taking over the whole of page 111! And there is also a witty cartoon illustration. I recognize the inimitable style of a talented illustrator, Vagrich Bakhchanyan. He is well known for his wry sense of humor. His work often appears on the pages of "The 12 Chairs Club"; he illustrated a few of my own stories as well. I have met him there, at the club. He is a short Armenian man with a long, artsy hairdo. His elongated face with big, brown eyes and prominent dark brow is usually sad but from time to time he wears a mischievous grin.

To show that the protagonist's career has ballooned, he replaced the head of a man dressed in a business suit with a trumpet. A bubble coming out of it reads, "You have to blow on it! Blow!" I rejoice: What a clever graphic interpretation of my story!

However, when I read the galleys, my festive mood disappears at once. Slavkin, the editor, has rewritten the story. He has left part of the protagonist's career in but cut it short at the point where he becomes the head of the technical ideas department. Now, there is nothing left of my text about the man reaching the higher governmental sphere.

The editor has also changed the hero of the story. Instead of an incompetent ignoramus, Slavkin has made him a college graduate. The young man arrives at the government-assigned place of work where, instead of doing engineering, they make him work as an office clerk. He punches holes in paper day in and day out . . .

Thus, instead of ridiculing the army of Party instructors, those ideological loafers, the story satirizes low-level mismanagement, a target on the Soviet publications' "okay" list.

In the edited and rewritten copy, not a trace of sarcasm regarding the Party officials is left. It looks like the only thing of any worth for them in my writing is that I have come up with some comical situation involving some laughable character. What they do with it is none of my business.

I am disappointed, but, after thinking for a while, I play along. After all, I should have known better. It was silly of me to hope that a satirical piece aimed at ridiculing the Party would make it into the pages of any Soviet publication, no matter how liberal its reputation might be. One more lesson learned.

I proofread the galleys, sign them, and leave. After all, I need the money. It is no use playing Don Quixote fighting windmills.

(Now, many years later, thinking back about that episode of my life, I concede that it might well be that I made concessions myself and rewrote the story. After all, I wanted to be published by such a prestigious press outlet again. But it does not change the essence of what has happened. Satire, the way I designed it, was not allowed to see the light of the day.)

A few days after I have signed off on the galleys of my rewritten story, the most curious thing takes place. Slavkin phones and invites me to stop by his office. What has happened? That does not sound good. Is my work still in trouble?

When I appear there, he gives me the tear sheets I have signed and says, embarrassed, "I'm sorry, buddy, but Boris Polevoy, our editor-in-chief, has axed it. Do you know what he said?" He grinned bitterly. "He said, 'If we believe Abramov, Russia is a country of fools.'"

Now Slavkin throws his head back and laughs out loud, inviting me to revel in how funny the reason for the rejection is.

I am astounded. No matter how much has been done to tone it down, to hide the initial satirical sting in my story, Boris Polevoy, an experienced writer, still has smelled a rat, figured out what kinds of people the author of the story has in his crosshairs. Even in a much subdued form, he has sensed that I make fun of how the Communist bosses run the country.

~

Six months later, however, the story sees the light of the day. It appears not in the pages of another Moscow magazine or paper but in a provincial publication. One day, on a business trip to Kazan, the capital of the Tartar Autonomic Republic, I stopped at the offices of the local spinoff of Moscow's *Crocodile*, called *Chayan* (Scorpio). It is a satirical magazine aimed at local targets; they also publish humorous stories. I dropped off the original typescript of "Brainstorming," and a month later a copy of the magazine with my story appeared in my mailbox in Moscow.

When I read it, I see that, though the editor has preserved most of my original text, he has also euthanized my original idea—to make fun of the nincompoops ruling the country. The editor has stopped the protagonist's career growth early on, when he is promoted to head a department of technical ideas. And they rewrote the ending, too. After making a whirlwind of a career, one day the protagonist realizes that, in order to move up, he needs to work with people who possess at least some knowledge needed for the business at hand. And so, he hires his former boss. In its regurgitated form, the story puts me to sleep.

I realize what has happened to my story again. The editor has used the comic setup but emasculated the satire. In fact, he has castrated it; he has turned it into a toothless humoresque. The editorial interference makes me feel disgusted with myself. It makes me feel like I am just whoring out my apparent ability to create comic characters and situations while leaving others to make whatever they feel like making out of them.

Well, where do I go from here in my writing career? That is the question that torments me now. . . .

20

For the Desk Drawer

Finally, I give up on playing the game. The day comes when, against my better judgment, I scribble pieces whose satirical intent is hardly hidden. I cannot help it, but whatever comes off my pen is unpublishable; it violates one or more taboos of writing for the Soviet press. No matter how hard I try to cover it up with some humorous setup, I fail. It looks like the story does not give a damn whether or not it sees the daylight. It is like, no matter how a pregnant woman feels about it, she will give birth to her baby eventually. . . .

For example, one day I recall one of the fact-based satirical pieces I wrote for *Crocodile*. The piece was about the slow pace of new technology adoption in the country. What I have learned by now is that the engine of the Soviet economy runs more or less smoothly only if you grease it well. That is how I come up with an idea for a short story titled "Damn American Technology."

The story is shaped as the inner monologue of a warehouse manager. Being in charge of spare parts for agricultural machinery, he muses about the fact that some people think his job is of no importance. As he sees it, they are dead wrong.

> "If you want to know," he reasons, "I should have armed guards protecting me. I'm sitting on a gold mine. That's how much the spare parts, which are always in short supply, are worth when it's the time of sowing or harvesting. Tractor drivers, auto mechanics, grain combine operators—they all come crawling on their knees. During those feverish times, these spare parts mean more to those people than their mothers do."

One day, they install an American-made, computerized inventory registry in his warehouse. Now anyone, with a push of a button, could see which spare parts and how many of them are available.

This act delivers a momentous blow to the warehouse tsar. Because of the innovation, he is no longer the master of his domain. Now, it is not up to him to disclose whether he has a particular spare part in his store. There is no need for desperate mechanics to bribe him anymore. This new development not only threatens his well-being. The way he sees it, it throws a monkey wrench into the entire way of life in his area. The frustrated manager considers the disastrous ripple effect of the situation at hand:

> Well, let's assume that, with this American watchdog in my store, I'd somehow survive on my salary of ninety miserly rubles—no extra income! So, what good is this machine doing for me? I was about to buy a Finnish-made sofa for my home. Can I do it now? Not on your life! And my bed's falling apart, so now I sleep on a dog mat.
>
> So, Nikolai, the furniture store manager, who's built a summer cottage for himself selling sofas "on the side"—what would he do if he lost customers like me? Continue living on his one-hundred-and-twenty-ruble salary? Could he buy his favorite filet mignon from under the table at our butcher shop? Not a chance! Filet mignon, yeah, right! How about cabbage and potatoes, like everybody else?
>
> To make ends meet, he'd have to sell off his summer cottage, along with the vegetable garden. He used to make a pretty kopeck selling strawberries in the town's market. So, with his garden gone, can someone tell me where the children in the city would get their strawberries? From the state stores? Are you kidding me? If their parents counted on it, their kids would develop a vitamin deficiency in no time. They would get scurvy, no doubt about it. . . .
>
> Now, if that's how things turn out, what in the world should Uncle Vasily, who runs our butcher shop, do? If he no longer has customers like Nikolai, could he buy the French-manufactured color TV set he spoke about recently with a twinkle in his eyes? Hell, no! And, mind you, he needs a lot of dough for what is

coming up for him. He still has to marry off his daughter Mashka and get his son Tolik settled in college.

"So, what's the overall picture we have?" the warehouse tsar is petrified. "This bloody piece of American technology is about to destroy the simple order of things, our whole way of life. All we have to expect now is the dramatic impoverishment of the masses and the collapse of our Soviet economic system as we know it!"

This discovery sends a chill down the warehouse manager's spine:

Oh, my God! Now, I understand what I haven't fully been aware of when I read about "imperialist ideological subversion" in the papers. That's what it means! Oh, you bastard Yankees! They sent us what they say is state-of-the-art equipment, but it's nothing but a Trojan horse. Oh no, Uncle Sam, we all should stay vigilant. They use all kinds of fancy words, like *detente* and *rapprochement*, while trying, in one fell swoop, to send our entire Soviet way of life tumbling head over heels to the devil! No way, you smart-ass Yankees! You won't get away with this! You haven't taken on fools, you know.

To put an end to this American act of "hidden sabotage," the manager rushes to his young nephew, a computer geek. After some struggle, the boy makes sure the American machine that has brought so much disarray into his uncle's life will be dead as a doorknob for quite a long time.

~

On another occasion, I am inspired by a source other than my own journalistic experience. I get not just story ideas but stories themselves as they happen in real life, still pulsing and kicking. My source is Natasha, a young woman I have met and fallen in love with. A graduate of the Moscow Institute of Steel and Alloys, she works as a junior researcher at one of Moscow's scientific institutes.

With her coming into my life, the anguish of not being able to write publishable stories anymore subsides. I try to enjoy life as fully as I can. But, listening to my lover talking about how her day at work has been, I cannot help but reach for my pen again.

During one of our leisurely Sunday breakfasts, she tells me about something that happened in her research lab the other day. Her story touches upon a forbidden topic—the hidden unemployment (or underemployment, if you wish) in the country. One of the glorified advantages of the socialist system is that it cures unemployment, the "most pervasive evil of capitalism." In many Soviet settings, there are far more employees than needed. It results in overstaffing and people killing time on the job. They do anything to escape boredom. So when, the other day, the boss caught my woman and her coworkers sitting idle and chatting in their lab, he steamed up. He berated them, but they quickly shut him up by suggesting he give them something to do.

Like the tale about the Trojan horse of American technology, I write the story down—and file it away. I cannot even think about taking it to any of the editorial offices. If I were to do such a thing, they would think that, despite being just in my mid-thirties, I am losing it, that I am no longer able to censor myself, to sense the bottom line of what one can or cannot write about in the Soviet press. It would be inconsiderate of me to show this piece to an editor. Moreover, it would be outright careless. Not only could I get in trouble if it got into the hands of some snitch, but they could also accuse anyone who read it of not reporting anti-Soviet propaganda to the authorities.

The same thing happens again when my beloved relays another episode of her daily life. Every year, on November 7, on the occasion of the anniversary of the October Revolution, it is expected that every Soviet establishment should take part in the street parades. It is a show of loyalty to the powers that be. You would not find any report in the Soviet press on what usually takes place on the eve of these activities:

THE PARADE

A week before the October celebrations, there is an air of excitement in our lab. The girls discuss their plans for the holiday. Not that it is such a big deal, but, whatever you say, it is still two extra days without rushing to work, getting crushed to death in buses. These days off do feel like holidays. As usual, Nina Ivanova will visit her friend Zina Petrova to bemoan the fate of being dumped by her husband. And, for sure, Irena Sidorenko's festive mood will be spoiled. She is dead sure her hubby, Fedka, will again get stinking drunk and she will drag him home from the sobering-up station.

So, we make ourselves comfortable, chat and count our miserable rubles. We try to see whether we will make it until payday.

Right at that moment, the chief of the division creeps in, avoiding eye contact. He looks so sad one would think his wife's presented him with twins again. He chews on his mustache and stares at the floor. Then, he takes a piece of paper out of his pocket, scrutinizes it, and squeezes out: "Ivanova, Petrova, and Sidorenko! You're assigned to take part in the parade. Assemble at the entrance to the Institute at 7:30 a.m.!"

Everyone is silent. This mustached mouse always spoils everybody's mood.

"I can't." Nina Ivanova raises her hand as if she were still in high school. "My husband's walked out on me. I don't feel like a parade."

"It doesn't matter," yaks the mouse. "Go there and enjoy yourself. You may even meet someone."

"I have a valid reason," says Zina Petrova.

"What kind?"

"I can't say it in front of everybody."

"Fine. Tell me later."

"I can't later either. It's private."

"Tell it to a woman, say, to Nikolaeva. She's in charge of the parade assembly."

"She wouldn't understand. She's an old maid."

"Go to the regional Party Committee!" The mouse rages as if it's getting ready to bite. "You'll find someone to tell it to there!"

"Do you think so?" Zina wiggles her chest.

"Petrova! That's enough of your dilly-dallying. Just go!"

"I can't either," I say, tumbling over on my side. "I have appendicitis, chronic. I never know when it will grab me."

"To hell with all of you!" the chief yells and runs out of the laboratory, red like a boiled lobster.

But later he comes back, smiling.

"Well, okay, comrades. You know I'll be the one to get it. They'll say no one showed up from our department. They'll saddle us with extra political education courses. Is that what you want?"

"Ask Kouzin from the metal shop," we say almost in unison. "He'd never pass up the chance to get away from his bitch of a wife into the fresh air."

"I asked him already," the mouse answers. "'The fresh air by itself,' he tells me, 'isn't enough. A bottle of vodka with something to snack on,' he says, 'would do the trick.' And where would I scrape up the money for a bottle for him? We have already gobbled up our bonus funds, which they made us contribute to the director's banquet."

"Okay," says Zina. "I'll go to your parade if you give me a day off. I have to go out of town, to Ismailovo Fair. I need a macramé handbag. I have the jacket for it, but my handbag to match looks terrible. There are more chances of finding what I need on a weekday. On Sunday the fair is crowded like hell. They could make macramé out of me over there!"

"I can't do with anything less than three days," sighs Nina Ivanova. "I have to visit my mother-in-law. She lives in a village near Tula. Perhaps, a mother's dressing down will affect my worthless runaway hubby."

"Okay," the chief chews on his mustache one final time. "You have no conscience, but so be it. I'll put down you have gone to an auxiliary factory for a day or two. On an exchange program. But be at the parade, from the beginning to the end! I'll check on you. Otherwise, forget about getting any days off!"

Now, one day, when I no longer think about writing publishable pieces, I discover that my internal censor, whose presence in my consciousness I took for granted since I started my satirist's career, has left me without advance notice.

It did not happen overnight. First, he has taken some days off. Then, he seemed to enjoy a long vacation, I assume, flying south to bask in the sun at some Black Sea resort. In his absence, I felt unusual, even worried, as if I walked the streets with my eyes closed, expecting to stumble and fall face down right after the next step.

Soon I stop caring about the internal censor's whereabouts altogether. Perhaps this is why I no longer focus on this or that oddity of everyday life but muse over what the Soviet society at large is all about. I see it not only vacant of the proclaimed equality and harmonious relationship among its different strata. I see that people have long adjusted to the demands of the ideology. The system produced plenty of human beings confident they possess the ultimate truth, which is no subject for discussion or even occasional probing.

One day, lost in my reveries, I stroll along Petrovka Street. Some passerby asks me what time it is. I stop to look at my watch. As soon as I tell the man the time, a gray-bearded, middle-aged fellow dressed in a heavy fur coat looks at his watch and corrects me out loud. He does it with such an authoritative air, as if he were the uppermost source of truth in the world.

I chuckle to myself. As I walk along, I wonder where the reproving tone of the stranger's remark comes from. . . .

The next morning, I find myself jotting down another piece, knowing well it will not see the light of the day:

Moscow Time

"What time is it?" someone asked me at the bus stop.

"Twenty to two," I said.

"Ten to," said the person next to me in line.

"One forty," I said, after looking at my watch again. "Moscow time."

"One fifty-one," said the same man, using the tone of a radio announcer so convincingly that a few people adjusted their watches.

"Wait a minute, comrades," I said. "The exact time is now one forty-two and thirty seconds. I checked it out at the post office."

"One fifty-two exactly," the man said. "Don't confuse people."

"What do you mean?" I flared up. "You! I . . . What makes you so sure your time is accurate? My watch is brand new. I bought it the other day. It has a two-year warranty."

"Big deal!" said the man. "I don't care if it's a ten-year warranty! . . . One fifty-three," he added, pontificating to the crowd.

"It's unbelievable!" I was furious. "It is one forty-five only, but you are so pigheaded. I've met no one so stubborn in my whole life."

"C'mon, comrade!" he said. "Calm down! Don't get excited. It's just that I love truth more than anything in life. You could say it's the one thing I live on. Now it is one fifty-four and thirty-one seconds."

"So," I said, squeezing the handle of my briefcase. "What an opinionated guy you are! Who gave you the right to misinform the public? In wartime, they'd court-martial you for such things."

"Let's assume you've frightened me," said the impudent fellow. "But this one," he pointed to his watch, "is impartial. One fifty-five, dear comrades," he reported again in his announcer's tone.

"No, I won't leave it like this," I said. "It's a challenge to society, that's what it is. Everyone lives by the same clock, but this guy has set one up just for himself. And it's fast, almost as if he wants to be sure he'll always be the first one out there."

"Nonsense," the man said. "I love the truth. And I'm willing to suffer for it if needed."

"Look at this truth-lover we've found!" I shouted, and in passionate fury I grabbed him by the sleeve of his coat. He jerked his arm, trying to free himself.

Just then, a busybody rushed up, an ageless, round-faced, rosy-cheeked man with white eyelashes. He grabbed the truth-lover by the strap of his coat.

"Not so fast, pal," he said. "Call a cop," he nodded. "I'll hold him. Some Mister Orator! Why are you disturbing people?"

"But I . . ." the truth-lover gasped.

"Give it to him," someone from the crowd suggested, in a wheezy voice, as he jumped up and down waiting for the bus. "What makes him so special?"

"People have gotten too rowdy." Varka, the well-known neighborhood alcoholic, ran up and joined the growing crowd. "Would anyone have thought of things like this in Uncle Joe's time? Why are they bothering this guy!" she squealed. "Let him go, you skunk."

"Go ahead, scream," said the fellow with the white eyelashes, continuing to smoke as he held onto the strap of the coat. "Maybe he'll toss you a ruble for some hair of the dog."

"Let him go," Varka whimpered.

"Go away, slut."

Blowing out smoke, the fellow with the white eyelashes sniggered: "Look, she found herself a man." He turned to the crowd, "She's the type who thinks anything in pants will do."

While this was going on, the lover of exact time wilted and turned a little gray.

"Huh, huh," he coughed as if he had a tickle in his throat.

I felt sorry for him.

"Listen," I said to the fellow with the white eyelashes. "Forget · about him. He's just a stubborn dude."

The fellow measured me with his eyes and wound the coat strap around his hand even more.

"Don't worry, we've tamed horses wilder than this one," he said.

"Look at that dissident," a voice came from the crowd. "He makes a thousand rubles—he's a fat cat, and here he is making trouble."

"I'm just an ordinary engineer," my rival said with some effort. "They give us 120 rubles—you could just scream, but it won't get you more."

"You make 120," an old woman in a babushka said. "Look at how clean he is. And I make just 80. Am I any worse than you? He has the nerve to complain, and I must sweep up trash after him."

A tall intellectual, dried up like a smoked chub, cleared his throat and called out: "You, old hag, you make twice that much. These days, you're lucky to find a cleaning lady."

"Oh!" Putting her hands on her hips, the old woman swayed from side to side. "He's jealous of my money. Would you like to spend your days bent over as I do? You're not the type for dirty work."

"Yes, all kinds of people are giving orders these days," a worker wearing a cap said in a hoarse voice. "But as soon as you need help, there's no one around."

"Maybe he's a Jew?" someone said in the crowd. "Let him go to Israel if he doesn't like it here."

"What's happening, citizens?" A cop on duty appeared and saluted.

"It's nothing," I said. "We just got into an argument about whose watch is accurate."

"About what?" the policeman asked again. "Okay, you, breathe out," he said to my opponent.

Then he made me do the same. We breathed by turns right under his nose.

"It smells like gasoline," said the policeman. "Do you guys get high on gasoline?"

I breathed in from my palm. My breath did smell like gasoline.

"We all have smog in our lungs," said the intellectual. "It's not surprising. We don't protect our environment. What can we do? There is no money to clean it up."

"You're right," said the policeman, pulling up his belt. "When there's no money, there's not much you can do. The Museum of Eastern Art was robbed the other day. We don't have enough money to station someone there."

He waved his hand as if to say it was a bad business, this problem of money, and leisurely walked away.

"But what should we do with this guy?" the fellow with the white eyelashes called after him, still holding my opponent by the strap of his coat.

"Oh, enough about him!" said the policeman. "Maybe he's a drunk. But he is steady on his feet. I have no right to arrest him."

"Oh," the fellow with the white eyelashes groaned in disappointment, releasing the strap of the man's coat. "Some police we have nowadays!"

"You see how people are getting out of hand," another voice came from the crowd again. "In Uncle Joe's time, such an outrage would never happen."

Little by little, the crowd began breaking up.

Like other stories I have composed lately, this one I write down and file away. I console myself with the thought that I am not alone in writing unpublishable stories. I know many authors do it with no hope their work will see the light of day in their lifetime. They write "for the desk drawer." I witness the birth of a special literary genre called "nonperishable lit" (*netlenka*), literature that its authors hope will survive longer than they do. They work hard, muttering to themselves Mikhail Bulgakov's pronouncement in *Master and Margarita*, "Manuscripts don't burn!"

(It is a case of wishful thinking, however. Manuscripts do burn, and how! Nikolai Gogol destroyed the second volume of his novel *Dead Souls*. Anna Akhmatova did the same to the full version of her poem "Russian Trianon," and Boris Pasternak to his book *Three Names*.)

Well, my case is much more modest. I need time to accept the new reality. For ten years, I have become hooked on seeing my work in print. It's clear that my satirical career has run into a wall. I jog my mind day and night. What, *what* could I possibly write to be published again?

21

A Jewish Writer?

Much distressed by the setbacks on the satirical front, one day I realize that what has happened to my writing career is for the best. Maybe it is a sign I should put aside the whole bag of satirical tricks, all that writing-between-the-lines business, forget all those allegories and parables, euphemisms and circumlocutions. After all, topical satire is perishable; with the passage of time, it becomes obsolete. Perhaps now is the time to return to my earliest passion. Why not compose some lyrical stories instead? About love, longings, and dreams. . . . Satires no more!

Some time passes, and a story forms in my head, a story that comes from my old Odessa memories. I jot it down, rewrite it a few times, and decide I have the best shot at getting it published in *Youth*. I remember the guilty expression on Victor Slavkin's face after he tried but failed to push my "Brainstorming" story through.

Victor greets me warmly, and, since my story is short, he sits me in an armchair at his desk and reads it.

It's Not a Simple Thing

Why do you look at me, young man? You're wondering how come on a Sunday an old man is sitting in a cemetery, wearing a big cap, hurrying nowhere, and waving his foot back and forth. . . .

Yes, young man, it's strange. I'm surprised, too. You remind me so much of myself some sixty years ago. Why do I have such an impression? Because I see you're unhappy because you aren't in love with anyone. . . .

But do you understand this? They introduce you to a young girl, and, well, you don't like her too much. You respect her, yes. But you don't love her, at least not the way we all want love when we are young. So, you don't love her. . . . But how do you say such things? It's not so simple. You're delaying it and delaying it. . . . Well, you say, I'll tell her the day after tomorrow. . . . Okay, I'll do it on Sunday. . . . After that concert in the city park . . .

In short, you're dragging it out for such a long time that you learn from your parents you're engaged! But you're an honest man; you want her to know you, well, don't love her. Now you vow to yourself that right before the marriage date you won't be such a wimp anymore and you'll tell her *all*. But it's not such a simple thing—to say to a girl you don't love her. . . .

Okay, you decide, I'll get married, and then when there is no love, quarrels and fights will start, and we'll get divorced. And that'll be the end of the whole story.

But imagine to yourself a crazy thing. You get married. You wait for quarrels, but there are none! None and none! You haven't anything to complain about! Well, you, as an honest man, open your mouth to tell her, "Excuse me, my dear, but I don't love you." But you only open your mouth. It was she who had her say: "We have to wait with that new sofa. We will have a baby."

A baby! A new thing now, a baby! Now try to tell her what you would say when she's already breastfeeding the baby. Tell her such a thing, and her milk will dry up. The baby will be hungry. And is it his fault you don't love his mama?

Okay, you say to yourself, the baby doesn't feed on his mama anymore, he's eating his cereal. But now the baby has chicken pox. Keep your mouth shut until the baby gets well. And then . . .

And then you have to go on a business trip again. And when you come back from the business trip, you are told that soon you'll be a papa again.

Making it short, my young man, imagine that you are an eighty-three-year-old, you have seven children, three grandchildren, and one great-granddaughter, named Masha! . . . But how can you live with a person and not tell her the truth at last? You gather all your wits. You go to her. . . . But, my young man, she's not feeling well. She is ill. She, my young man, is dying. You ask her to forgive you and admit on her deathbed that . . .

But she doesn't give you a chance. She smiles, nods with a happy face, and whispers, "I always knew it." You don't understand but try to explain to her you didn't love her, you did *not*. . . . She dies in your arms, smiling.

Now do you understand, my young man, why every Sunday an old man sits in a cemetery in his old cap, hurries nowhere, and waves his foot back and forth?

It's strange, very strange. . . .

What was I thinking?

Slavkin finishes reading and gives me that look, which, combined with his apologetic smile, can mean nothing else but *the sentence is final, not subject to appeal.*

"I'm sorry, Emil," he sighs, "we can't publish it. It's a good story. Both humorous and sad at the same time. But it won't get published."

"May I know why?"

"Because it's Jewish."

I do not ask him what I would ask an editor in America today, "So what?" Now, in the early seventies, they remove anything that could appear Jewish from the pages of the Soviet press. It is not popular to be a Jew.

Come to think of it, it has hardly ever been fashionable in my lifetime. I have shied away from my Jewish identity for as long as I can remember. However, since Israel's Six-Day War of 1967, a new anti-Semitic campaign was launched in the country. They reissued Trofim Kichko's slanderous booklet *Judaism without Embellishments* (Iudaizm bez prikras, 1963) and Yuri Ivanov's defamatory *Beware: Zionism!* (Ostorozhno: sionizm, 1969). These books are nothing more than modern iterations of *The Protocols of the Elders of Zion*, the infamous pamphlet about an alleged Jewish conspiracy to conquer the world. The Soviet media feed this conspiracy to the masses. They present the ongoing Polish workers' unrest and the attempts at creating "socialism with a human face" in Czechoslovakia as nothing but "Zionist schemes."

Slavkin finds my story not kosher enough from a political point of view (pun intended). No matter how innocent it is, its appearance on the pages of the magazine might spell trouble for the editors. They would risk being accused of "pouring water on the mill of the Zionist propaganda."

To make things worse, Slavkin himself is Jewish. If he does not kill that kind of story and instead passes it right off to the managing editor, he risks being accused of "gathering up his Jewish Kahal." In the anti-Semites' lingo, this means Jews favoring their own. He could lose his job.

Slavkin's pronouncement that my story is Jewish catches me off guard, however.

"What makes it Jewish?" I say.

Slavkin shrugs, as if it is self-evident and he should not even waste time explaining it.

"It's Jewish, Emil," he sighs with a sad smile. "Trust me on that."

I leave the editorial office of *Youth* in dismay. How on earth am I writing Jewish stories without even knowing it?

For a long time after that, I revisit the tale in my mind and ask myself the same question, "What's Jewish about it?" There are no Jewish names (or any names at all!) nor any religious references associated with Judaism. Not a word is spoken in Yiddish or Hebrew. However, Slavkin came to his conclusions right away. Maybe because of the literary association? In one of Isaac Babel's *Odessa Stories*, there is also an old man sitting in a cemetery and talking. Well, growing up in Odessa, I saw people acting like that.

Perhaps, in my story, the way the old man expresses his thoughts and feelings betrays his Jewishness. But that's not *that* critical. If that is the only problem, the story could be saved by rewriting the old man's speech. Slavkin is a professional writer. Since he liked the story, he would have suggested I do that. There is something much more critical in the old man's behavior than his lexicon, something that cannot be changed without ruining the whole story. But *what*, what trait of his personality makes the story so Jewish?

I have been trying to understand for a long time what being a Jew means—since my first day of school, when, upon hearing my surname (which is Jewish to the Russian ear), my classmates attacked me, calling me a "kike." It puzzled me. What was Jewish about me? Was having a Jewish surname enough to be Jewish? There must be something more substantial!

Yes, in our family, my father, my mother, and my grandmother sometimes exchanged phrases in Yiddish. Yes, a few times a year, our family celebrated holidays with strange names. They called one of them Rosh Hashanah, the Jewish New Year. It took place not on the first day of January but in September and, to make it more confusing, on a different date each year.

There was a Jewish holiday for children; its name was also strange—Hanukkah. My cousins and I received gifts—candies, nuts, and a few rubles. It was not much, but back then, at a time of overwhelming poverty, it made us children feel filthy rich.

On one spring day, my mother would bake triangular cookies with jam filling. She explained that they call the holiday Purim. It was easy to see that she was not just cooking because it was to be done on that Jewish holiday but that she did it with a special joy, which I, an adolescent, could not fathom. "But of course!" Her face flushed from the heat of the stove, she answered my unuttered question. "It's Purim, after all!"

During Passover, you were supposed to eat some flavorless baked product with a name that was also strange to the Russian ear—"matzo." There is also Yom Kippur, the Day of Atonement, when the adults fasted the whole day and then made up for it at a table laden with delicacies.

These special holidays aside, however, we lived just like the rest, no better and no worse than our Russian neighbors. Did celebrating the Jewish holidays make you a Jew? That is all?

They situated the synagogue of my childhood (the end of the 1940s and the beginning of the 1950s) on the outskirts of the city. My parents visited the temple seldom, mostly on Yom Kippur. They took me there only twice—once when my grandmother passed away and then another time when my Uncle Abrasha on my mother's side died. As I understood much later, they took me to the synagogue rarely so as not to "soil my reputation" as a young Soviet pioneer.

I know no Hebrew and only a smattering of Yiddish, just a few phrases and expressions I heard at home. Judaism as a religion is, by and large, unknown to me, as is the millennia-long Jewish history. Except for the story of the Exodus. . . . When I was a kid, my mother told me why, during Passover, I had to consume tasteless matzos. . . . Of the Jewish writers, I read only Sholom Aleichem in Russian. Once, in conversation, my father mentioned Mendele Mocher Sforim, whose stories he had read as a child. Those are my only connections to all things Jewish.

As I was growing up, I saw that my father took to heart the fact that, by the circumstances of our life, I was alienated from the culture dear to him. He sighed on that account, but he could hardly do anything about it. I grew up in the postwar years, at the time of Stalin's anti-Semitic campaigns, which rolled over us, one after another, like tsunami waves, threatening to destroy everything in their way. It was not the best time to affirm one's Jewishness.

Even though my native language is Russian and I know Russian history and literature better than the history and literature of any other people, I have never thought of myself as ethnically Russian. The indignities of everyday antisemitism have not let me forget that, for the world at large, I am a Jew, period. As much as I have resented being treated as one, I have become used to it, as you get used to an ugly birthmark on your forehead. There it is, right in the middle of your face. It has been there for as long as I remember. What can you do about it?! But, unlike a birthmark, you cannot remove it.

After some time, another little story forms in my head. (I do not remember now whether I wrote it because something like this happened to me or whether I just gave a literary shape to one of the countless Odessa jokes I had heard in my youth wandering the streets of my native city.)

THE WATCHMAKER

I brought him my watch, which had seawater that had leaked into it. First, the watchmaker took time to examine my face. He did it as if he had to repair it, not my watch.

"So, young man, what happened to your piece?" the watchmaker asked, lowering his head as if addressing his belly, raised above his desk. With an imperceptible movement, he moved his watchmaker loupe from his forehead, where it was resting, onto his eye.

"It's slow," I said. "It's awfully slow."

The watchmaker sighed.

"And you're always in a hurry?"

Hardly stirring his hand, he opened my watch with a wry face, as if it were an undercooked clam.

He examined the clockwork and asked: "Do you have a job?"

"I do," I said, surprised. What does that have to do it with my watch?

"How's your health?"

"Thanks, I'm all right."

"You're married? How's your wife? No health problems?"

I replied that she was fine, too.

"Does she also have a job?" The watchmaker continued questioning me without raising his head and while, as it seemed, examining the innards of my watch with disgust.

"Yes," I shrugged. "My wife has a job."

"And how are your children doing? You have children, right? Are they doing well in school? No need for tutors?"

"Thank you; they're all right." He was getting on my nerves with his line of questioning.

The watchmaker lifted his head finally, looked into my eyes, and smiled, as if his smile, having begun on his lips, should reach the tips of his ears at all cost. And when it happened, he latched the cover of my watch and extended it to me:

"Then, here's my advice to you, young man. Buy yourself a new watch."

When, a few days later, I reread the story, I realize that it has something in common with "It's Not a Simple Thing," the story rejected at *Youth* magazine. In both pieces, the protagonist thinks first of someone else's well-being, even if it is to his detriment. In "It's Not a Simple Thing," a man marries without love—and stays married for the rest of his wife's life—just because he cannot bring himself to hurt a young girl's feelings. In "The Watchmaker," after the title character finds out that a customer can afford to buy a new watch, he advises him to do just that because fixing the old one would cost him more.

On one of my trips home to Odessa, I pay a visit to my cousin Yan Tentser, who lives with his grandfather. As far as I know, he is the only observant Jew in our extended family. They even employ him as the treasurer at the local synagogue. While waiting for my cousin to finish fixing us snacks, by chance I pick up one of the old volumes lying around his house. It turns out to be the Talmud in Russian. No wonder I have never seen it in my life; it was published a long time ago, back in the 1920s, when some private publishing houses were still allowed. I scroll through the tattered pages and skim. I understand a little, but one passage attracts my attention. It is concerned with some moral rule. Something like, when visiting a shop, do not ask the shopkeeper about the price of his wares unless you are considering purchasing them. The rationale for such a prohibition is that an idle inquiry raises, in vain, the seller's hope that he can make a sale.

This Talmudic call for extraordinary consideration for the seller's feelings astounds me when I try to apply it to my current life. An average Soviet store clerk could not care less whether you purchase anything. Wages are meager and hardly ever based on commission. No wonder salesclerks are gloomy and as inviting as a tundra in the winter. I figure that, in Talmudic times, the first few centuries of the Common Era, the situation was different. The well-being of the seller (who was often the store owner) and his family depended on whether he sold something. That is why the appeal to be careful with his feelings was a call to respect your fellow human being's right to survival.

And here, for the first time, I realize why Slavkin felt my story is Jewish. Though I have met Russian people who are respectful of the feelings of others, in the Soviet cultural fabric of the time, sensitivity and consideration of others are perceived as Jewish.

It begs this question then: Why do I assume my character's consideration for other people's feelings is characteristic of all humanity?

Little by little, it comes to me. I was born and raised in a Jewish family, and, as children always do, I assumed the moral world of my immediate surroundings was the norm.

Our family's budget depended on my father's earnings. As I have informed the reader already, he was a highly skilled housepainter who worked privately, putting himself at risk of being caught by Soviet financial police. His work arrangement could cost him a huge fine or even jail time. Still, he charged his customers according to their income. If his client was a well-to-do man, he made him pay full price. However, if an underpaid schoolteacher came to him, he would say, "Let's do this. I'll freshen up your apartment, and you'll pay me whatever you can afford."

As for my mother, a strong woman, when somebody asked her why she had not given hell to some bitchy neighbor who had annoyed her greatly, she always said the same thing, "If you must break it off with someone, do it in style." If you end a relationship, do it without offending the other person, even if your anger tempts you to do it. My other relatives, aunts, and uncles acted similarly.

My guess about the reason the editor felt that "It's Not a Simple Thing" was a Jewish story is confirmed when, later, I come upon a quote from the ancient Jewish scholar and sage Hillel the Elder. When asked about the essence of Judaism, he replied, "What's hateful to you, don't do to your neighbor. That is the whole Torah; the rest is the commentary—go and study it!"

The way I understand Hillel, a person who disregards this ground rule cannot consider himself truly Jewish. Even if he *is* a Jew in his documents, observes Jewish holidays, and eats gefilte fish and matzo . . .

~

My fiasco with "It's Not a Simple Thing" depresses me. My last hope for moving on in my writing career turns out to be stillborn. If I will write what I feel like writing, not just what I know the Soviet presses will publish, then I must face the fact I have written myself into a corner. If Jewishness is so natural to me that I am not even aware of it, no matter what I write, it will inform my work, whether or not I want it to. It means my fiction writing will get the same cold shoulder as the story submitted to *Youth*.

I resist facing the truth of this situation. I do not know how to handle it. What is next? Is this the end of my writing career as I know it?

PART VI

Jumping into the Abyss,
1974

22

Flipping a Coin

The thought of running out of options in my writing career does two things—it depresses me and it shifts the focus of my attention from my inner world to the outer one. It brings me back to earth and wakes me up to reality. It is as if the viewfinder in a camera focuses—I notice something unusual in the faces of my friends and journalistic acquaintances. Their expressions have changed. They no longer resemble people bogged down with everyday concerns, such as where they can buy kefir or that much-sought-after Vologda butter. Now their faces seem detached, bearing an otherworldly look.

One day, I hang out at the café of the House of Journalists with my friend Grisha Kremer. As we are sipping our coffee, I nod toward Matvei, a tall, dark-eyed fellow with a bush of curly hair. He is another café regular who joins us at our table and indulges in our journalistic gossip and trading the latest underground jokes. Today, he keeps to himself; he shies away from us, acting much more reserved than before.

I ask Grisha, "What's with him?"

The man's face is pale, as if he hasn't had a good night's sleep in days. He stuffs his handkerchief in his mouth and pulls it back out; it is some strange anxious habit he has developed lately. He does not speak much, sits next to us, and then leaves, without his usual "So long, guys!"

"Don't you know, man?" Grisha says, "They've denied him permission to emigrate. He has become a refusenik now."

I realize that, for quite some time, I have been trying not to pay attention to the unusual goings-on in the country. Meanwhile, TV anchormen have been talking about the "Zionists' subversive activities against our country," which "aimed at provoking Soviet citizens among the persons of Jewish ethnicity." From time to time, they broadcast rallies featuring sullen-looking older men. It seems they have been handpicked to fit the Semitic stereotype. One by one, the sad men climb onto a podium, wave their fists toward the camera, and shout, their voices hoarse with anger, "We do not and could not have any other homeland besides the one we have already—the Union of Soviet Socialist Republics!"

Instead of just saying "the Soviet Union," they spell out the full name of the country into the microphone. Bad actors, they try hard to reassure the public that they are respected members of society, not some second-class citizens. That they are head over heels in love with their Soviet homeland.

After seeing these broadcasts, I cannot help but look back on my life. I recall all the things I have tried to leave in the past so I could move forward.

My school years in Odessa. . . . Just because your surname did not sound Russian or, at the least, Ukrainian, people assumed you are some second-rate human being. Childhood bullies yelled, "A kike, a kike's running along a pike!" (*Zhid, zhid, po verevochke bezhit!*) It was as if you were an insect, some cockroach. At recess, they tripped you for no reason. Your peers' unsympathetic, even hostile gaze sticks forever in your subconsciousness. And you ask yourself, "Why? What've I done wrong?" While never uttered, this question has never left your mind, either. It has been swelling with pus, becoming an abscess in your heart. WHY?

A drunken voice in the line for vodka during the postwar years in Odessa shouting, "Hitler's left his business unfinished!"

My mother's eyes, filled with bitterness and pain on the day she returned from a meeting at our District Board of Education after discovering the ominous extra commas in my essay, written in by the enemy's hand.

The stuffy summer of 1955. . . . When trying to get into college, my Jewish peers and their parents fought the many-headed hydra of the Soviet authorities.

How Boris Protopopov, editor of the newspaper *Soviet Russia*, chewed his lip before telling me I had to change my byline because my surname was "not quite for the newspapers."

How editors of feuilleton departments of various newspapers that published me patted me on my shoulder when I asked about being hired, replying, "Well, don't you already know why?" That was an injustice I not only had to accept but also had to be complicit in.

How I got a job at a publishing house just because they assumed that I must have blood connections to their director's Jewish wife. . . .

And recently they have discovered the notorious Jewish mentality in my stories. They treat the Jewish sensitivity toward the feelings of a fellow human being as if it is a malignant germ in a blood test. Well, it looks like I am a Jew much more than I thought.

I remind myself that, for as long as I can remember, together with my Jewish friends and colleagues, I have heard out, laughed at, and passed along many jokes that delivered the same message—it is a rotten fate to be a Jew in the Soviet land. The jokes remind me of what I know firsthand: that hiding your Jewish identity is a primary psychological preoccupation.

> A telephone rings in the communal apartment.
> "May I talk to Moishe, please," the voice says.
> A neighbor responds: "We have no one like that here."
> Another phone call: "May I talk to Misha?"
> The neighbor shouts: "Moishe, come over! It's for you."

In fact, many jests make it clear that being a Jew in Russia is worse than being a convicted felon. Being identified as a Jew alone is a punishment:

> They proposed a new penalty for traffic violators. For the first offense, one gets a hole punched in his driver's license. For the second violation, he gets another. After the third offense, the ethnicity in his passport is to be changed to "a Jew."

Out of the multitude of other quips of the same kind, there was one that seemed directed at any Soviet Jew holding onto the hope that, in time, things would change for the better:

> A question to the Armenian Radio: "Will there be the fifth item in the passport under communism?"
> Answer: "No. But there will be a sixth, 'Were you a Jew under socialism?'"

Well, what is to be done now? Is there no other choice but to leave the country where I was born and raised?

I recall that infamous televised press conference of the so-called All-Union Anti-Zionist Committee held four years ago, in March 1970. I did not understand what was so frightening about Zionism and why Soviet papers treated it as being as reprehensible as Nazism. A military commander, a two-time Hero of the Soviet Union, David Dragunsky, headed the group. During the broadcast, he did not show much emotion. The face of the Colonel-General of Armored Forces was as impenetrable as tank armor. His service to the state and his hard-won awards spoke for themselves as proof of his unquestionable patriotism.

The most recognizable face among the committee members was that of comedian Arkady Raikin. During his recent tour of Europe, the Western press had dubbed this superstar of the Soviet entertainment world the "Man of a Thousand Faces." One look at any of them made people chuckle.

That is why his visage during the press conference made me anxious. What had happened to him? Why was the king of laughter, whom the whole country loved and adored, so gloomy? Now, his facial expression was as inviting as Moscow skies in late February, when wet snow turns into a dirty-gray slush under the passersby's feet.

I do not remember whether he said anything at the press conference. But his look spoke. *Nay*, it shouted, *Don't be fooled, people! God is my witness, I'm here not of my own free will. They've dragged me here. They need not even my face so much as my name, my renown.*

Watching that press conference sent a cold shiver down my spine. If the powers that be could make these famous people appear on the All-Union TV screen and force them to repeat *Pravda* clichés, then what could they do to ordinary Jews? If they could force these celebrities to say these things, they would hardly have any scruples dealing with anyone else. They will knuckle you down, and you would not dare to produce even a whimper. . . .

I try not to think about what has happened in the country lately, but I cannot help it. It comes back to me again and again. The first warning sign that the world of tolerated satire was crumbling came more than two years ago, at the end of 1971, when they shut down a favorite TV show, *KVN*. They had tried taming the college students' irreverent laughter when they replaced the live shows with prerecorded ones. But that was not good enough, apparently, and they shut it down altogether. . . . Half a year later, in June 1972, through the jammed airwaves of the Voice of America, I learned that, in Leningrad, they had forced poet Joseph Brodsky into exile. And, just a month ago, in February 1974, they arrested Solzhenitsyn and then expelled him from the country. . . .

~

From time to time, I visit "The 12 Chairs Club," if only to chat with its editor, Ilya Sulsov, an upbeat and energetic fellow, the club's spiritual mastermind. Lately the club's publications have become tamer than they used to be. Toothless, from a satirical point of view. . . . What could it possibly mean? One day, when I find myself near the *Literary Gazette* editorial offices, I stop by to say hello.

I enter the big room where the club members convene. I look around, but I do not see Ilya. There are a few others there, including Vitaly Reznikov and Vagrich Bakhchanyan, the artist who illustrated my pieces in the *Literary Gazette* and the magazine *Youth*.

"Where's Ilya?" I ask. "Has he stepped out?"

From this point on, our conversation resembles a dialogue from a Eugene Ionesco play.

"No," Reznikov replies. Immersed in proofreading galleys, he greets me with a nod.

"Well . . . is he on a business trip?"

I know that, from time to time, Ilya joins a few renowned club authors, such as Grigori Gorin and Arkady Arkanov, when they give concerts around the country.

"No," says Vitaly.

"Is he vacationing?"

There is a pause, and this time Vagrich replies, "No."

"Is he sick?"

Vitaly tears himself from the galleys for a moment, looks at me as if seeing me for the first time, and says "No" again.

Here, I pause before asking the next question: "Do I understand you right?"

"Yes," both Vitaly and Vagrich reply almost in unison.

My heart sinks. The "yes" means one thing only: Ilya has left the country. He has emigrated. . . .

A bizarre situation has arisen in the country. Although all who emigrate do it with official permission, the people associated with them are assumed to be accountable somehow for the fateful decisions made by others.

(Getting ahead of myself, I will be pleasantly surprised when, on October 8, 1974, as my family and I land at the Vienna airport on our way to America, out of the crowd of people greeting the arrivals, steps out and warmly shakes my hand none other than Vagrich, the artist and my friend.)

The episode at "The 12 Chairs Club" makes me feel as if I have stepped on a slippery sidewalk. From now on, I must consider the next move in my life.

23

Bless Stanley Kramer!

The decision to leave my native land is the most difficult of all the calls I have ever made in my life. An agonizing one. Bringing my papers to an exit visa office means playing Russian roulette (in this case, it *is* Russian). It means spinning the drum of the metaphorical revolver and pulling the trigger with an unknown outcome.

My stomach turns in anticipation. Whatever response I get from the authorities, I am playing a fate-altering game. If the revolver's cock strikes the cartridge capsule, that is, if they turn me down, I am in big trouble. The act of applying for emigration to a capitalist country is a political act, a statement of disloyalty to the system. Just as film exposed to light is ruined forever, to file documents for emigration is to destroy one's present well-being. No matter how pitiful it may be, my job provides me with a minimum of sustenance. As an unlucky petitioner for an exit visa, I may lose my position. In that case, to survive, I would be lucky to be hired as a street sweeper or an elevator attendant.

But that is not all. They could subject me to public ridicule. Would-be émigrés are being hissed at and booed by the whole country. Public ridicule serves as a preventive measure intended to intimidate others, those who might follow your suit. "Scum of society" (*otshchepentsy*); this is what the newspapers call anyone who applies to emigrate. The root of the Russian word is *shchepy*, "wooden chips." It hearkens back to Stalin's infamous pronouncement amid the mass persecutions of the Great Terror period. When asked by foreign correspondents why so many innocent people had been butchered, the "Father of the Nations," as Soviet propaganda dubbed him, sniggered and said, "When you cut a forest, chips fly." The derogatory term *otshchepentsy* signals how the Soviet authorities treat those who want to leave this best country in the world. Such people are rubbish; they are worth no more than some sawdust. . . .

However, the prospects for what will happen if the proverbial Russian revolver clicks on an empty chamber, that is, if they let me go, are no less wrought with anxiety—but for different reasons.

Today, when my American friends and colleagues ask me about leaving my native country, the Soviet Union, back in 1974, I tell them a popular joke of that time:

They call up Rabinowitz for military service. They train him as a paratrooper. The drill sergeant barks: "Listen up, comrade soldiers! Follow my instructions. First, we all get in that pickup truck, and I'll take you to our airfield. Second, you board a plane that will take your asses three thousand feet up in the air. Third, on my command, you jump and pull the main parachute ring. If it doesn't open, don't panic. Pull the spare parachute ring. Then, when you land, you get back into the pickup and return to the base. Questions?"

Together with others, Rabinowitz gets in the pickup. He goes to the airfield and boards the plane. The plane climbs three thousand feet. When it's Rabinowitz's turn, he jumps. He pulls the parachute ring. The chute doesn't open. He pulls the spare parachute ring. Again, nothing happens.

Rabinowitz rushes head-down to the earth, mumbling, "With my luck, I bet there won't be any truck down there either."

The black humor of this joke is an accurate reflection of the admixture of anxiety, aloofness, and hopelessness that swirls in my soul on the eve of the most pivotal moment of my life.

"Fear has huge eyes," says the Russian proverb; that is, it makes mountains out of molehills. Ancient Greeks represented the fear of the unknown, the primordial human fear, as what a person would feel wandering in a labyrinth in which the Minotaur, the mythical half-man half-bull, could strike at any moment. Soviet authorities have spared no means to cultivate the dread of leaving the country. Back in 1970, Mosfilm produced and released widely a movie titled *The Flight* (Beg). The action takes place at the end of the Russian civil war. On the run from the Reds, the protagonists of the movie, Russian aristocrats, flee to Turkey and soon hit rock bottom. Because they have no way to support themselves, they gamble on cockroach races in street-run casinos, selling off their fancy clothes.

Soon, all those who refuse to return to the bosom of Mother Russia wind up in nothing but their underwear. Literally.

The script was based on a play by Mikhail Bulgakov, the author of the anti-Soviet tale *The Heart of a Dog*. It circulated underground, retyped on onion skin paper; they called such underground literature *samizdat*. The movie seemed to tell the viewers, "If you don't believe the Soviet authorities, see for yourself what your adored writer warns you about. Decay and ruin await anyone who is stupid enough to leave our great Motherland."

However, I have hope. I tell myself that more than half a century has passed since the events in that film took place. Maybe the situation over there, beyond our border, has changed for the better? Perhaps now it is possible for someone like me to survive over there? Maybe I stand a chance?

One evening, at the café of the House of Journalists, when I see my friend Arkady Polishchuk there, I ask him whether he knows any foreign correspondents among the habitués. It would be good to talk to someone who has firsthand knowledge of life beyond the Soviet border. I want to hear about it straight from the horse's mouth.

Arkady looks around and waves to someone on the other side of the café.

"There is one of them right there." He nods toward a man in a beige suit, wearing a fedora. "Peter . . . but, well, buddy, you better leave him alone today. Give him a breather. He's just returned from Paris. He needs a week or two to come to his senses. You know, to get used to our Soviet way of life again. . . . When they bring Sputnik back to earth, they do it as smoothly as possible, don't they? Otherwise, the damn thing would burst into flames in the dense layers of the atmosphere."

True enough. I look at the "Parisian man." His glassy stare tells me he recalls strolling along the Champs-Élysées and the cancan kicks of the Moulin Rouge girls. I decide not to disturb him for his own sake. Even though he has reentered the orbit of our Soviet life, asking about his recent trip abroad may cause irreparable damage to his mental health.

On another occasion, Arkady introduces me to a man in his late thirties with a goatee who is smoking a pipe and sipping coffee. The man has recently returned from Canada. I ask him what impressed him the most on his trip there.

The man finishes drinking his coffee. He stuffs his long pipe with tobacco again, lights it up, and takes his time to answer me, waiting while his pipe gets going. Then he lifts his eyebrows as high as he can and immerses himself in thought for a long time. I see him sifting through haystacks of his Canadian impressions, searching for one that someone like me who had never crossed the Soviet border could comprehend without his going into too many details. When he realizes the utter futility of his search, he narrows his eyes, thinking about how best to articulate his response.

"Well, you know, man," he utters finally, "their supermarket doors open and close automatically."

His coffee cup and his pipe travel toward each other in midair slowly until they touch. . . .

After one more try, I conclude that Soviets who travel abroad lose their minds. Any attempt to recall what they have seen in a Western country shuts their brains down.

My single stab at foreign travel had taken place about twelve years prior. After I graduated from Odessa Polytechnic Institute, they sent me to Kiev to supervise the installation of telephone lines along a new gas main. One day, while visiting our management offices, I spotted a poster advertising a cruise along the Danube River. The ship would stop at ports of call in several countries. By taking the cruise, I could visit not only socialist countries (Bulgaria, Romania, Czechoslovakia, and Hungary) but also capitalist ones—Austria and West Germany. Could that be true?

Well, I thought to myself, you never know! As a Russian saying goes, "Only God knows what the devil might have up its sleeve!" (*Chem chert ne shutit!*) I submitted my application to the authorities, and they quickly turned me down. Their reasoning—"Comrade Draitser's experience of working within a collective is not long enough"—seemed strange only at first glance. What they really meant was that I had not had enough Soviet life experience to know that they do not let people of my kind travel abroad. Given an opportunity, a single person, unencumbered by a family, is likely to defect.

So, now I face a formidable task: to learn about real life on the other side through conjectures and suppositions. To gain some sense of that alien day-to-day existence, I sort through the glimpses of images of that life. The glossy magazine *Amerika*, published in the States, has a limited circulation; only a chosen few can get hold of it. Nobody takes the magazine seriously anyway. It is all too clear that it is no more than a tourist prospectus. It portrays "real" American life the way Soviet books in the style of socialist realism portray Soviet life.

I had met foreigners in my early youth when I lived right in the center of my native town, Odessa, with my parents and my younger brother, Vladimir. Spanish, Italian, Greek, and French cruise ships moored year-round in our warm-water port. They brought tourists from all over the world. The foreigners strolled our streets, stepping down from huge foreign-made buses. You could never mistake them for my fellow citizens. Not just their clothes and gait, even how they smelled set them apart. The raincoats those tourists wore were of subdued colors, ranging from the color of brewed coffee with milk to pale blue, the color of the early-morning Odessan summer sky. We, Soviet citizens, wore Chinese raincoats, all dark blue with rubberized checkered lining; we reeked of newly manufactured tires.

The tourists' faces were well groomed and bronzed year-round. The makeup on the women's faces was hardly noticeable. Because Odessan women used low-grade Soviet products to bring out their beauty, our overseas visitors developed false impressions about our city's public mores. In seaports throughout the globe, whenever a ship enters the harbor, professional sirens appear preying on the hearts of sailors. But here in Odessa, it seemed these sirens flooded the streets. . . .

The foreign tourists were not young people but retirees who had at last found time to travel around the world. We struggled to believe they were not wealthy people who owned yachts or even steamships; they were people of the usual trades, from bookkeepers to steelmakers. But to us, they were filthy-rich folks. How else could we explain that they even smelled different? (Now, in hindsight, I realize they used deodorant, a substance unknown to any Soviet person.) All female foreigners had their nails done. Even in the winter, no matter how cold it was, all the men appeared on our streets with no hats or earmuffs. And the hair of both sexes was combed and greased with brilliantine.

What impressed us even more than the way they were groomed was the way the foreigners carried themselves. Though they were in the territory of an unfamiliar country, they behaved as if they had walked our Odessan sidewalks and looked over our poor and ugly shop windows for a hundred years. They did not tilt their heads in surprise. They did not curl up as we always did in unfamiliar situations. They were quiet and full of modest dignity, which was what bothered my young conscience the most. These people arrived from the countries partaking in the cruelest exploitation of man by man, and yet they did not look like slaves.

Instead, the tourists appeared happy with their lives. Why else were they so calm and sure of themselves? Where the hell did the affability and goodwill their faces expressed come from?

These mysterious people appeared from the world I knew only from foreign movie newsreels. Besides strikes, riots, and street protests, these newsreels were packed with tornadoes, hurricanes, and earthquakes. It looked as if our planet's countenance suffered from a tooth flux on its Western side only. All natural disasters hit the capitalist countries only as if to punish them for their moral trespasses. (There was no mention ever of hurricanes or earthquakes that occurred on Soviet territory.)

~

Just like other departees (*ot"ezhanty*; the great and mighty Russian language gave birth to such a word as well), I am squeezed between the Scylla of my Soviet life and the Charybdis of the unknown American one. I know the Scylla perfectly well, but I have rather shaky ideas about the Charybdis. What is awaiting me on the other side of the Soviet border? I do not have the faintest thought about what I should do with myself in the country with the most advanced technology. Even the Soviet propagandists concede it through clenched teeth.

With emigration cracked open since 1968, a few thousands have taken advantage of this rare opportunity. Most of them have settled in Israel, some in the United States or elsewhere. Sometimes, their letters to their Soviet relatives and friends slip through the censors' hands and reach the addressees. Those contemplating following suit hunt for those letters. How does a Soviet person survive out there, in a world so different and, in many aspects, much more developed?

I read as many of those letters as I can lay my hands on. No matter how hard I try to place myself mentally in American life, zilch comes out. Upon arriving in America, a violinist, a graduate of the Leningrad Conservatory, joined the Los Angeles Symphony Orchestra. A friend of a friend, a chess grandmaster, recently took part in an international tournament in Canada, already under the banner of the new country. One day, I learn through the jammed Voice of America broadcasts that they have invited some Soviet ballet stars who defected while performing in New York to join an American theater troupe.

However, what would *I* do over there? What am I able to offer? I am neither a gifted violinist, nor an outstanding chess player, nor a ballet star. . . . Yes, I earned a BS in electrical engineering some years ago, but now it is hardly more than a piece of watermarked paper in a dark-blue cover embossed with gilded lettering. In the past, I worked first as a foreman on a gas-line construction site for a few years, then at a research lab, but then I abandoned my trade. Since then, I have made a living editing technical literature. It is out of the question that I could get such a job in America. My English is poor, within the limits of our high school program. Thus, I hardly have any skills that would make me employable in America. I have already married Natasha; we have a year-old baby son, Maxim. How will I provide for them on the other side of the Soviet border, in a new world that I hardly know?

When my desperation reaches its apogee, a letter from Pittsburgh winds up in my hands. When I read it, I see a glimmer of hope. The letter describes what had happened to a young Muscovite with Asperger's syndrome when he arrived in America with his wife. A distant American relative of hers made some phone calls, and they set him up to work on some assembly line that produced gas meters. The young man learned to screw in bolts and tighten up nuts in the assigned places, and now the young couple has no worries about their daily bread. They are happy as a clam in their Pittsburgh home.

I cheer up. Wonderful! Although my manual skills are not that hot (perhaps, if I try hard, I could hammer a nail into a wall straight), it doesn't matter. In time, I would figure things out. If a person with disabilities has learned how to work on an assembly line, God willing, I would manage it too. But then again, I have no one in America who could make that fateful phone call to secure even an assembly job for me.

Desperately scanning my mind, I recall that, back in my student years, I interned with a team of skilled technicians and learned how to connect wires and read blueprints. Watching the *Foreign Newsreels*, I have noticed that, in America, they have plenty of vending machines selling soft drinks. Hopefully, given a chance, I could land a job as a repairman for those machines. American-made or not, they are bound to break from time to time, right? Somehow, I would figure out their circuitry. I would learn where and how to replace a fuse or reconnect a loose wire. Though I had never seen the entrails of an American vending machine, I decide they are like the ones that sell seltzer on the Moscow streets. (I have no idea, at the time, that American tourists visiting Moscow were disgusted at seeing the way glasses are washed in the street vending machines. We put the glass on a metallic perforated gadget and press a button that lets little spurts of water spray the glass from all sides. Only after stepping onto American soil did I discover disposable paper cups.)

~

To get a better grasp of what life in America is all about, I try to watch as many American movies as I can. Thanks to my membership in the Union of Soviet Journalists, I have the privilege of watching every American film screened at their club.

They Shoot Horses, Don't They? . . . Jane Fonda plays Gloria, a young woman of the Depression era. Together with another wannabe, she enters a grueling dance marathon. She becomes so tired and bitter that she convinces her partner to put her out of her misery by shooting her. The picture depresses me. What an inhumane place America is! How could people over there treat each other that way!

It's a Mad, Mad, Mad, Mad World, directed by Stanley Kramer. . . . The movie seems to be produced as if on cues from a Soviet propaganda department—to illustrate capitalist "money grabbing" (*pogonia za nazhivoj*). In search of buried treasure, a motley bunch of Americans rush headlong into the desert, losing their minds and trying to outsmart one another.

Easy Rider. . . . I watch it and am at a loss. I wonder why these young men roam the country on their bikes. Shouldn't they be gainfully employed to support themselves and their families?

Midnight Cowboy. . . . A young Texan fellow arrives in New York for the first time hoping to become a real hustler, bilking rich women through his sexual prowess. But he finds he is the one getting hustled. The movie introduces me to a pet American gadget—a TV remote control. During a love-making scene, the channels flip by themselves while the couple rolls back and forth over the device lying on the bed. I am flabbergasted: Why would anyone need a remote control to begin with?! How hard could it be to walk to the TV set and change the channel? What a lazy lot those Americans are! The only thing I can say to explain my reaction then is that there were only *four* channels on any Soviet TV set.

~

One day, in the House of Journalists, I see another Stanley Kramer movie, *Bless the Beasts and Children*. It makes me forget about all the practical things I am worried about while contemplating my move to America. It

pushes me over the edge. Since my mind is racing day in and day out
trying to decide what I should do—to leave or not to leave—I see the
film as a fable about opportunities for freedom ignored.

In the picture, they have sent several emotionally disturbed teenagers
from broken homes or dysfunctional families to a summer camp, hoping to set them straight. On a field trip, the boys witness a phony hunt of
surplus buffaloes. For sheer entertainment, the hunters shoot the fenced-
in, peaceful animals.

The animals die in agony, kicking their legs. Horrified, the boys scream
"Killers!" at the adults.

Back in their camp, shaken up by the slaughter they have witnessed,
the boys have nightmares of their parents shooting them point-blank.

They break out of the camp that night to save innocent animals from
the butchery. They must do it overnight, before dawn, when the next party
of shooters arrive.

The boys rush through the night. First, they ride their horses. Then
they hotwire a beat-up utility car. When they run out of gas, they reach
the reserve on foot.

Setting the buffaloes free turns out to be a formidable task. They are
locked up behind a fence.

Time is pressing. The boys are desperate. What the hell are they supposed to do?

One boy throws himself behind the wheel of a small car in the parking
lot nearby and rams the corral fence, creating an opening.

Now, the buffaloes can escape. "*Hey,*" the boys shout, "*you're free now!
Run!*"

However, the buffaloes do not move a muscle. They have no intention
of escaping. They ignore the opportunity to free themselves. Their cap-
tivity has its advantages. It feels safe. It is predictable. Giving up freedom
means they no longer have to be always on guard.

The boys turn up their radios. They hoot, halloo, and cheer. Finally,
the buffaloes walk out of the corral and stop nearby and graze peacefully.

The boys are mortified. They fear witnessing another bloodbath. They
scream to the beasts, "Move! The hunters are coming!"

Nothing helps.

One boy gets into a truck and, blowing the horn, drives into the buffaloes, making them run away. Trying to shoo the animals, the boy drives
over the edge of a ravine to his death.

The closing scene of creatures running for freedom has a profound effect on me. It makes me sweat. My heart beats fast. An iron ball rolls up in my throat and gets stuck there. . . .

I am watching the movie with Grisha. I elbow him. He is puzzled. What is wrong with me? I am not known for being physical when expressing my feelings.

"What's the matter with you?" he whispers.

I know that, so far, Grisha does not think of leaving the country. Therefore, I do not do what I feel like doing—shouting to him, *Don't you see! The movie is not about poor beasts; it's about people like me! . . . How am I different from those dumb buffaloes? . . . The corral gate has cracked open for me, and I still sit on the fence. How am I better than those animals?*

I am disgusted with myself. Why do I still drag my feet! I need to stop beating around the bush. I must seize the opportunity, no matter how risky it is. It would not last forever. Enough is enough! I am a human being, for God's sakes, not some witless buffalo!

At this moment, I know I have reached the point of no return. I realize that, if I give in to my fears of the unknown, of whatever lies ahead after my fateful filing of an exit visa application, of whatever else I might encounter afterward, and stay, I would not be able to look at myself in the mirror. I will lose whatever modicum of self-respect I have been able to preserve throughout my Soviet life, the life full of big and little every-day indignities. I will despise myself. *I'm a coward! If it weren't for the boys, the buffaloes would not have understood they should run for their lives. Am I as dumb as these poor critters? I'm a human being, after all, am I not?*

The next day, I grab the pile of documents, which has sat there so long, and take them to the local exit visa office. If they reject me, I say to myself, at least I would not blame myself for not even trying.

After a long, long while, I am sound asleep the entire night. . . .

~

Years after the fact, every time I recall that episode of my life, I say to myself, "Bless *Bless the Beasts and Children!* Bless Stanley Kramer!"

24

A Small Iron Door in the Wall

"So, young man," the KGB major says, stretching his hand toward my briefcase, "let's see what you've tried to smuggle into the embassy of a foreign power."

It happens sometimes that way. You set off on a journey in inclement weather. Before stepping outside, you gather all your internal forces. Ready to fight the elements, you raise the collar of your coat and pull down your hat as far onto your head as you can, almost to your eyes. But, soon after you start, the weather changes for the better. The clouds disperse, the sun peeps out, there is a gust of a tailwind, a happy coincidence—and you reach your destination much sooner than you had expected.

That is what happened to me. It is May 1974, and I have filed my exit visa application for my family and me. I have been preparing myself for the authorities' decision for a long time. I tense up, thinking about what I would do if they turn me down. There is no reason to expect they would deny my request. I have never been privy to any state secrets. However, they turn people down at random. They refuse you just to annoy you. To let you know it is not a sure thing to apply and leave. Any applicant risks rejection, which means to be forever marked as politically unreliable.

To prepare myself for such an eventuality, I have made friends with a few refuseniks, people who were not permitted to emigrate. I have let their courage rub off me.

But something unexpected happens. After only three months of waiting, I get permission to leave the country. The reason for my lucky change of fate will become clear later. Right then, American lawmakers were discussing the possibility of amending the Trade Act of 1974. It concerned the granting of preferential status to Communist countries. Henry Jackson, a senator from the state of Washington, and Charles Vanik, a congressman from Ohio, thought it would be wrong to grant such a friendly status to countries that treat human rights, including the right to emigrate, like a doormat. During the debates, the senator has expressed his belief that, in such countries, people vote only with their feet, moving toward the state border.

Put yourself in the place of Soviet authorities. What should they do now? On one hand, the Soviet Union is the best country in the world, but, on the other hand, there are people who want to run away from it. No, no, ladies and gentlemen! Nothing like that! If there are oddballs, freaks, and yo-yos who apply for emigration, they are just a pitiful grudging few. Their ties with family abroad drive them to leave our great country. The ruling for the public at large is this, "Based on humanitarian grounds and in the interests of family reunification, the Soviet Union grants some ethnic minorities permission to emigrate to capitalist countries where they are the majority." They include Armenians, Germans, and Jews in this group. To be sure, there are plenty of Armenians and Germans happy to flee the country. Mostly, though, they have been added to this list just for show, to cover up the Jewish character of the movement for the right to emigrate.

So, I receive a message from the Office of Exit Visas. They inform me that I should pack up and ship off while the going is good, that is, within thirty days. With butterflies fluttering in my stomach—not just a few of them, a whole swarm rushing around in there—I head for the Dutch embassy.

What does the Dutch embassy have to do it with it? Like everyone else, I am leaving the country on an Israeli visa. However, for more than seven years, since the 1967 Six-Day War, the Soviet Union's diplomatic ties with Israel have been broken. Now, with the emigration ban lifted, the Dutch embassy steps in to help the emigrants with travel documents.

So, together with the butterflies, I set off to visit the Dutch embassy to process our visas and, if possible, ship my manuscripts out of the country. I believe that my writing life has ended. My desire to save a pile of papers with my writing serves no practical purposes. It is nothing more than a spasmodic willingness to preserve part of my old life on the eve of my future life, full of the unknown.

I could try to follow the established order. I could present my papers to the Glavlit, as the leading Soviet censorship office calls itself. (Its full name is "General Directorate for Protecting State Secrets in the Press under the USSR Council of Ministers.") They would check out my notes, and, if they found nothing seditious, they would stamp each page with their seal—and there you go. . . .

I have no desire to do that. First, if you hand over your papers to the authorities, God knows when you will get them back. If you get them back at all. . . . What Soviet institution, especially one as formidable as the Glavlit, ever abides by the country's laws and regulations? And for people who have turned down Soviet citizenship, the authorities could send the papers straight from the receptionist's desk into the office stove. At least some good would come of them—to warm up the gentle censors' fingertips at the stove tiles. Case closed!

Second, there are my diary entries, all too personal to be read by strangers. It would be like stripping naked in public. I have noticed no exhibitionist impulses in myself. Since childhood, my mother has reproached me for being too reticent.

And third, there are short satirical pieces from my most recent writing stint, the era of writing "for the desk drawer." The Glavlit could consider them provocative. Not only would they not allow me to take my papers out of the country but they might also allege that I harbor the desire to badmouth the Soviet state, just like the seditious authors I had read about in the papers. I am mindful of the possibility that, instead of being sent to the West, I might wind up going in the opposite direction in a freight car marked "40 people, 8 horses." They use such wagons not only to move troops during wartime but also to take prisoners to the gulag.

What could I do? How could I bypass Soviet red lines? The question is not new. It is as old as Soviet power itself. Since the USSR came into being, the whole population of the country has been thinking about this question from dawn to dusk. . . . However, it has become known among emigrants that, when visiting the Dutch embassy, you can ask to ship some of your papers across the border in diplomatic pouches.

~

It is mid-September. It is sunny, though it is on the cooler side. The embassy is on Kalashny Lane, near the House of Journalists. I enter the embassy yard. Lo and behold! A long line of people stretches from the lobby under a flat awning all the way to the gate. Because Soviet life has made me accustomed to standing in lines of any length, I gird myself with patience and ask the usual question, "Who's last in line?"

It is clear I will stand here for a long time. It is especially trying when you are a nervous wreck. You are about to leave the country where you were born and raised. You have never even put your foot on the other side of the state border. You know what the West looks like only because you have seen the *Foreign Newsreels* shown in movie theaters before the feature films. Those newsreels prove that living abroad is a nightmarish experience complete with flooding, tornadoes, earthquakes, and long lines for unemployment handouts. It is no wonder you feel like exchanging a few words with people in line. No matter what you say, you share a common fate now. They are your future travel companions. It is the eve of a decisive turn in their lives as well. They, too, have always been careful not to tell strangers they are filing for an exit visa. Who wants to become a pariah, an object of suspicion? Here, in line at the Dutch embassy, you can allow yourself to relax a bit. You are among comrades in arms fighting the same battle. You are among those who, just like you, their eyes squinted, jumped into the unknown without a parachute. Now, you are about to take your final step in the home stretch. Get your visas and tickets—and, as the great Russian poet Yuri Lermontov wrote more than a century ago on the eve of his exile, "Farewell, unwashed Russia!"

Some tall, squirrely man materializes next to me. Another émigré looking for someone with whom to shoot the breeze, to exchange meaningless phrases of the "fall has come quite early this year!" type. The man is lean; his face is wasted, pale, and wrinkled, like old linen after a sleepless night. Like me, he carries a briefcase. It is thin, worn out, and as crumpled as its owner's face. A briefcase identifies him as a man of intense intellectual labor, which has worn out both his face and his briefcase.

A cigarette in the corner of his mouth, Squirrely (as I nickname the man) chats with me. He has visited the Glavlit office and discovered that the line there to have your papers certified is too damn long. Where the hell can you find time for all these darn bureaucratic procedures! So many other things to take care of before leaving the country! I respond, nodding and telling him I would also like to get some of my papers out of the country, but here, at the Dutch embassy, the line is also a mile long.

The owner of the thin briefcase wastes no time—as soon as my words hit his ears, he drops the sympathy act. He does not nod, no moaning and groaning. At once, he straightens his body—he is much taller than me, almost like a fire tower—and motions toward the gates.

At the entrance to the embassy courtyard, there is a sentry booth with a phone inside. An aging mustached policeman, his face pocked, languishes nearby.

I turn around to see the guard already cutting across the yard. He moves at a leisurely pace, in a somewhat dignified manner, as if in slow motion on a movie screen. His step is that of a confident man carrying out his duties, which in and of themselves he hardly finds delightful. Well, they call me, and here I come. . . .

Finally, he approaches us and, his hands folded, stops, looking at me apathetically. He also shows no regard for Squirrely (I imagine that all uniformed policemen think little of their chameleon-clad coworkers). Apparently, assuming that, when a uniformed cop is present, his civilian clothes acquire the power of police get-up, Squirrely says firmly, "Come with us!"

To make me move, he touches me gently, as if I were a young girl, at my elbow and adds: "It's nearby."

The guards approach me from both sides, grab under my arms, and escort me out of the embassy courtyard.

Outside the embassy gates, once in Kalashny Lane, we first turn left, then right, and walk toward Suvorov Boulevard. We pass the House of Journalists, a vast mansion. We walk half a block and enter a small courtyard. It is walled off from the street by a stone fence overgrown with ivy vines, already kissed with fall's ocher. Sharp, black cast-iron rods peek out from under the leaves here and there. A quiet little Moscow courtyard; it is hard to imagine it is a place where any drama, let alone a tragedy, might unfold.

The guards lead me to a small iron door across the gate. That the door is iron-clad tells me that, as soon as it slams shut behind me, getting back to freedom would not be easy at all. "Abandon all hope, ye who enter here!" flashes in my mind like the sign over the gates of Hell in Dante's *Divine Comedy*. As soon as I see that door, Valentin Kataev's novel *A Small Iron Door in the Wall* springs to mind. Published several years ago, the book is about Lenin's life in exile and "the great man's struggle for the Party unity, for the coming revolution," as the reviewers wrote in awe.

As I approach the door, I am struck by the irony of the situation. In Kataev's work, a small iron door in the wall leads to Lenin's living

quarters on some quiet Parisian lane where he plotted the October Revolution. More than a half-century later, Lenin's secret police lead me, just
one of many others eager to leave his creation, to another small iron door
in the wall.

From his skinny briefcase, Squirrely pulls out a huge key that seems as
if it would open the gates to some medieval fortress. The architecture and
buildings here are not medieval but feel just as ancient, having belonged
to the Russian nobility in the early nineteenth century. I find myself
inside a small room now used as a place to interrogate people pulled
from the line in the embassy courtyard. It looks like the room has served
as a courtyard janitor's lodge. Only a few square feet in size, the place
could barely fit more than a few brooms and a wooden snow shovel.
There is also an armchair, for, I guess, the janitor to rest during his breaks
from cleaning.

Squirrely sits me down in the armchair. He lowers himself on a stool
near the door and announces: "You'll be waiting here until the KGB
curator arrives."

Wearing the same bored look on his face, the mustached policeman
leaves.

I have to wait in this tiny room with the armored door for the whole
of three hours. Why do I have to wait for such a long time? Because the
KGB curator has his hands full with other detainees? Or because he has
napped longer than usual after having lunch in his office? Or is it a way
to torment me with suspense? My anxious gut tells me it is the latter.
Maybe they will drag me straight to the Lefortovo, the notorious prison
in Moscow, or perhaps they will just beat me up and throw me out onto
some quiet street. After giving it some thought, I rule out these brutal
scenarios. I have not taken part in public protests. If I have written something less than flattering about the powers that be, I have done it not for
publication.

My heart skips a beat. My writing pieces are here, in my briefcase,
which I hold on my lap. Frantically, I sort out mentally what I have in
there. "The Wheel" . . . a grandma rushes around the country in search
of a baby carriage for her grandson. Well, it is just a satirical piece about
poor production and bad sales management. The Party ideologists have
left *some* space for public criticism, as long as it fits their propagandistic
formula, "less-than-perfect things, uncharacteristic of our system, still happen here and there in our country from time to time."

What else do I have with me? Ah, a short piece titled "The First Dialogue." I wrote it recently, recalling one of the Voice of America broadcasts I was able to catch. Some time ago, a certain American professor advanced the hypothesis that Russians endure tyranny and are used to oppression because they swaddle their infants too tightly. The babies grow up given to an inhibited life and the lack of freedom from a very early age.

I imagine a swaddled baby boy who can talk right after being born. Since he does not expect much fun in his life, the infant asks his parents to give him a good reason to go on in the world they have brought him into. They respond with the propaganda line that it is an upstanding citizen's duty to "fight for the happiness of the future generation of Soviet people."

"Oh, that calls for a standing ovation," the swaddled baby chuckles. "Sorry I can't oblige you, folks. My legs don't hold me up yet, and my hands are all tied up. Not much room for applauding."

Well, the spook should not give me a hard time about this piece. I am about to leave the country of my own will. This alone says loud and clear where I stand politically.

What else? Oh yes, there is another piece I wrote "for the desk drawer." It is titled "The Art Critic." This one could get me into hot water. The story pokes fun at the same organization that has snagged me out of the embassy line and keeps me waiting in this stone cage. In urban folklore, an "art critic" is a nickname for a KGB plainclothesman. When they send a Soviet artist abroad to show the superiority of socialist art over rotten bourgeois art, a KGB agent accompanies him as an "art critic" in case the artist tries to do something funny, like asking for political asylum. I strain my memory, recalling the text:

THE ART CRITIC

For quite some time, I had felt that this well-dressed, middle-aged man was shadowing me. He accompanied me everywhere, keeping himself at a distance. On the train . . . in the street . . . into a café . . . In the lobby of a building where I had dropped by to visit some friends, I could no longer restrain myself and approached him. He greeted me first.

"Hello," he said. "Allow me to introduce myself. I am Swordbeltov, an art critic."

"Comrade art critic," I said, "what on earth is going on? Why have you been following me around?"

"I'm studying."

"Studying? Studying what?"

"Everything. Your gait . . . your dress . . . the sparkle in your eyes . . . the tempo and rhythm of your life. . . . Everything about you interests me."

"What's so interesting about me? And why me in particular?"

"Every person interests me. You're just the first I began with."

"Began what?"

"The study of humanity. I'm taking night classes on art."

"Well then, study your art. And leave me alone."

"Excuse me," he said. "I didn't mean to offend you. It's just that art is the object of study in yesterday's art criticism. Today, the object of study for critics is the object of art itself, that is, man."

"Wait a minute. . . . Who gave you the right to follow another person around like a peeping Tom? It's both unethical and insulting."

"Oh no," he said. "Now you seem to be offended. But I haven't caused you any harm. I tried to get a little closer to you. Please don't move for a minute."

My whole body stiffened. I heard something click.

"Okay, that's it, thank you," he said. "You know, I've never seen your full face. You're quite a restless person," he smiled. "You're either reading a book or talking about something with your friends. Oh, I know all about your friends—our evening class sorted them out—who's gotten who. . . . But what kinds of things do you read?"

He thrust his hand into the outside pocket of my briefcase and pulled out a book.

"Excuse me . . . Aha, Chekhov, Anton Pavlovich. Great! It supports my hypothesis."

"What hypothesis?"

"That sometimes people read the classics, too."

"Well, that's great," I laughed. "Does that mean there are other opinions?"

"You're funny," he said. "And even likable somehow. Our observations tell us that people read God knows what. But it's not only God who knows; we art critics do too."

"What kind of science is this!" I cried. "Poking around in another man's briefcase!"

"If you're interested, go ahead, check out mine. You can ask questions."

He threw open his shabby briefcase, which he had been holding under his arm.

Inside was a hunk of bread, an aluminum cup, and the portrait of a man with a goatee. I had no more questions.

Well, the piece could spell big trouble for me. For a fact, I know the major will get offended. It is not too difficult to see that the things in the art critic's briefcase are ominous emblems of life in the gulag. All of them! A loaf of bread . . . an aluminum cup . . . and whose portrait could that be in the KGB guy's briefcase other than that of the fierce founder of the Soviet secret police, Felix Dzerzhinsky?

The thought makes my blood curdle. Over my whole Soviet life, I have been lucky not get into the paws of the secret police, and here, on my way out of the country, they have gotten me. May I be damned! Why, I ask myself, didn't I think twice about what to take along? What a dupe!

Then I remember Squirrely's battered briefcase . . . I realize, before I had composed the piece, I knew the spooks carried worn-out briefcases to resemble intellectuals. It seems I had forgotten about it.

I look at Squirrely. He stares at the ceiling. He is bored to death hanging around in the caretaker's lodge with a detainee for hours on end.

Finally, the door opens and a man about my age, in his mid-thirties, appears on the lodge's threshold. His straight blond hair moves from side to side across his forehead every so often. Light-blue, goggle eyes, plumpish lips . . . a familiar face. Where have I seen this man? Well, but of course! The same well-tailored suit, a stylish nylon shirt complete with malachite cufflinks, the same lobster eyes . . . Ha! The café at the House of Journalists! I have seen him over there. He hung out there often! So, he is an operative attached to the journalist brethren.

But wait, where else have I seen him before? Suddenly I remember. About ten years before meeting him at the café, at the start of my literary career, I had attended a few sessions of a young writers' group affiliated with the newspaper *Moscow Komsomol Member*. And there, among others, was this blond man with the bulging blue eyes. I guess that if he himself was not an "engineer of human souls," as Stalin nicknamed Soviet writers, then he was at least their supervisor.

At the meeting, he introduced himself to the group as Leonid. Now, this man sits in front of me on a stool that Squirrely has offered him, wearing a suppressed Mona Lisa smile on his lips (that is, the smile earmarked for use at the café of the House of Journalists).

Squirrely takes a position at the entrance, his arms crossed as if to remind me again: "Abandon all hope, ye who enter here!" Leonid flashes his burgundy leather-bound ID, confirming he is a KGB major. In stark contrast to the face he has used in the café, the one in his ID is unsmiling. (In all my Soviet IDs, I have the same somber, depressed facial expression, the kind you expect to see in American mug shots. In the Soviet Union, it was assumed that smiling faces have no place in official documents!)

What do you know! A KGB major, to boot. . . . Maybe if he were some lieutenant, I would have some hope to wriggle out of the situation somehow.

In what I can only imagine is an attempt to prove that his ID picture is of him and not of someone else, Leonid wipes the Mona Lisa smile from his lips. It is almost as if he said, "I'm not some customer at the House of Journalists café. I'm a KGB major carrying out my duties of national importance." The phrase he utters makes it clear: "Well, young man. Let's see what you have tried to smuggle into the embassy of a foreign power."

As if I were having an out-of-body experience, I wonder to myself, since when has Holland become a foreign power? Well, the USSR is a state power, all right. According to Soviet propaganda books, there are also imperialist powers—America, Great Britain, and France. But Holland, a country the size of a Moscow region? It is clear that the spook uses the term "power" to underscore the gravity of my alleged crimes. "An attempt at smuggling sensitive documents into the embassy of another country" seems dangerous enough, but "smuggling documents into the embassy of a foreign power" should make me shake in my boots. Well, what about a state like Liechtenstein? Or Luxembourg? There is also Monaco, where they have casinos in Monte Carlo.

I reply with a shrug: "Well, some sketches and notes."

Leonid also shrugs.

"What for? Over there," he utters, "nobody cares about all this stuff. It's a different world out there. . . ."

He says it in a hopeless tone, one unbefitting an interrogator, and looks not at me but somewhere off into the distance. It seems like, at some point, he may have toyed around with the same idea for himself. To leave behind his previous life, to cross over into the world on the other side of the Soviet border . . .

It may sound strange, but, for a moment, the fact that the spook confirms my doubts calms me down. Really, why did I schlep all these papers nobody but myself cares about to the embassy?

Squirrely dumps my briefcase on a folding table, and Leonid rummages through my papers. My throat dries up at once. It tickles. I am seized with anguish. What will happen to me? Not in the coming day, but the next minute. . . .

Suddenly, it hits me that most of my papers are handwritten. They are chicken scratch; they are barely legible. To tell you the truth, sometimes even I have trouble deciphering my own writing. Who knows what I have scribbled there? Back in my school years, my father reproached me for my bad penmanship from time to time. He told me more than once it would do me a lot of good if I took the time to improve my handwriting. I have never gotten around to doing it for lack of time. And now, by sheer serendipity, that fault of mine may well save me from trouble. God willing, Leonid will not read "The Art Critic" or anything else that the authorities might find offensive.

My body stiffens as I watch the major. At first, trying not to lose the physical composure a major ought to have, he strains his eyes, squinting. Then, grunting, he raises one sheet after another to the dim light bulb hanging from the ceiling. With an annoyed expression on his face, he pulls out a small eyeglass case from the inside pocket of his jacket. He opens it up and takes out a pair of horn-rimmed glasses resting on a blue velvet lining. Both the eyeglasses and the case are designed so elegantly it is clear they are a non-Soviet make. I cannot help thinking, *I bet he's snatched them up from some foreign tourist while shaking him down under some pretext.*

The spook puts on his glasses. I freeze. He hacks, clears his throat, and hacks again. Unable to make any sense of my papers, irritated, he throws the glasses back on the folding table. His face assumes an angry and disgusted expression, the kind a dog wears while it sniffs a brand-new galosh that still reeks of rubber.

I sigh in relief. It looks like I am in the clear. Leonid turns to my other papers, the ones I have typed up on my Olympia typewriter. I am not worried about them. I have typed up only the pieces I thought about showing to some editor. There is no subversive material there. Leafing through them for a while, Leonid pounces on a piece titled "An Open Letter."

As I understood later, the stool pigeon's single task was to weed out anyone who carries protest letters or pamphlets. Refuseniks' struggle for the right to emigrate was already at its height. Publicity was their only weapon in fighting human rights suppression.

The spook reads this "open letter" piece, but I could not care less. What he is reading is just a draft of one of my lampoons that did not make it to print. In that piece, I used the format of an open letter as an ironic device. If my memory serves me right, it was something like an open letter written by the director of one of the Black Sea resorts, in which he reveals that he has taken bribes from vacationers he accepted into his establishment.

The officer sifts through the rest of my papers. He finds nothing incriminating. Frustrated by this waste of his time, he gives me a disapproving look and declares: "Well, if you want to take all this stuff out of the country, you must take it to the Glavlit and get their permission."

With that, they let me go. The major leaves the lodge, and Squirrely tags along behind him, mumbling and wearing a rueful countenance.

My legs made of gelatin, still not having processed that I got off with only a scare, I walk down Suvorov Boulevard. I pass the House of Journalists and, trying not to jump for joy, I head to the Nikitsky Gate subway station. I go home.

On the train, I check behind me every so often to see whether I am being followed. I get my first breath of fresh air when I am on the streets again. The danger is over. . . .

~

My encounter with the KGB in the Dutch embassy courtyard was not my last run-in with the frightening agency. Before I boarded my plane at the Sheremetyevo International Airport, a customs official—a tall, unsmiling man of about fifty—rummaged through my suitcases and came upon my scrapbooks. Since I had trouble finding any decent ones in Soviet stationery stores, an acquaintance of mine, a bookbinder, made them to my specifications. The scrapbooks were large, a foot and a half long and a foot wide, their covers upholstered with a dark-green cloth. I filled their

pages with clippings of my work that had appeared in papers and magazines throughout my writing career. I had no specific reason for doing
this. I just wanted to have some keepsake, some memento of that volatile
part of my life when my excitement was often followed by disappointment and joy by frustration.

On the eve of my emigration, I was convinced I should say farewell
to my writing life once and for all. I was sure that leaving the country
where my native tongue was spoken meant I would never take to my pen
again.

The author's scrapbook page vandalized at Moscow customs, October 8, 1974

The customs official showed no emotion when he discovered my scrapbooks. In a business-like manner, he pulled them out of the suitcase, placed them on one of the inspection tables, and pressed a button. Soon, through the side door of some makeshift partition, a uniformed KGB lieutenant in his mid-twenties emerged. He approached the inspection table and, without even looking at me, scanned my scrapbooks, page by page and tore out my clippings. It seemed the officer did it randomly. He crumpled them in his fist and threw them into the nearby wastebasket.

When he finished, he returned my half-torn scrapbooks to the customs official and, in the same way as before, without ever looking at me, walked away and disappeared behind the same partition through which he had emerged. My stomach empty, I felt violated and robbed, as if the KGB man had torn out and crumpled up pieces of my past life.

Yet, his actions did not surprise me. All throughout my Soviet life, I had gotten used to the fact that the authorities, especially those representing the most formidable agency, can do whatever they feel like doing to you. The only thing that seemed to be odd was the KGB officer did not tear out all my clippings, one after the other, but did it selectively.

Most of the torn-out materials consisted of my satirical pieces published in *Lenin's Banner*, a regional Moscow newspaper. He also destroyed a few other articles—from *Crocodile*, from *Izvestia*, from *Komsomol Pravda*. But he did it randomly, apparently, out of sheer spite, just to annoy me.

So, it was strange. Why the hell had he cared so much about my pieces published in *Lenin's Banner*?

It took me a long time to get to the bottom of that mystery.

Epilogue

When I left the Soviet Union, I was convinced my career as a Soviet satirist would die a natural death. After settling in with my family in Los Angeles, I discovered my *Crocodile* correspondent ID card #267 in my papers. I treated it as a memento of my past journalistic life, of all its exciting and disappointing moments.

Back in 1971, they had forced me to return it after the scandal caused by my satirical article in *Crocodile*. Out of the blue, after I had already shored up all my inner strength and jumped headfirst into the abyss of the unknown (that is, applied for emigration), a phone call from *Crocodile* came. They invited me to visit their editorial offices in the *Pravda* high-rise, where, with little ado, they returned my ID and asked me to write another piece for the magazine.

To this day, I have no idea what made them do it. There was hardly any need even to pretend that the magazine shed its proverbial "crocodile's tears" (pun intended) over one lost correspondent. As the teeth in the jaws of the real-life beast of prey are replaced in time, the magazine had an abundance of eager freelancers ready to step in. Had Manuil Semyonov, the editor-in-chief, been tormented by guilt over having punished a writer for his own oversight? After all, it was his job to make sure his magazine did not step on the toes of those deemed untouchable by the Party head honchos. Or maybe he had received instructions to make amends with whomever he had offended, since letting that anger sit fuels the enemy's propaganda?

I am also tempted to think the editor's clemency toward me was a result of his clairvoyance. As became known later, my nemesis, the minister of culture, Yekaterina Furtseva, fell from grace with the powers-that-be the next year. Addicted to alcohol, first she was punished for her lavish lifestyle and had to pay a hefty fine. Then, she was not reelected to the Supreme Soviet, the most substantial sign of her fall from grace with the top brass.

I will never know the truth. Whatever the reason for the return of my *Crocodile* ID, the magazine had extended its expiration date to December 31, 1974. Since I had landed in New York on December 30 of that year, I arrived in America still a correspondent for the Soviet satirical magazine. This circumstance turned out to be symbolic on several levels. Even though I thought that, when leaving Russia, I was leaving my Soviet satirist cap behind me for good, my former literary involvement caught up with me in the most unexpected ways. Its ripple effect took me in unforeseen directions.

My disregarding the wishes of the Soviet authorities paid off. I ignored the KGB spook's instructions to take my papers to the state censorship committee for approval. Instead, as soon as I came to my senses after being detained by the KGB at the Dutch embassy, I called my brother, Vladimir. He lived with our parents in Odessa; they had already filed their applications for exit visas. I told him I would mail him all my handwritten "for the drawer" pieces and added: "When your time comes to get your visas at the Dutch embassy and you stand in line over there, *do not talk to anyone. About anything! Not even about the weather!*"

Thankfully, my brother listened. A year later, after also settling in Los Angeles, he handed me my manuscripts. The Cold War was still in full swing, and several of those pieces appeared in the op-ed pages of the *Los Angeles Times* and, in the original language, in the New York–based *The New Russian Word* (Novoe russkoe slovo).

In America, I caught up on my literary education, which I had not been given a chance to do in my native land twenty years earlier. When the time came to pick a dissertation topic, it was only natural for me to fall back on my decade-long experience in writing satire. This work, which eventually appeared as *Techniques of Satire: The Case of Saltykov-Shchedrin*, determined the direction of my scholarly interest. Both *Taking Penguins to the Movies: Ethnic Humor in Russia* and *Making War, Not Love: Gender and Sexuality in Russian Humor* were indebted to my Soviet-era professional interest.

To my surprise, the satirical spirit I had developed back in the USSR did not die a natural death after I left the field of Soviet journalism. While greatly appreciative for the opportunities I took advantage of in the new land, I penned several satirical pieces on American topics. They subsequently appeared in the *Los Angeles Times*, the *San Francisco Chronicle*, the *Los Angeles Daily Examiner*, *Confrontation* magazine, and *Studies in Contemporary Satire*.

~

The lives of my former comrades-in-satirical-arms also took sharp turns. The time for Soviet-style satire seemed to be over. Ilya Suslov, who emigrated to America a few months before me, worked for the Voice of America and the Russian-language illustrated magazine *Amerika*. Before his untimely death in 2017, he published six books of humorous prose.

Before leaving the country in 1977, Arkady Polishchuk joined the human rights movement in the country. He advocated for the religious freedom of Christian believers—Evangelists, Pentecostals, and Baptists. In the West, he continued his fight in defense of persecuted religious believers in the USSR. Since 1984, Arkady worked for Radio Liberty. In recent years, he published two memoirs—*Dancing on Thin Ice: The Travails of a Russian Dissenter* and *As I Was Burying Comrade Stalin: My Life Becoming a Jewish Dissent*.

Grigory Kroshin left Russia in 1996 and settled in Germany. Having ten books of satirical prose to his name, Grigory also developed his newly found talent for humorous cartoons. In recent years, several personal exhibits of his artwork took place in German cities.

~

In the late 1970s, a small Los Angeles–based immigrant publishing house, Almanac-Panorama, produced a weekly paper with ads for Russian-speaking doctors, dentists, and lawyers. The publishers entrusted me, a former servant of the Soviet satirical muse, with putting together a sampling of Soviet underground jokes. We titled it *Forbidden Laughter* and included jokes the Russians told about Stalin, about Khrushchev and Brezhnev, about the endless Party meetings, about whether there would be World War III ("No, there won't be. But there will be such a struggle for peace no stone will be left unturned").

When the booklet was produced, we knew next to nothing about how to publicize and promote it. The slim volume would have gone no further than the bookshelves of the Almanac employees had it not been for lucky (albeit hardly joyful) circumstances. Soon after the book's publication, the Soviet Politburo elders decided to strengthen their friendship with the neighboring Afghan people. They did it through a surprise visit to the country with a large contingent of Soviet troops. A collection of Russian underground jokes gave American people hope that the Afghanistan invasion was just a prank that went sour. The *New York Times* and the *Washington Post* wrote about *Forbidden Laughter*. The *Los Angeles Times*, *Atlantic Monthly*, and several other American periodicals reviewed it. As the volume's editor and compiler, I received my lifetime portion of the proverbial fifteen minutes of fame.

Predictably, the Soviets were not amused. *Crocodile*, now run by a different editor-in-chief, responded with an enraged editorial write-up. In the Orwellian tradition of rewriting history post-factum, they denounced me, the *Forbidden Laughter*'s editor and compiler, as a nonentity, an imposter, and a modern-day Inspector General of Gogolian sorts, who had hardly any affiliation with the Soviet satirical scene. They also accused me of providing grist for "Washington's propaganda chiefs" who "had extracted [me] from the pile of immigrant trash" and showered me with dollar bills. A UCLA Slavic Department grad student at that time, with a wife and a baby son on my hands, what could I say in my defense? Perhaps, just that I wish the part about the dollar showers were true. . . .

However, I was destined to meet my denouncers face to face. In the spring of 1987, in the spirit of Gorbachev's newly implemented policies of glasnost' and perestroika, a delegation of Soviet satirists from *Crocodile* visited America. They made several public appearances, including at UCLA. My alma mater called on me to help with interpreting. Reluctantly, I obliged. . . .

A few months later, taking part in the symposium "Political Humor around the World," I met Art Buchwald, whose work I had long admired. *Pravda* loved to reprint his syndicated Pulitzer Prize–winning political satires. During a break, I told him that the Soviet satirists had asked me, with an air of disapproval, why I had left my great Soviet Motherland. Art thought for a second, raised his thick brows, and asked, for a moment stopping to chew on his cigar: "And what did you tell them, Emil?"

I had been part of the hosting party, I explained; I had to be polite.

Art flicked the ashes from his cigar and said, articulating every word, as if dictating the line to his secretary: "You should have told them you left the country because they didn't provide you with a parking space."

With Art Buchwald and Mark Russell at the symposium "Political Humor around the World," June 1987 (courtesy of Joel Buchwald and Mark Russell)

I laughed hard. His joke was even funnier to me than to him. Over my whole Soviet life, not only had I never had a car, I could not even dream about it. . . .

While the Soviet knee-jerk reaction to *Forbidden Laughter* was to be expected, I took a long time to solve the mystery of what had happened at Soviet customs right before I boarded the plane. Why had the KGB officer pounced on my writing scraps? Why had he torn out certain clippings but left others intact?

The answer came years later when I researched the biography of a former Soviet intelligence officer, Dmitri Bystrolyotov, for my book *Stalin's Romeo Spy*. Back in 1973, I had met him by chance, and he told me his life story. Now I recalled some details of his spy work. After the Soviet foreign intelligence in 1920s Prague had recruited him, a destitute young Russian émigré, his first assignment was to scan the local Czech publications. They charged him with "open source" scouting. He fished out bits of information about local plants and factories, their products, the directors' names, and other business-related minutiae. They added this data to the intelligence database for possible further use.

When I examined the ravaged pages of my scrapbooks, I saw again that most of the destroyed clippings were of pieces I had published in *Lenin's Banner*, the Moscow regional paper. Why had the KGB cared so much about that publication?

Now I realized that the KGB officer at the border had destroyed those clippings as part of Soviet counterintelligence procedures. In my satirical pieces, I mentioned the names and positions of people responsible for careless work, violation of financial discipline, and other business-related offenses. (As I understood later, it was pointless to tear out clippings of my publications from the national periodicals, such *Izvetsiya, Komsomol Pravda,* or *Crocodile.* They were available by subscription outside the Soviet borders.)

On my first trip to Washington, DC, I visited the Library of Congress. While browsing through the catalog, I discovered microfiches of many Soviet newspapers, *Lenin's Banner* among them. It looked like Soviet counterintelligence was not aware that the Library of Congress had those newspapers. Like many other Soviet institutions, the KGB worked sloppily; the left hand did not know what the right one was doing.

I took the *Lenin's Banner* microfiches of the issues with my publications to the library Xerox room. Upon returning home, I pasted the copies of my articles back into my scrapbooks, in the same places where they had been before they were snatched up by the KGB goon's hand.